SOLDIER, SAILOR & AIRMAN TOO

THE FIGHTING LIFE OF
GROUP CAPTAIN A.B. 'WOODY' WOODHALL

SOLDIER, SAILOR & AIRMAN TOO

THE FIGHTING LIFE OF
GROUP CAPTAIN A.B. 'WOODY' WOODHALL

ISBN: 978-1-906502-21-8

Published by

Grub Street Publishing Limited,
4 Rainham Close, London SW11 6SS, England
sarah@grubstreet.co.uk | www.grubstreet.co.uk

Cover design and layout by Mark Andrews for
Willson Scott Publishing Limited
design@willsonscott.biz - www.willsonscott.biz

Foreword

HOUSE OF COMMONS,
LONDON. S.W.1.

From: — Wing Commander P.B "Laddie" Lucas, D.S.O., D.F.C., M.P. (Commander of 249 Squadron during the Battle of Malta in 1942 and Member of Parliament for 10 years during the 1950's, serving under Churchill, Eden and Macmillan. Laddie Lucas is also the author of several books including Flying Colours, Thanks for the Memory, Malta – A Thorn Rommel's Side, Out of the Blue and Wings of War.

"As an officer in the Royal Air Force I was personally associated with Group Captain Woodhall throughout the greater part of the late war. In particular I served with him in Fighter Command during much of this period, and came under his control for eight months in Malta, in the dark days of 1942. I claim, therefore, the right to say I know him well.

Both as the Sector Commander at Tangmere in 11 Group of Fighter Command during 1940 and 1941 and, later, as the officer upon whom the control of the fighter squadrons in Malta in 1941 and 1942 directly fell, Group Captain Woodhall proved himself to be a balanced and competent administrator whose forthright decisions reflected not only a fine judgement, but also a paramount sense of duty.

He was essentially a leader who, without attempting to do so, compelled others to follow him. Indeed the squadrons over which he exercised control had a loyal and devoted faith in his ability and would obey spontaneously his sometimes exacting commands.

He made those under him contented and happy, and he was blessed with the faculty for making the men and women who carried little responsibility feel important.

He was able to delegate authority, and yet retain a decisive grip over his whole command. I never saw him flustered even in moments of great operational stress. As a squadron commander under his command I found him co-operative and approachable, and he always seemed to have time to listen. I look back now and can see even more clearly how considerable was his executive and administrative ability.

I doubt whether the Royal Air Force ever produced a better operations controller of aircraft. Nature had, of course, given him the advantage of a striking and distinctive radio voice. It injected confidence and stability into the heart of many a pilot at times when the circumstances might well have promoted a measure of confusion. He could nurse home an inexperienced pilot who was in difficulties, not because he knew necessarily more about controlling aircraft than most, but because his intuition told him what was in that pilot's mind and what therefore he should be instructed to do.

Group Captain Woodhall was honest and upright. His integrity, like his courage, was unquestioned."

P.B. LUCAS.
November 1957

Foreword

Supplementary Foreword by Squadron Leader Jeff West, Hamilton, New Zealand. (Squadron Leader West, as a Sergeant-Pilot, was Douglas Bader's wingman the day the legless ace was downed in 1941. (It was originally anticipated that separate forewords would appear in United kingdom and New Zealand editions.)

I have known Group Captain Woodhall for over seventeen years. In 1940 and throughout 1941 he commanded Tangmere Sector in 11 Group Fighter Command, R.A.F. The writer was a member of 616 Squadron at Tangmere during this period. Tangmere sector embraced the South-eastern part of England, the counties of Hampshire, Surrey, Sussex and Kent, i.e. the most forward and busiest sector in the Air War at that time.

When the Fighter sweeps over the Channel and northern France started, the Group Captain personally took over the Ground Control — no matter the hour - and much of the success of the Wing was attributed to the skill with which Ground Control was conducted. The Wing was led by the famous legless Douglas Bader until 9th August 1941. In the flights, after hectic sorties, never once did I hear one word of criticism over the quality of Ground Control whilst the Group Captain was on the air. He was responsible for the safe homing of many a crippled machine. The Group Captain had a very good "voice" over the ether. He spoke clearly, concisely, humourously - was never flurried - and the sound of his voice when we were in the thick of it, was most reassuring. Group Captain Woodhall was also very human and understanding. He always made a point of meeting every pilot - Sergeant or C.O. - when landing from a sweep.

In February 1942 when Malta was taking the major weight of the German Air Force - plus Italians - the Island was in dire straits. The fact that the R.A.F. saw fit to send Group Captain Woodhall there to command the Ground Control of the Island Defence is ample proof of the confidence they placed in him. Like a clot I volunteered and went along too, and this nightmare period was negotiated in no little measure through the manner in which Group Captain Woodhall personally controlled operations, moved among the Airmen and Pilots, all of whom gave him their complete confidence and assisted in re-organizing defence and tactics. Things were pretty chaotic there in early 1942. Despite this very heavy strain, (and after a long spell at Tangmere), the Group Captain stood up to it better than younger men carrying infinitely less responsibility.

Personally I cannot speak too highly of the Group Captain as a man, and as a Controller I hold that he has no peer.

Squadron Leader J.G. WEST.
September 1958

Acknowledgements

My thanks to all the following who have helped provide detail for this book.

I have to single out Hans Houterman in the Netherlands for his contributions. Until I came across his website (www.unithistories.com), I despaired of finding names, initiials, ranks and dates of some comrades referred to in Woody's original manuscript. Many of my queries meant his searching through Navy, Army and Air Force lists going back to early 1916.

Among others who contributed information (in no particular order) were:

Basil Vickerman
Dave Homewood
Franek Grabowski
Michal Havrda
Brian Cull
Heather Prins
David Skyrme
Frederick Galea
Audery Mattison
Angus Mansefield
The Times of Malta
Dave Homewood
Dave Wigley
Hugh Turner
Mike Short
Larry Hill

Particular thanks to Jan Brown (Christchurch) who typed the original manuscript into a computer document and thus saved me many hours.

Contents

Introduction

Woody was the second-youngest of four children and was born to Job and Clara Woodhall (formerly Richards) on January 9, 1897. He had an older brother Herbert and younger sisters Mabel and Dorothy. His birth certificate states he was born at Laburnum Cottage, Kirkby R.D. In the 1901 Census his father's occupation is listed as stock and share broker and later there was apparently some financial scandal that resulted in his being posted to a branch office of his firm in South Africa. We also know that Woody attended Bolton Grammar School from August 1909 to June 1912, but he gives no details of his schooling nor any other information about his childhood save the opening two paragraphs of his story. His service papers state he was at the School of Mines, Johannesburg, in 1913 and 1914 where he was studying to become a mining engineer – a career he totally abandoned for military service.

His birthplace, Kirkby-in-Furness was in the north-west England county of Lancaster but in the area that is now Cumbria. Kirkby was a collection of small hamlets in mostly rural surrounds and most of the houses are described in the 1901 Census as labourer's cottages. The nearest town of any size was Ulverston, but Barrow-in-Furness some 12 miles away was already a heavily-industrialised city built around iron-ore and steelworks and with a growing shipbuilding base. One of the largest employers at Barrow-in-Furness was the Vickers Engineering Company which not only built warships and the Maxim and Vickers machineguns but eventually conventional and later nuclear submarines. To the north of Kirkby is the Lake District, now a major tourist destination and nearby is Coniston Water where John Cobb, and Malcolm and Donald Campbell were to successively set world water-speed records. In modern times, it is the Sellafield nuclear-processing plant to the north of the Duddon Estuary and also feeding into the Irish Sea that garners most publicity. Barrow-in-Furness now has major unemployment as a result of the decline in defence spending following the end of the Cold War.

Chapter 1

A Marine at the Somme

My first love was the sea, yet although I was born in Kirkby in Furness on the shores of the Duddon Estuary, the latter was so full of shifting shoals and sandbanks that I was never able to satisfy my longing to sail as a small boy. All I could do was to sail models in ponds and streams.

However, when my mother, my sisters and I went out to join my father in Johannesburg, to my joy I found a mine dam called the Wemmer Pan within a mile or two of our house. Here, the McKinnon brothers, two Highlanders from Skye, taught me to sail in a traditional clinker-built dinghy they had built and rigged themselves. The McKinnons were reserved and fairly taciturn men whose native language was Gaelic and who spoke English rather haltingly with an attractive accent. They were fine sailors who had learned their art in fishing craft in the Hebrides. Yet they took an interest in me and they not only taught me to sail but also to build boats with the result that boat building and sailing are my chief hobbies to this day.

When Britain declared war on Germany in August 1914, I was 17 years old and serving in the South African Defence Force, with the exalted but unpaid rank of Acting Lance Corporal. Volunteers were called for to fight for the British Empire to expel the Germans from their territorial possessions in German South West Africa, the area which is now the independent country of Namibia. To my astonishment I failed to pass the medical examination for entry to the Army owing to a dose of malaria I'd had some two months before. I was invalided out and like most people in those days, I thought the war would be over in a matter of months, so I decided to get back to England to join up there. With my values and upbringing, it would have been shameful to let such an opportunity for both adventure and service to my country pass me by. It was a time of great patriotism and hope and we all felt it imperative to fight for our ideas of freedom and our way of life and government.

All passages to England were booked up for months ahead (largely for reservists being recalled) but I was determined and after a few days exploration of the Capetown docks and a lot of door knocking, I managed to sign on as a deckhand in the SS Ingoma, homeward bound with reservists and horses. As a passage worker, I was paid three shillings a month. The fo'c'sle disapproved of me because I was looked on as a black leg (non-union labour) and they showed their disapproval by throwing my mattress over the side. However, I filled two fodder sacks with hay intended for the horses, sewed the mouths of the sacks together, and had quite a comfortable bed.

The "fo'c'sle"(short for forecastle) was the collective name for the crew of a merchant ship in those days as they were invariably segregated from the officers and lived in the forecastle of the ship. In the Navy they would have been called the lower-deck as compared with the officers being upper-deck. It was most likely my private schooling and relatively upper-class upbringing (and therefore my lack of regional accent) that most raised the ire of the crew.

On our first Saturday at sea, rum was issued to the crew and the fo'c'sle bully, an unpleasant, belligerent and antagonistic type, got rather drunk and decided to beat me up. Luckily for me, he was drunk, and also there was an iron stanchion in the middle of the fo'c'sle. I had done a certain amount of boxing at school, so by dint of dodging round the stanchion, and side stepping his drunken swipes at me I was able to avoid any serious hurt. I waited until he was practically breathless then hit him hard in the stomach and winded him. As he doubled up I stepped back and a friendly hand came on my shoulder and a Cockney voice said "Good for you, boy that's fixed the bastard."

The owner of the voice was a short thick set little Londoner, who had been a professional pugilist in his day. "Shorty" (I forget his real name) took me under his wing thereafter and practically every evening would produce a dilapidated set of gloves and proceed to knock me all round the fo'c'sle. He would then drop his hands, and say "Your turn now, have a fair go at me." Although he didn't attempt to guard, I very rarely managed to hit him. He was one of the toughest, quickest little chaps I have ever met, and a most delightful character. He taught me a lot about boxing.

After three weeks of scrubbing decks, washing down paintwork with "soogy moogy" (caustic soda), painting the funnel with "crab fat" (grey paint) and tarring down the stays, my hands and clothes were in a disreputable condition by the time we docked at Southampton. I landed in England looking like a tramp. To add to my troubles, someone (I suspect the bully whom I had laid out) rifled my suitcase, and stole my money, only 10 pounds, but it was all I had.

However, I sold a suit of dungarees for 1/- and sent a telegram for help to my brother, Herbert, who was married and lived in Bramhall, Cheshire. It was too late to get a reply that night so I slept on some straw in a railway truck because I was not allowed to sleep on the ship as the crew had been paid off.

(Later that year, the SS Ingoma was put into service as a troopship and was used in that role until 1917. In one of those curious twists of fate, she was sold to an Italian company in 1937 and torpedoed by Malta-based RAF aircraft in late January 1942 while en route to Tripoli. I was by then stationed on Malta and read about the sinking in a pilot's combat report. She stranded near Tagiura after a towrope broke and was refloated, towed to Tripoli and scuttled in the harbour entrance to prevent her falling into British hands. After the war she was refloated by a British salvage company and broken up for scrap.)

Next morning, Herbert wired me 5 pounds, and all was well. I still remember the luxury of the bath, the shave and the enormous breakfast I bought myself before taking the train to the north.

After about a dozen attempts to enlist (I think I tried every recruiting office for miles around) I nearly gave up. I was turned down medically each time. Eventually my perseverance paid off when in August 1915 I was accepted in the Manchester University Officer Training Corps and before the end of the year I applied for a commission in the Royal Marine Light Infantry and was accepted.

By this time, I suppose I had thrown off the effects of the malaria. When I was medically examined at the Admiralty I never mentioned it and studiously avoided saying anything about any previous service except in the OTC. Of course they may have lowered their standards a little by this time as the war had taken on a much more ominous character than envisaged at the outset. Britain and her allies had suffered huge losses in the Dardanelles and on the Western (European) front. In fact most of the regular Army that started the war a year before was either wounded or dead. There were already calls for conscription in Britain at this time and it was introduced the month I started service with the Royal Marines simply because there were not enough volunteers to replace the casualties.

On January 8 1916, I reported to Forton Barracks, Gosport, resplendent in a new khaki uniform, with highly-polished Sam Browne belt and boots. At the Guardroom where my taxi paused, an enormous Sergeant gave me a cracking salute and told me to report to the Adjutant's quarters. The Adjutant, Captain Cuthbert Goode, greeted me courteously, led me over to the officer's mess and introduced me to the Senior Subaltern, Edward Bamford a tall red headed veteran of about 30 years of age. Bamford, a fine officer, greatly impressed me. As his life and career had so much influence on us all, I make no apologies for describing in detail the events surrounding him that became so much part of both my and the Royal Marines' history. Rather shy and reserved, Bamford was a born leader, and a great gentleman. He was awarded the VC at Zeebrugge in 1918, and subsequently, to the grief of the whole Corps, died of pneumonia on board HMS Cumberland when serving on the China Station, Wei Hei Wei, in 1928. His grave was in the Bubbling Road Cemetery, Shanghai which now no longer exists.

Although German U-boat operations were largely contained by 1918, they remained a serious threat to Allied shipping, particularly in the English Channel. Many enemy submarines were based at the occupied Belgian seaports of Zeebrugge and Ostend, which were both connected by canal to the inland port of Bruges, where more U-boats and destroyers were accommodated. The British Admiralty had long considered ways of neutralizing these bases but action was not taken until Vice-Admiral Sir Roger Keyes came up with a bold plan for a blockading operation. Some 75 ships, under Keyes' command took part in the raid, which began in the early hours of 23 April 1918.

A diversionary attack was mounted against the mile-long Zeebrugge mole, with 200 Royal Marines and Naval personnel being landed from the old cruiser HMS Vindictive and two requisitioned Liverpool ferries, the Daffodil II and the Iris II. The landing party was to destroy the German gun positions and blow up the magazines and installations but immediately came under heavy fire and was unable to achieve all objectives. There was partial success in this phase of the attack when the bridge connecting the mole to the shore was destroyed by an old submarine that had been packed with high explosive.

At the same time three obsolete coal-fired cruisers filled with concrete - Thetis, Intrepid and Iphigenia – steamed into the inner harbour under heavy German fire. Thetis did not reach the canal entrance, she was scuttled prematurely after hitting an obstruction and while the other two ships were sunk at its narrowest point they failed to block the channel completely as they were not positioned correctly.

After the raid the Germans claimed the attack had not achieved its objectives and that their engineers had quickly been able to clear a passage around the block ships. The Kaiser awarded bravery medals to many of the defenders, claiming the operation a German victory. This German version of events was accepted by many people, particularly those in England who had disapproved of the young Admiral Keyes' aggressive action. At that time, many senior naval officers felt that strong action against the Germans should be discouraged, since it would only provoke damaging counter attacks.

Keyes was convinced the raid had been a success and most of his supporters and allies agreed with him. The evidence seems to support his view of events. Aerial photographs taken soon afterwards showed two of the blockships in position across the mouth of the canal preventing it from being used by German submarines. It was later discovered that several German submarines and motor torpedo boats had been trapped in the canal and had remained there for the rest of the War. After the War the Liverpool Salvage Company took more than a year to clear the canal using the best of modern equipment.

Captain Bamford received one of 8 Victoria Crosses awarded for the raid. As with several World War I actions where so many officers and ranks distinguished themselves, such as 'The Six VCs Before Breakfast' won by the Lancashire Fusiliers at Gallipoli, the Royal Marine Zeebrugge VCs were awarded by ballot, whereby those involved in the action voted for the person they believed most deserved the award. The other Royal Marine VC at Zeebrugge was Sergeant Norman Finch who was selected as the non-commissioned recipient form the Corps. He was the sole survivor of the "fighting top" or machine-gun nest that provided covering fire from the Vindictive for the landing party.

Edward Bamford had already been awarded the DSO for his gallantry aboard HMS Chester at The Battle of Jutland. Bamford (by then Major) died of pneumonia in 1928 en route to Hong Kong and was buried in the English cemetery in Shanghai. A 1930's photograph in the RM Museum shows a picture of his grave and headstone but all cemeteries containing 'foreigners' were destroyed in the Cultural Revolution of the late 1960's and a shopping centre now stands on the site. No trace of the cemetery remains.

The two Liverpool ferries were to receive more fire and glory when they took part in the evacuation of Dunkirk in World War II and in recognition became Royal Daffodil II and Royal Iris II.

Although I was a very nervous, raw and extremely probationary Second Lieutenant, Bamford made me feel as though I really belonged. His example and his quiet efficiency helped to instil in me that Esprit de Corps for which the Corps of Royal Marines is so justly famous.

Forton Barracks was very crowded so I was instructed to find myself a billet and I was very lucky to find most comfortable rooms in Parham Rd, Gosport, within 200 yards of the barracks. The owner of the house was a delightful old lady whose grandson was a cadet in the Royal Australian Navy. She welcomed me warmly, treated me as one of the family, and needed a lot of persuading before she would accept the billeting allowance. Coincidentally, I later served with her grandson, then a midshipman, in HMS Agincourt in 1918.

The first morning on parade was rather shattering to us newly caught subalterns. There were eight of us, and for some reason or other I was the senior of the batch. I was instructed to fall in the "young officers" in front of the Officer's Mess, and after calling the batch to attention, report to the Adjutant.

This entailed marching almost the entire width of the parade ground in front of a whole battalion of RMLI who were fallen in for inspection prior to Colour Hoisting.

Cuthbert Goode, the Adjutant, was mounted in front of the parade, and after I had reported to him he turned and called "First Drill Gibbs!" Gibbs, a lean Warrant Officer 2nd class, standing nearby, sprang to attention, gave a cracking salute and said "Sir."

The Adjutant, in a tone that had both intent and judgment, said ominously, "Take the young officers, First Drill, and do your best to make them Royal Marine Officers."

Gibbs, "Very good Sir" turning to me with another cracking salute, "Stand the Young Officers at ease, sir, then fall in yourself on the right."

When I had done this, Gibbs, with a word of command that almost literally lifted us to attention, said "Young Officers 'shun Good morning Young Officers Young Officers stand at ease." Then in a conversational tone he went "My name is Quartermaster Sergeant Instructor of Infantry Drill Gibbs commonly known as First Drill Gibbs and don't you forget it, gentlemen don't you forget it!" And we didn't. Gibbs was our guide, mentor and friend he taught me everything from infantry drill to field training, his lectures on the history of the Royal Marines, and on Esprit de Corps were never forgotten. He obviously loved the Corps (his father and grandfather had served in it before him) and he taught us to love it too.

He instilled into us young officers the basic principle of leadership "always look after your men - your first care is their comfort and well being."

For six months we were put "through the hoop" of infantry drill, bayonet fighting, musketry, field training and physical training. Once a week we went out hunting with the Gosport and Fareham Beagles and were as fit as fleas. Our pay was 7/6d a day, out of which we had to pay 5/6d a day mess bill and yet I never felt poor. We were fed like fighting cocks, our time was fully occupied, and we had all the amusements we needed practically within the confines of barracks.

The old mess at Forton will always be dear to my memory. The ante room with its comfortable leather armchairs and enormous fireplace, the library with its hundreds of well-worn leather bound books, the pleasant breakfast room where we had all our meals except dinner and the lovely dining room. The latter was an enormous high-ceilinged room, with portraits in oils of famous Marines in the uniform of their day and a beautiful old dining table so lovingly polished by generations of Marines that you could see your reflection in the ancient mahogany.

Leading up to the dining room was a wide staircase, and opposite the dining room was the musicians' gallery where on guest nights our famous band played during dinner. On such occasions the wide folding doors of the dining room were thrown back. With the light from the enormous silver candelabra reflecting on the table, the darkness of the stairwell, and the dim lights beyond the well over the music stands in the musicians gallery the whole scene was like something out of a previous century. After we had drunk the King's health, the bandmaster would join us and take his glass of wine with the president, while the string quartet would come into the dining room, and play soft music, as the nuts, fruit and liqueurs were circulated and cigars and cigarettes lighted.

Our senior officers were some of the best men I have ever known. Widely travelled, well-read, strict disciplinarians, yet withal courteous and kindly; they all bore the stamp of the famous Corps in which they had served so many years. In those days, a Major was at least 36 years of age, a Lieutenant-Colonel over 40 - vast ages to a Subaltern of 19 as I was then. Such names as Brigadier-General Roe, our Commandant, Colonel Chichester, Colonel Lywood, Colonel Darley and Colonel Evans come to mind, amongst many others. They all entertained us youngsters in their homes and in the mess and went out of their way to help and advise us.

Colonel Chichester was a particularly fine character, who had been a great athlete in this day, but who, because I believe he had over trained and strained his heart in earlier life, was debarred from active service to his lasting grief. He was Chief Musketry Instructor at Browndown Camp, near Lee on Solent, and was one of the finest officers I have ever served under. Later, for no reason that I could think of, he used to send me most welcome parcels from Fortnum and Masons when I was in France with the 2nd Battalion Royal Marines.

My particular pal was Freddy Garnett, a lovable Irishman, who strangely enough had also come from South Africa to join the Corps. A year or two older than me, he was much more mature and sophisticated. We served together in France, were wounded in the same action, met subsequently for brief intervals in Barracks until he was demobilised in 1919 and returned to South Africa and I went out to China. I last heard of him indirectly in the 1920s, when adventurous as ever he was in trouble for poaching elephants. I wrote to the last address I knew, but the letter was returned.

After six months we were considered fit to take our place in the field, and were sent to France as reinforcement officers to the much depleted Royal Marine Brigade which as part of the famous 63rd Royal Naval Division had gone to France after the evacuation of Gallipoli.

The Royal Marine Brigade of four battalions was reduced to two battalions owing to heavy casualties. Typical of the Corps, they had to be the first ashore in raids, among the first in the main landings and the last to leave. Many of the survivors had a feeling of loss and betrayal that was shared with the Anzacs. They saw their withdrawal as forced on them by politicians rather than military commanders, they had withdrawn from positions many had died and bled for and they had abandoned the graves of their comrades.

We were among the first batch of newly-trained reinforcements and after a few strenuous days in the "Bull Ring" at Etaples joined the 2nd Royal Marine Battalion which was in billets just behind Vimy Ridge. The Battalion Commander was Colonel Hutchison, a very fine soldier, who later became Adjutant General of the Royal Marines. My Company Commander was Captain St Clair Morford, a real fire eater and a very gallant gentleman. Other names that come to mind are "Joe" Thorold, Jimmy Stokes, "Jarge" Welman and "Jerry" Weeks.

Thorold was the Battalion Bombing Officer as well as second in command of the Company, a quiet, unassuming and very brave officer. He was very musical, and a great admirer of Kipling. He knew most of the Barrack Room Ballads by heart and I believe composed music of his own to sing them to. In our dugout in the front line, in our Company mess in billets, Joe would have us all singing *Road to Mandalay, Ladies, Song of the Banjo, The Ballad of East and West* and the like. A particular favourite of the men was Soldier an' Sailor Too which was the informal anthem of the Royal Marines. I still know the words and can play most of the songs but I never heard Peter Dawson sing them to the same tunes! I particularly remember him cheering us up when the sun came out briefly after a long, cold and noisy day when there had been heavy artillery fire, some casualties and we had been digging trenches in the mud and the rain. Without preamble he just began singing..

"I've taken my fun where I've found it

I've rogued and I've ranged in my time

I've 'ad me pickin' of sweet'earts

And four of the lot was prime .."

(opening lines of "The Ladies" by Rudyard Kipling)

Alas, Jimmy Stokes, Gerry Weeks and Jarge Welman all were killed at Beaumont Hamel in November 1916. St Clair Morford was seriously wounded on a night patrol in mid-August, he was awarded an MC before this however. Morford and Welman were the only Regular Officers in the Company then, the former a "veteran" of about 28 who had been through the Gallipoli campaign with the Battalion before coming to France. When he recovered from his wounds, Morford was seconded to the Royal Flying Corps and flew for the rest of the war, being further decorated as a pilot. We met again after the war, during the "trouble" in Ireland, and again in the last war by which time he was a Major General.

"Jarge" Welman we called him "Jarge" because he looked just like a farmer with his thick set muscular body, ruddy complexion and rather slow speech - had a fund of stories, always wore a rather lugubrious expression and could tell the funniest tale without the vestige of a smile. The men loved him, he was a great companion and comrade and a great loss to us all when he was killed leading his men "over the top."

"Jimmy" Stokes was a very gallant boy (I think he was just 19) who took life and the war very seriously, and was utterly conscientious. He was religious but never obtrusively so and he always volunteered for the most dangerous jobs. He was small, compact and amazingly fit and strong. In thinking of him and all those other boys who were killed I can only say "what a waste". It was in the days when the average life of an infantry subaltern at the Front was three weeks at the most.

Knowing as many of those young men as I did in both World Wars, I cannot help thinking that this miserable world we are condemned to survive in now, with it's senseless economic, atomic, scientific and generally horrific threats to humanity would be a much better place if all that grand youth had been allowed to grow up and influence events. In others words I'm a firm believer that in any war, the best of our manhood and womanhood gets killed or irrevocably maimed first (whether mentally or physically or both). And so much discord, misery and war is in the name of religion.

Because I happened to be a rather good shot with the rifle, and also I suspect because having been a few years in South Africa they expected that as a "Colonial" I might know something of scout lore, I found myself in charge of the Battalion Scouts and Snipers. This little unit - 20 strong - was originally organised in Gallipoli by a famous Colour Sergeant (I regret that after all these years I have forgotten his name) who had led the RMLI shooting team at Bisley in pre-war days. The unit he had organised was first class, each one was a marksman, and with the exception of about three or four, had served a very hard apprenticeship as snipers in Gallipoli. They taught me a lot, and I was very proud to learn.

Most outstanding was Corporal Howard, when I met him he was a veteran of 19 with at least five years service. He went out to Gallipoli as a Bugler with the 2nd Battalion Royal Marine Light Infantry in 1915, from a boy to Private RMLI on his 18th birthday and by the time he reached France in June 1916 was a Corporal.

Howard was so typical of many of the backbone of the Corps of Royal Marines that I must tell you about him. His father and his grandfather had both reached the rank of Sergeant Major in the Corps and so did young Howard eventually. Don't tell me there is nothing in heredity! He was a marvellous shot, could move over rough ground as silently as a snake and for such a big man (he was over 6 feet tall) could make himself more invisible than anyone I've ever met. Corporal Howard was a tower of strength, he was a loyal and supportive comrade, a credit to the finest Corps in the world.

This Scout and Sniping business was, as you may imagine, a rather specialised affair In order to do his job properly, a sniper in trench warfare must have a hundred per cent concealment; otherwise the sniping post he occupies (and he himself) will only last for two shots at the most. The construction of the sniper's post is the first care. It must have the requisite field of fire, show no sign of newly-turned earth or other disturbance and there should be no unusual activity in its vicinity.

We would first select sites for sufficient posts to cover the battalion front, then try to take advantage of some object that had been visible to the enemy for some time, and make use of this object as camouflage.

For instance, there was an old ammunition box with the lid off lying on its side just in front of the trench parapet in one place. We dug through the parapet and used this box as a loophole. If one shot was fired a day from each post we were satisfied. After two days or at most three, that post would be given a rest to avoid it being spotted by the enemy through too much use. Once the enemy spotted or suspected a loophole, retribution in the form of concentrated trench mortar fire and even artillery fire was swift. We used regulation short Lee Enfield rifles fitted with Ross telescopic sights, and they were very accurate.

Just to the north of us in the Souchez sector, there was a large slag heap thrown up by a coal mine. Although this slag heap was behind the trenches held by the Welsh "Bantams," Corporal Howard and I decided that from the top of it we should be able to look right down into the enemy trenches, and shake them up thoroughly.

(At the outbreak of war, the British Army refused to accept recruits under 5ft 6in tall, and coalminers were exempt from call-up altogether. In 1914 the MP for Birkenhead, Alfred Bigland, pressed the War Office for permission to form a battalion of men who were under regulation size but otherwise fit for service. Within a few days, some 3,000 men had volunteered, many of whom had previously been rejected as being under height. The original men were formed into the 1st and 2nd Birkenhead Battalions of the Cheshire regiment, later redesignated the 15th and 16th Battalions. Other regiments such as the Welsh Regiment, Lancashire Fusiliers, West Yorkshires, Royal Scots, and most famously the Highland Light Infantry, similarly recruited "bantams". Many of the recruits were miners who were particularly valuable as tunnellers and trench builders. Eventually these bantam units were formed into the 35th Division. Another, the 40th, had a mixture of bantam and regulation units, although it is generally recognised as a bantam Division. The bantams were very popular at home, and were often featured in the press. However, by the end of 1916, it was found that the general fitness and condition of men volunteering as bantams was no longer up to the standard required. It is worth noting that the recruiting posters for the Royal Naval Division in 1915 stipulated 5ft3in as a minimum height.)

After blacking our faces and hands, we climbed the slag heap from the rear one night, and when dawn broke were positioned on top of the eastern slope so we could look down into the enemy lines with ease. They were not more than three to four hundred yards away and we were over 100 feet up.

We watched the Germans come to dawn "stand to" and realised that in this particular sector at least, the front line trenches were only manned by a series of sentries placed about 75 to 100 yards apart - we'd spotted three of them by the glow of their cigarettes before dawn broke. All that happened at "stand to" was that their daytime reliefs were marched up and for about half an hour each sentry post was double manned. The main body of troops "stood to" in the support trenches. We carefully marked the positions of these sentries on our map and this information was exceedingly valuable in subsequent raids we carried out.

By some steady sniping we then managed to completely disorganise the Huns' breakfast. Eventually we were spotted and just managed to slide and scramble down the rear of the slag heap without being hit by the heavy barrage the enemy concentrated on it.

As we fell into a trench behind the slag heap we were greeted by the irate Colonel of the Welsh Battalion, Lt Colonel C.J.Wilkie. He was justifiably angry because we had not asked his permission to snipe in his sector, in fact we'd asked nobody's permission. I got another "Raspberry" from my own Colonel but when our scouting information was produced I was a little more popular, at least with my own Colonel. In retrospect, it was strange that in the training we'd received nobody had seen fit to warn us that sniping brought retaliatory consequences, particularly for troops other than ourselves.

I must also mention two other friends of mine; Privates Taylor and Wilkinson. Taylor was my MOA, Marine Officer's Attendant. He was a tough, stocky chap who could turn a hot appetising meal out of a tin of "bully" and a few "hard tack" biscuits under the most impossible conditions, and the speed with which he could organise a hot Dixie of tea (usually well-laced with rum) when we came back cold and wet and muddy from a patrol in "no man's land" was a miracle.

Wilkinson was my "Runner" and on most occasions my shadow. He was always on hand ready to take urgent reports, either to Company or Battalion Headquarters, and had an uncanny way of getting there and back in spite of shelling, trench mortar fire and sniping.

Although he was wounded by the same shell that laid me out at Beaumont Hamel, we were to meet again many years later. After this period of time, details are rather hazy (I never kept a diary, more's the pity) but amidst all the mud, wet and discomfort that seemed to be the main part of our existence in that period I have the undying memory of real comradeship, loyalty and bravery that was all around me, and above all, the esprit de corps that inspired everyone.

A large percentage of the battalion were veterans of the actions at Antwerp and Ostende in 1914, and afterwards Gallipoli (February-April 1915). When the Germans first moved into Belgium at the outbreak of war their prime objectives were the ports of Ostende and Antwerp. A formidable force of five divisions and 173 guns including 'Big Bertha' (a giant 420mm howitzer mounted on a railway wagon) laid siege to the old fortress city of Antwerp. To assist the Belgians, an immediate force of 2000 Royal Marines was sent to Antwerp and this was followed up by sending the ill-prepared but battle-keen Royal Naval Division of 4000 men to Ostende. As Belgium surrendered to the overwhelming forces of Germany on October 10, they were too late to have anything but a delaying action which did, however, gain a valuable few days for the British forces to move to Flanders and set up their positions in France. Many of the my Battalion were Regulars and many were pensioners who had been recalled to the Corps on the outbreak of war. Having served with them, I know exactly what the expression "seasoned troops" really means.

I learned more about the essentials of leadership in those days than ever since, not only from my senior officers, but from many a humble private of Marines. As for the non-commissioned officers, they were incomparable, I cannot say more.

When we first arrived in France we started in the support trenches and our training involved dispersal among other companies of regiments that had been there for several months. By mid-July 1916 the Royal Naval Division was relieving the front line trenches and we spent from four days to a week at the front before being relieved (usually by the 1st Royal Marine Battalion). By this time the summer offensive had begun. Looking back, I am surprised at how astonishingly keen and optimistic we still were at that time. We knew that there had been some setbbacks such as the Newfouundland Regiment losing nearly 700 men and officers from a regiment of 800 in an abortive attempt at taking Beaumont Hamel on the first two days in July. We also heard that the New Zealanders and Australians who had been with the naval division at Gallipoli had also been sent forward with many losses. As we heard later, the July 1916 action which opened the Battle of the Somme had cost 58000 casualties with very little gain. Yet we never lost the belief that we would eventually carry the day.

We were suffering minor casualties on a daily basis in the various scouting raids being carried out. Often, platoons would be sent forward to replace barbed wire cut by mortar fire and as this involved getting out into No Man's Land, there was a risk of being caught by machinegun or mortar fire. Some days we huddled in the bottom of our trenches as the enemy probed with artillery fire and our artillery fired back. A typical few days might bring no casualties but then a patrol of 8 men would fail to return from a night raid and if we were lucky they would reappear a day late but often with someone missing or killed. Sometimes, nobody returned. Occasionally we saw aircraft, either ours or theirs and I do recall thinking that up there was a better place than down where we were. On a few occasions we watched the aircraft duel and we saw a couple of machines fall but they were too far away for us to see who they were or investigate.

When we were relieved at the Front, there would follow a few unreal days of relative quiet but our was time taken up with with close order drill, inspection of arms, bayonet practice and occasionally the chance to clean and bath. (Hot baths were rare.) Then we would go back out to repairing trenches, repairing roads, laying wire and sometimes laying out gas cylinders ready for an attack.

Of course while this was going on, our side was also shelling the opposite lines, cutting their barbed wire with mortars and generally trying to make the enemy more uncomfortable than we were.

There was an incident on one scouting mission that has haunted me all of my life since. Not continuously, but it has come back as a recurring dream whenever I have been feverish from an illness and the events resurfaced as a sharp-focus memory in the second war when German tactics seemed particularly brutal during the Battle of Malta. I was an unobserved witness in a forward trench when a wounded Prussian officer asked one of my marines for a drink of water. The marine propped his rifle against the side of the trench and went to unfasten his waterbottle in what was a humane and sympathetic response to an injured and apparently non-combatant victim. As the marine held the bottle up to the officers lips, the Hun produced a revolver from behind his back and shot my man dead, right in the forehead. I saw red, there is no other way to describe it. Immediately after that I had no clear recollection of the past few seconds but I had the marine's rifle with fixed and bloody bayonet in my hands and the German too was dead and a nasty sight. That whole scene has replayed in my nightmares and I am not sure which is worse - the look of disbelief and horror on the marines face, or my own feeling of absolute impotence at being unable to stop the deaths. I cannot say I was sorry for killing the German. If the wind was from the north or north-east we would be on gas alert and would often don gas helmets. That was always a miserable feeling, breathing was restricted, vision was impaired and I wondered just how I would deal with a real gas attack. Would I gain anything if I tried to hold my breath or would it be best to gulp it in and get it over?

Sadly, because the enemy was using gas against us, we often retaliated in kind. There was one period in August or September where we spent several days on and off gas alert and it culminated in our letting gas go within a couple of hours of attending divine service as the wind was favourable. This resulted in a heavy German artillery bombardment of our front and second lines. We lost an officer and eight men. The next morning we were again under trench mortar and howitzer attack as we were relieved by the 1st Battalion RMLI. Another officer and 10 men wounded. Back in billets a day or two later and Joe Thorold was singing Kipling's "In the Neolithic Age".

'But my Totem saw the shame; from his ridgepole shrine he came,
And he told me in a vision of the night:-
'There are five and forty ways
Of constructing tribal lays
And-every-single-one-of them-is-right'

During the last week of September we spent several days practising advancing from trenches in waves. The first and second waves attacked a line (represented by one company in a defensive line), the third wave then advanced and held that position until the next two waves came up and moved through to the next advance point. Put simply, the waves of troops leapfrogged each other.

This idea was the result of our learning from previous failures at the Somme. In the early advances, the front line took an objective and then pushed forward without fully clearing the captured area with the result that the enemy could come out of their dugouts in the uncleared trenches and shoot the advancing troops in the back. Or worse, they pushed our troops forward into machinegun fire.

We also developed a new way of utilising artillery support. There was a softening up bombardment as before, but we infantry were to advance close behind i.e. within 50 yards of a creeping barrage in the hope of catching the Germans with their heads still down. In the earlier system the artillery tended to increase their range to well beyond the advancing troops and the Germans who were generally dug in deeper than imagined had time to come out and catch us in the open with machinegun fire. This new plan did of course rely on good communication and accurate artillery and I think the major problems sometimes experienced still were a result of a breakdown in this area. One of the new things we tried was signal communication with an observation aeroplane – a signal was taken in from us by an observer in an aeroplane then passed on to the 63rd Royal Naval Division HQ. As the signalling was visual we did not have a lot of confidence in using the system in battle conditions.

In the aftermath of the huge loss of life in the trenches of World War I it is often suggested that there was little regard for life. At the field level where we were, all our officers took the casualties very much to heart and all actions were painstakingly analysed in their aftermath. And remember, we were fighting a determined and well-equipped foe with well-prepared defences.

On the night of the October 12, 1916, senior staff officers of the division visited the trench system east of Colincamps. A German 5.9 inch shell (15cm Krupps) landed amongst them, decapitating Major E.F.P. Sketchley DSO RMLI and severely wounding our commander, Major-General Sir Archibald Paris in his back and left leg, which was later amputated. A firing party of 200 Marines from the 1st Battalion Royal Marines attended the funeral of Major Sketchley at Forceville Military Cemetery the next day. The whole of our division was greatly saddened by these two casualties.

The importance of General Paris to us was well chronicled by Douglas Jerrold in *The Royal Naval Division* published in 1923 (Hutchinson):

"General Paris had been with the Naval Division since the day when it was first concentrated in Antwerp. He had commanded them in their most unfortunate as well as in their most successful adventures, and he had never failed them. But he was something more, in the eyes of the Division, than a respected commander: he was an institution. He was the last relic of the days when the Division had fought under orders from the Admiralty: he was the last bulwark between the Division and the Army. And he was a very effective one. He was recognized by those in authority as an officer of pre-eminent caution and prudence. So long as he remained, there would be no attempt to interfere with the internal organization, which meant so largely the fighting efficiency of the Division. It was not, perhaps, realized at the time, how much the Division owed to General Paris in this respect, though it did not take them long to learn it. If he had never erred on the side of over-enthusiastic praises, he had shown his unswerving confidence in the capacity of the Division to do credit to itself as a fighting force, by putting no limit on promotion from within the Division, and by leaving to his subordinate commanders a reasonably free hand in the discharge of their responsibilities. The result had been that it had gathered strength from one reorganization to another, and yet had always preserved its identity."

Much to our disgust, General Paris, who obviously been a father figure to us all, was replaced by Major-General Cameron Shute, an Army commander with no feel for the naval traditions and spirit of the Royal Naval Division. One of his first directives was that naval ranks and insignia be replaced with the Army equivalent. A.P.Herbert later wrote a very unflattering poem about Shute. It was a song that Joe Thorold would have enjoyed. The commander inspected the division for the first time after a period of heavy rain and much discomfort and wrote an extremely critical report about the general state of the naval men. Herbert's poem was called simply "Schultz."

"The General inspecting the trenches
exclaimed with a horrified shout,
I refuse to command a Division

Which leaves excreta about.
And certain responsible critics
Made haste to reply to his words
Observing that his Staff advisers
Consisted entirely of turds.
But nobody took any notice
No one was prepared to refute,
That the presence of shit was congenial
Compared with the presence of Shute.
For shit may be shot at odd corners
And paper supplied there to suit,
But a shit would be shot without mourners
If somebody shot that shit Shute."

If someone had written such about one of our own officers, we would have been horrified and anyone singing such a song would have been on charge, but because it was about an Army man it was different. Later, so I'm told, Major General Shute came to respect the Royal Naval division and spoke of them with fondness and pride.

After about five months of static trench warfare, enlivened by trench raids, gas alarms, shelling and sniping, we went south to the Battle of the Somme, or more exactly the planned Battle of Ancre. (As Ancre is French for Anchor, it seemed then a fitting battleground for Royal Marines and the Royal Naval Division as a whole).

The entire area around the Ancre valley and particularly the well-planned and ably-manned fortifications at Beaumont Hamel had withstood all attempts by the British to take it, and it was only after the fall of the Thiepval Ridge on September 28th that another attack could be launched with any degree of real confidence.

The Battle of Thiepval Ridge was the first large offensive mounted by the British Reserve Army of Lieutenant General Hubert Gough during the Battle of the Somme. Beginning on September 26, the battle saw the capture of the German fortress of Thiepval which had been an objective on July 1, 1916. Also overrun and captured was the redoubt of Mouquet Farm by the 11th (Northern) Division, which had been attacked without success in August and September by Australian, and later Canadian, divisions. On the right flank of the Reserve Army, the Canadian Corps advanced about 1,000 yards north from Courcelette.

This British push ended on September 28 with the capture of the Schwaben Redoubt, north of Thiepval, another first day objective that had been the site of fierce fighting by the 36th (Ulster) Division. Later we would realise that about five square miles of territory had been gained for the loss of some 12,500 lives. General Gough was keen to continue the pressure on the German defences and so the Battle of the Ancre was planned. We received our first orders for the attack on October 23 and the plan called for us to support the 1st Royal Marine Battalion and alongside us, the

Anson Battalion of the RN division would support Howe Battalion. Behind us were the Hood and Hawke Divisions and behind them Nelson and Drake Divisions. Backing all that would come the Dublin Fusiliers and the Bedfords with the Honourable Artillery Company and the 7th Royal Fusiliers in the final wave. Three other divisions including the 51st Highlanders were to attack to the north and there was to be an attack by the 19th Division towards the south of the Ancre. A further division would be held in reserve and used where needed.

On October 28, the importance of the coming battle was underlined when the Commander in Chief, General Sir Douglas Haig visited the battalion. It was a surprise for most of us, we had just moved from waterlogged billets into a slightly drier area when we were fallen in as sections outside our bivouacs for the general's inspection.

The weather was appalling when we marched up to the battle trenches and we then had to dig attack trenches and also a set of jumping-off trenches at right angles to the main line of attack to make sure the troops did not veer off course. Made worse by the heavy rain, the ground was already muddy due to the high water-table from the River Ancre. These factors (and I believe lack of supplies) meant several postponements of the original attack date but on November 10 we were told it was "W" day which meant the attack was on November 13 ("Z" day). Our artillery had been maintaining a series of "softening up" barrages since November 6.

There was talk that tanks were to be in support but probably due to the conditions, there was no sign of these semi-secret weapons. (I read later that three tanks did come into the action on November 15. Although they became bogged well short of their proposed objective, they were instrumental in taking out two particular German strongpoints which initially pinned the RMLI down during the advance.)

On the morning of November 12 we were given an extra days rations, flares, bombs, 4 sandbags each, and extra ammunition. The company commanders issued the final orders for attack at briefings in the afternoon. After checking all our equipment we were all moved to our jumping-off positions by 2030. The Germans appeared to realise something was planned - they shelled our frontline and communications trenches heavily and there were about 70 casualties overnight.

Our orders were to fix bayonets in the dark and have all men ready for attack at 0450 on the morning of the 13th– we were in clear view of the Germans on the ridge ahead and obviously did not want the sunlight glinting on hundreds of bayonets to give our game away. As it happened we need not have worried, the day dawned with a thick mist obscuring our positions as our artillery started the opening barrage. The Germans replied by shelling No Man's Land and the support trenches and they swept the whole area in front of us with machinegun fire.

Perhaps luckily, I have only a few hazy recollections of the action from then on. Our first Battlion went over the top as planned at 0545. (Immediately following the explosion of a 30,000lb mine under the Hawthorne Ridge to the north of us.) The land sloped gently down to the German trenches which were the first objective but it was very muddy and pocketed with shell holes which hindered any chance of a fast charge. I was laid out by artillery fire within seconds of getting into the open, I don't believe I even made it to our front wire. (Apparently I was buried by a blast that killed several of my comrades.) Later reports showed that all of our first battalion commanders and most of their officers had been killed before reaching the German lines and most of our casualties occurred in the open just beyond our own wire. With few officers left, the responsibility of command passed down to the NCO's with the worst of the fighting still ahead. That the attack continued without faltering demonstrated the toughness and discipline of the Corps and showed what leadership from the front meant (and cost). The 1st Battalion took the worst fire from the German trenches and machineguns but in the 2nd Battalion we were caught in the open as the artillery barrage intensified. History shows that the Hood and Drake Battalions of the Royal Naval Division achieved their objectives in taking the German front lines on the right of us but the Hawke and Nelson Battalions were shelled and machine-gunned to near oblivion from a strongpoint unknown in our planning. Like so many of the villages occupied by the Germans, all the houses and visible structures had been obliterated by artillery fire but hundreds of cellars remained and it was from these the enemy seemed so often to emerge unscathed as soon as the barrage stopped.

We did however, achieve our objective. Both the Royal Naval Division and the 51st Highlanders succeeded where others had tried and lost and despite the fearful losses achieved an important victory. At the end of the battle our two RM battalions had only their commanders (Lt Colonels Cartwright and Hutchison) and two other officers left. Recent figures put the dead at 169 other ranks and 13 officers with 410 other ranks and 22 officers wounded – or in broad terms, 375 returned from a strength of about 980 starting the battle.

It was in this action that Colonel Bernard Freyberg, in command of Howe Battalion, Royal Naval Division, was awarded the Victoria Cross for his personal leadership and bravery. While wounded several times and under fire he continued to lead his and two other battalions to the final objective, Beaucourt, where the Germans surrendered in hundreds.

Most of the dead from the action have no known grave and are commemorated on the Thiepval memorial with others buried in cemeteries at Ancre, Hamel and Serre and areas around the battlefield. Although I was wounded in those first moments, I was not in fact officially reported injured for another 21 days, on December 6. I cannot imagine what the scene on the battlefield must have been like for the medical orderlies and stretcher bearers but I know we lost eight of our medical unit who were killed trying to help the wounded.

(Although I can state with certainty that I was wounded on November 13, it was not until December 6 that my unit records me as "officially declared wounded". Like so many others I was simply "missing in action" in the meantime – a term that meant killed but not identified for a sad majority of our men. In the few days following our action a further 5000 men were lost for little gain – post-war figures put the overall losses at Beaumont Hamel at 10,000 plus and our "victory" was in fact the final major act in the Battle of the Somme.)

The next thing I knew was that I was in a Casualty Clearing Station. Apparently I had been dug out of the mud "with a severe wound as the result of a shell explosion." I had a shrapnel wound in my lower back which had been cleaned and strapped (an orderly cheerfully told me I had a hole "yer could put your fist right in" that had just missed my spine). In bouts of going in and out of consciousness while being probed and examined I heard someone say "This poor chap won't be walking again." I couldn't move my arms or legs and I lay there in a state of stunned paralysis but with frighteningly clear thoughts about what those words might mean. Eventually, despite very severe pain, I managed to wriggle my toes on both feet. I was going to see if I could drag myself to the latrine but a medical officer saw me try to move and came over and restrained me. He gave me an injection and I passed out again. My next clear memory is of being in a hospital train, being fed a delicious chicken broth by a lovely girl in a nurse's uniform.

I was in the top bunk and had finished my soup when I heard curses coming from the lower bunk. I couldn't move sufficiently to look over the edge so I called out "What's the trouble?"

"Trouble!" came the reply "You'd be in trouble if you had to try to eat lying on your tummy. A blasted sniper literally caught me bending and now I've got five holes in my backside."

This caused a chuckle from all in hearing who were not too ill to appreciate it.

I next woke in the hospital in what had been the Casino Palace Hotel at Vimereux and shared a room with an army doctor recovered from his wounds who was allowed out of bed. Bless him, he looked after me and even brought me bedpans when there was no response to my bell because the hospital was so overwhelmed with the number of wounded and dying.

I am rather hazy about this period, because there was a certain amount of pain and the dope I was given to dull it may have fogged my memory. However, just before Christmas I was transhipped across the Channel in a hospital ship, and found myself in a hospital train on its way north from Dover. Some time in the night there was an air raid, Zeppelins we presumed and the train was held up for a couple of hours or so. Anti aircraft fire could be heard in the distance, but it was so far away that none of us patients were at all concerned after the hell we'd just come from.

We eventually arrived in Manchester and were taken by ambulance to a hospital in Withington. To my astonishment, my brother Herbert was at the station in Manchester to greet me and to see me off in the ambulance. Goodness knows how he found out that I was arriving at that particular place and time. In due course I was sent home on sick leave (my father and mother had by then returned to England and were also living in Bramhall). Eventually, early in 1917, I was ordered to report for light duty to the Royal Marine depot at Blandford, where the training battalion was stationed.

It was bitterly cold when I arrived, with four inches of snow on the ground. I didn't last long at Blandford. Whether it was because of the cold or because the duty wasn't light enough I don't know, but I passed out when supervising musketry training on the range one day, so the medical officer ordered me back to Forton Barracks, Gosport for really light duty.

The highlight of this transfer was that I acquired as my servant, Private Stevens, who remained with me until the end of the war. Stevens was a pensioner who retired a month or two before war broke out, and was recalled to the colours almost immediately. He served with the RM Brigade at Antwerp and after recovering from wounds received there, was posted to the Reserve Battalion. A burly Hampshireman, Stevens was a first class Marine, and a most loyal attendant. I held him in the highest esteem and affection. He was quite a character with a tremendous capacity for beer. I once asked him how many pints he consumed in one of his weekly sessions and his reply was "twenty five before I lost count, sir!" Of course in those days beer was, I think, only 3d a pint in the canteen. Stevens and I served together continuously until the end of the war. I have never known a more loyal, efficient and resourceful person and we became great friends.

Just about this time I met another well known personality Major Thomas Orde Lees who had been with Shackleton to the Antarctic as the motor sleigh expert and stores officer. His diary is regarded as the most reliable and detailed account of the 1914-16 expedition, especially when recounting their epic small-boat voyage to Elephant Island after Endurance was trapped in the Antarctic ice and the subsequent stranding until Shackleton returned in a rescue ship. Orde Lees returned to civilisation to find it in the middle of a war. Because he had been away from the Corps for so long, he was apparently considered to be out of date, and was relegated to training duties.

One of his less military accomplishments was to ride a bicycle balanced only on its back wheel while he dismantled the front forks and handle bars and then assembled them again. The story went that when he was a subaltern, Queen Victoria had insisted on seeing his trick cycling performance. (This apparently made him very unpopular with the other officers of the Corps – such behaviour was totally unbecoming of an officer.) He actually took a bicycle with him on the Shackleton expedition. "My greatest loss with Shackleton was having to leave my bicycle behind," he told me one evening at dinner. "It was the best Rudge-Whitworth that ever lived."

He was also a fine horseman, and frequently took me out hacking with him when we could borrow horses from a nearby remount depot. There is a saying that "the horse is the friend of man and the enemy of the Marine Officer." Needless to say I was a typical Marine officer, but I had a lot of fun when I went hacking with Major Orde-Lees between falls! I was surprised to read in later accounts of the Shackleton expedition that he was considered stand-offish and an outsider. He certainly was not like that with me or any of us at the barracks. Not long after I last saw him, he managed to get himself to the Western Front with the Balloon Service. He then transferred to the Royal Flying Corps and was one of the pioneers of parachute jumping, in fact it was through his efforts that pilots in the RAF were eventually allowed parachutes. Initially, the non-flying commanders thought that pilots should not have any means of abandoning their aircraft – they should go "down with the ship."

After the war, he became involved in teaching women to jump from aircraft in a newspaper-sponsored scheme. This did not endear him to the high command and he was pressured to resign from the service (by then the Royal Air Force). His enthusiasm for parachutes saw him eventually teaching parachute jumping to the fledgling Japanese Air Force as a member of the British Naval Air Mission in the early 1920's. (He stayed in Tokyo until 1941, by then he had spent nearly 20 years reading English news on Japanese radio. When war was imminent, he and his family were evacuated to New Zealand. Sadly, I was unaware of these last facts when I was working for the Civil Aviation department in Wellington in the mid-1950's, Thomas and I probably walked past each other regularly without knowing it.)

There is another fine officer who comes to mind Major Dave Gowney quite a character who had risen from the ranks, had served in Gallipoli and France, and at this time was Adjutant of the Portsmouth Division RMLI.

We all loved Dave, in spite of, or perhaps because of, the way he used to "chase us around the parade ground." He was a superb trainer, training the football team, the regimental Field Gun team, and the tug of war team. There wasn't a single sporting activity in the division that he did not take part in, in spite of the fact that he must have been well over 50 at the time.

They were happy, strenuous days during which I rapidly recovered fitness, but unfortunately not fit enough to pass the Royal Flying Corps medical tests. One at least two occasions, the examination seemed to be going fine until the doctor saw he scar in my back. However, I had several friends in the RFC at the School of Special Flying, Gosport and after much persuasion managed to secure a flight.

The flying training base was commanded by the famous Colonel Robert Smith Barry and of course the Gosport system of flying training instruction he evolved at that time is still the basis of flying training to this day. In this system, one instructor would stay with a particular group of students throughout primary flight training and the training stages were overlapped. The instructor had a 'Gosport tube' – a simple tube based on the traditional naval voice-pipe - to enable him to talk to the student.

I had my first flight with Vernon Castle as my pilot in an old Bleriot monoplane not much different from the machine used by Bleriot to make the first flight of the English

Channel in July 1909. In the passenger's seat I was exposed to all the winds of heaven, because the fabric covering on the fuselage stopped at the back of the pilot's seat and my bucket seat merely had struts and wires around it. I was thrilled of course, and even this short half hour's flight whetted my appetite for more. In sailing, I had always loved the feeling of being accelerated by the wind. Here, in an aeroplane, we were riding on the wind and you could feel the very essence of it.

Vernon Castle and his wife, Irene, became famous before the war as probably the first exponents of exhibition ballroom dancing and they were among the first to make a successful career of it. They invented the foxtrot and popularized a graceful yet energetic style of dancing that made them equally famous and loved on both sides of the Atlantic. Vernon was a delightful, quiet and modest type, extremely good looking, very fit and a magnificent pilot. He was unfortunately killed later in the war (February 1918) in a flying accident at Benbrook Field near Fort Worth, Texas, where he was teaching American air force pilots combat flying.

My enthusiasm at that first flight lead to a second flight in a BE2C (BE stands for Bleriot Experimental) which had dual controls. And then, very unofficially, I was taught to fly. I spent all the leave time I could get, every Saturday afternoon and Sunday at the aerodrome at Gosport (called Fort Grange in those days).

Fort Grange was a fascinating and interesting place for me and it was to become very familiar in the years to come. In those days the officers' and other ranks' accommodation was in the old stone fort, a relic of the post-Napoleonic French invasion scares of the 1850's. There were in fact two old forts, Fort Grange and Fort Rowney, about a mile apart with the aerodrome to the west of them. Each fort had officers', NCO's and other ranks' quarters which had obviously changed very little from the 1850's. Being totally underground, they were very damp, but with electric light and large fires, the quarters had a charm of their own. The dining room and ante room were rather like a section of the underground railway in London, but with windows at each end.

(Between 1853 and 1863 five forts with supporting batteries of guns were built on the western side of Gosport to protect Portsmouth harbour from any invasion force attacking from the land. Disguised by earth and grass banks, the forts had circular keeps and 83 guns each and were protected by moats, although Fort Grange's moat has been filled in. The forts, along with the Portsdown forts and a number of others were successors to the Martello Towers, which were fortified towers built in scores along the south coast of England in response to the threat of an invasion by Emperor Napoleon in 1802.)

In World War II when Hitler and the Germans again prompted a similar fear of invasion, forts had of course been replaced by fighter squadrons of the Royal Air Force and Gosport's aerodrome among others was back in service as part of a defensive line. During the time I was learning to fly, one of the RFC pilots had an amazing escape when he flew into one of two very high wireless masts near Portchester at the back of Whale Island. The pilot remained in his cockpit with the engine of his aircraft wedged into the girders very near the top of the mast, some 200 feet from the ground. Eventually a very stout-hearted sailor climbed the mast and brought the pilot down, a feat worthy of the sailing-ship seamen of old and one that would test even the most experienced steeplejack. I did not see the actual rescue, but I saw the remains of the aircraft at the top of the mast. I never heard how they got the aircraft down. The crash was so typical of the vagaries of flying in those days; the pilot had a headwind at the time of the accident so his speed of impact would only have been a few miles an hour otherwise the collision would have killed him. Being in a light and relatively delicate machine you were very much at the mercy of wind gusts - and this was still before service aircraft carried parachutes.

Chapter 2

A Fleet Surrender

Pride goes before a bad landing, or maybe the word was getting around that young Woodhall was having too much fun on his time off. Whatever the cause, my illicit flying training came to an abrupt halt when in August 1917 I was ordered to join HMS Cardiff, a newly completed C Class Light Cruiser commissioning at Fairfield's yard in Glasgow.

At short notice, I took over my detachment of about 35 Royal Marines, marched behind the Portsmouth Divisional Band to the harbour ferry and crossed to the Portsmouth Harbour Station. There, to my astonishment, the rest of the ship's company was added to my command - about 350 seamen and stoker ratings. I was given a veritable sheaf of documents and told that I was responsible for the safe arrival of the whole ship's company at the other end of the British Isles.

The only other officer was a young Surgeon-Lieutenant. Luckily we were sent by our own special train and meals for the whole journey had been ordered at pre-arranged railway refreshment rooms at stations en route.

As sailors will, several of the ship's company managed to lay in an assortment of alcohol at these stops with the result that five of the party had to be practically carried on board when we arrived at our new ship. Expecting a reprimand for allowing this to happen, I found to my relief that I was given quite a good mark for not losing any of my charges en route.

Unfortunately I had a very short stay on HMS Cardiff because it was decided that she should be the flagship of her cruiser squadron. This meant that her Marine Officer had to be at least a Captain so I was relieved by the Squadron's Marine Officer and I returned to Forton Barracks accompanied of course, by my faithful batman, Stevens.

We were almost immediately posted to Stromness, one of the coastal batteries defending the entrance to the naval base at Scapa Flow in the Orkney Islands off the northern coast of Scotland. Once again, we had to travel almost the entire length of Britain by train – for Marines we seemed to have developed an uncommon affinity for railways.

Our emplacement was on Hoy Sound about a mile outside Stromness, sited on high ground which covered this western approach to the fleet anchorage. It was a bleak spot and most of our energies were devoted to keeping the men and ourselves fit when not occupied by watch keeping. Apart from normal gun drill, a certain amount of field training, musketry, and manning the guns and the Battery Commander's Post, we played a lot of soccer, staged our own little concerts and did a lot of gardening in our spare time. The potatoes from our gardens saved us from near starvation that bitter winter of 1917-18 when we were completely cut off from ration supplies for nearly three weeks by snow and almost continuous blizzards. Early in the New Year of 1918, Stevens and I were sent back to Forton Barracks because I was posted to a naval gunnery course at HMS Excellent on Whale Island and a torpedo course at nearby HMS Vernon.

I believe the Naval Gunnery School is very little changed since those days. Of course, there must be tremendous differences in the training given, but the lay out of HMS Excellent when I last saw it from the air in 1944 seemed very little changed since 1918.

But the HMS Vernon I knew ceased to exist. The torpedo and electrical school, still known as HMS Vernon, became a shore establishment at Gosport on the west side of Portsmouth Harbour. In 1918, HMS Vernon was in fact three ships, three old line of battle ship hulks, moored head to stern in Portsmouth harbour. The hulks were finally replaced in the early 1920's.

I cannot help feeling regret at the passing of those sailing ship hulks with their lovely tarry smells, their massive low deck beams and well-scrubbed teak decks. When I first explored the old ships I half expected to meet pigtailed sailors dressed in the rig of Nelson's day, in spite of the fact that the 'tween decks and gun decks had been turned into lecture rooms, torpedo and electrical workshops and engine rooms containing the most modern generating plant.

Our course in gunnery in HMS Excellent was strenuous in the extreme. Every movement was carried out at the double. Being wartime, we had to study hard to absorb the instruction which was compressed into a much shorter time-frame than afforded in peace time.

As a result of hard cramming, I passed out of the courses in Gunnery and Torpedo with high marks, much to my own astonishment. To my further gratification, I was granted a permanent commission in the Corps. (Gaining the permanent commission was a real achievement for me. Since being wounded off the battlefield of France and the subsequent collapse at Blandford I felt there was something I had to prove, if only to myself.)

In June 1918 I was appointed to HMS Agincourt and after yet another train journey the length of Britain I duly reported on board the ship back at the naval base of Scapa Flow. The story of the Agincourt with its tragic-comic political intrigues and possible results on history and humanity would make a great plot for a Shakespearean epic, or perhaps a Gilbert and Sullivan musical.

Argentina, Chile and Brazil had been locked in an arms race since the turn of the century, a race based on simple pride rather than any territorial ambitions or insecurity. Battleships were the ultimate status symbol of power and national prestige. After a series of acquisitions by all parties, Brazil finally reached the stage where two dreadnoughts were under construction in Britain but they had already been trumped by Argentina ordering bigger, more powerful battleships from the United States. So the Brazilian Naval Minister, Admiral Alexandrino de Alencar decided his country must have something bigger still – he wanted a fast battleship armed with twelve 14-inch guns, fourteen 6-inch guns and fourteen 4-inch guns. The contract was won by Armstong Whitworth of Newcastle who were already building Brazil's previously-ordered battleships. Work started in October 1911 on the Rio de Janeiro, at that stage simply known as Design 690 and with a three-year delivery date. Tyneside workers could look forward to full employment for at least that period. The contract did have a slight hook that none at the builders' had foreseen as a problem – it stated that the new Brazilian government would have to ratify the contract under a new Navy Minister, Admiral Marques Leao. And while Armstrong Whitworth had been finalising the design for the Rio de Janeiro, Leao had been touring Germany where the armament company Krupps, knowing about the escape clause, embarked on a systematic campaign to lure the contract away from Armstrongs. One of Krupps' key arguments was that their 12-inch naval gun could penetrate any armour known, so why waste money on 14-inch guns? They then produced a plan for three scaled-down battleships with 12 –inch guns which would be far cheaper to build and arm and also maintain. Krupp's final persuasive effort was arranging for the Brazilian admiral to have an audience with Kaiser Wilhelm who was, of course, enthusiastic in his endorsement.

After taking office as Navy Minister, Leao delayed ratification of the British contract and unveiled the Krupps' designs to his government. In response to this disastrous news, Armstrong Whitworth immediately sent their chief designer, Tennyson d'Eyncourt, with hastily drawn-up new designs for various ships smaller than the original 31,600 ton Design 690 and with weaponry ranging from 13.5inch to 16-inch guns. After discussions with Leao, d'Eyncourt reaised that the cost and efficiency of the 12-inch guns were an important factor but that the new naval minister was still very keen for Brazil to have the world's biggest battleship. In an extraordinary overnight feat both of naval architecture and salesmanship, d'Eyncourt worked up a new design based on a lengthened hull of Design 690 but with no fewer than fourteen 12-inch guns as the main armament and twenty 6-inch guns as a secondary armament. This meant that for several hundred thousand pounds less than the original Armstrong ship, Brazil would have a vessel with the most main and secondary guns and would also be the world's largest battleship in displacement and length. The contract was signed and Design 690A was born. Now Newcastle could really celebrate – more construction workers were hired from all over Britain and overtime and nightshifts were the order of the day because the Big Battleship, as she was now nicknamed, was still due for completion in 1913.

When a British company smuggled rubber trees out of Brazil in the 19th century there was little idea of the consequence. The trees were cultivated at Kew Gardens and eventually transferred to Malaya where they flourished with the result that in 1912 Brazil lost its international monopoly on rubber.

However, ignoring the economic problems at home, a large delegation of Brazilian dignitaries came to England and were in Newcastle for the christening and launching of the Rio de Janeiro on the scheduled date, January 22, 1913. But within six months, the British-owned rubber plantations in Malaya effectively bankrupted Brazil, resulting in the great but unfinished battleship being auctioned to the world with a reserve price of almost 3 million pounds.

Meanwhile, back in the Mediterranean, Turkey after losing the Balkans war in 1912, was still posturing with Greece over the Aegean Islands – an obvious arena for battleships. With British naval experts advising both sides, Turkey took the advice of Rear Admiral Sir Douglas Gamble and on December 29, 1913, became the proud owners of Sultan Osman I, the largest battleship in the world, known formerly as the Rio de Janeiro. Greece immediately ordered two dreadnoughts from France (a battlecruiser was already under construction in Germany) but as a stopgap bought two older battleships from the United States.

Back in Newcastle, 900 men had been laid off in August 1913 and the unfinished hull 960A had earned the new nickname of HMS Rust for obvious reasons. But in January 1914 employment again boomed as a rush job was need to complete the battleship for her new owners by July. When the Sultan Osman I went on sea trials in the North Sea in the first week in July of 1914, a Royal Naval legation was training a 500-man delivery crew of Turks in Constantinople. Among the crew were some Turkish officers as well as a shipyard crew and a Royal Naval advisory crew. But Europe was obviously heading towards war and the First Sea Lord, Winston Churchill was not alone in his extreme misgivings at handing over such a ship to a potential enemy. Deliberate delays were engineered to push back the delivery date including a diversion north after the sea trials and three days at anchor in the Firth of Forth, Scotland.

(The catalyst for the war, the assassination of Grand Duke Ferdinand of Austria, had occurred in Sarajevo on June 28. Although the Turkish Navy had links and sympathies with Britain, the Turkish Army was openly on the side of the Germans in any forthcoming conflict.) Such was the political climate that the Royal Navy ordered its Grand Fleet to stay at a state of war readiness during the royal review at Spithead on July 15-20, 1914. Everything came to a head on August 2, 1914 when with one gun short of the full 12-inch complement, the ship was finally seized by the Royal Navy on the direct orders of Churchill. On the same day they also seized the Reshadieh the smaller battleship being built by Armstrong Whitworth for Turkey. These actions polarised Turkey and in the face of such humiliation the entire population threw their support behind Germany and against Britain. It was said that they would even have fought on the side of Greece to get their battleships back.

And but for this ship, would the stage and setting exist for the horrific events on Gallipoli and the loss of all those lives? (For the record, the Gallipoli operation cost Britain 21,500 dead; France 9,798; Australia 8,709; New Zealand 2,701, India 1,358 and Newfoundland 49. Not to forget the Turks, they lost 86,692.)

The modifications to the ship for Turkey had included a fitting-out with the finest wood veneers and furnishings and the ship had separate and spacious cabins for the officers as well as generous crew accommodation. By Royal Naval standards, the armour was less than desirable and all that space and splendour had been at the expense of watertight bulkheads. Once seized, the ship was quickly renamed HMS Agincourt. It was immediately obvious that some foresight had been exercised - most of the nameplates and instruction plaques which had been engraved or written in Turkish had the English equivalent on the back so they simply had to be turned over and screwed back into position.

The nucleus of the original delivery crew had been drawn from the crews of the Royal Yachts and the core of Agincourt's commissioning complement consisted of almost the entire crew of the royal yacht RY Victoria and Albert including the commander, Captain Douglas Nicholson. With her unheard of luxury within the Royal Navy, HMS Agincourt was quickly (and affectionately) nicknamed "The Gin Palace" by both her crew and the rest of the fleet.

The crews of the Royal Yachts were specifically-picked men from the navy, mostly long- service pensioners who had volunteered for additional service. Most of these "Riggers," as the seamen were called, served in the ship throughout the war and although originally looked down upon by many of the rest of the navy, soon established themselves as equal to any. With her final gun in place and with the removal of a massive and ungainly structure known as the Marble Arch which originally spanned the number three and four turrets, HMS Agincourt entered service on August 25, 1914.

Initially, the main armament of Agincourt was beset with problems. Many of the 12-inch shells fired in early trials broke up in flight and none of the originally-installed electrical firing pins worked. There was also widespread and persistent apprehension that a full broadside of fourteen 12-inch guns might destroy the ship.

If ever a man had faith, it was Agincourt's gunnery officer, Commander Valentine Gibbs. Under his tireless and enthusiastic instruction, all those teething problems were overcome and he used every chance to give both the crew and machinery practice until on a memorable occasion, Agincourt fired a full salvo in the Irish Sea.

Reportedly, over half the Turkish glassware and crockery aboard was smashed with the concussion and for days afterwards the crew were cleaning up the coal dust that escaped the bunkers and infiltrated the entire ship.

By the time HMS Agincourt took part in the Battle of Jutland on May 31, June 1, 1916, the crew had a reputation for aggressive and accurate gunnery. Agincourt fired ten full salvoes of the 12-inch guns during the battle, 144 rounds in all. Although she did not hit anything (that battle was mostly a skirmish at extreme range) the sight of her firing was apparently awe-inspiring. With each salvo she disappeared behind a sheet of flame and smoke to the extent that some eyewitnesses believed a battlecruiser had blown up. Hits were recorded on two German destroyers with the secondary 6-inch guns towards the end of the fight.

When I joined the ship, Agincourt was basically part of a deterrent force that was kept at readiness and largely at anchor in Scapa Flow. As long as our fleet was in position guarding the North Sea, the German fleet was effectively trumped and dared not leave harbour.

The Royal Marine detachment, composed of R M Artillery and R M Light Infantry troops (known respectively as "Blue" Marines and "Red" Marines) manned two of the 12in gun turrets. The aft superimposed turret was commanded by the Major of Marines. This turret would take over the fire control of all the main armament if the Director Control were damaged. The other turret manned by Marines was commanded by the Senior subaltern, Brockman.

To my pleasant surprise, I was given command of the aftermost turret on the quarterdeck which was manned by seamen. And what a grand turret's crew they were. With the exception of a few "hostilities only" ratings, they were all seasoned long-service men, most of them 40 years old or more.

Although the main turrets on ships of the Royal Navy were traditionally numbered or lettered from bow to stern, on Agincourt, they were called after the days of the week. The configuration (seven) was too obvious to ignore. The fore turret was Sunday and my particular turret was Saturday.

As Officer Commanding Turret, I was given charge of a morphine outfit after being instructed by a young doctor how to use it and when. We also had some new and very strict procedures for handling the cordite charges for the guns. It was a cloosly guarded secret at the time that many of the major British casualties at the Battle of Jutland were regarded to be partly as the result of the way we handled and stored our explosives. Damage control had apparently been better on board the German ships as many had withstood severe direct hits without sinking whereas our battlecruisers, HMS Indefatigable, HMS Queen Mary and HMS Invincible had all exploded after single critical hits.

In an earlier clash of the war , the Battle of Dogger Banks, one of the most important outcomes was the German discovery of the vulnerability of ammunition-handling chambers to the flash of bursting shells. They lost no time in fitting anti-flash, devices to them. The post mortems on the British losses at Jutland found the demise of the battlecruisers very likely to be due to unprotected magazines and to some extent the number of older unstable charges being used.

Even more worrying to those of us handling ammunition and high explosives were the losses of ships and men not due to enemy action. The battleship, HMS Bulwark, blew up in Sheerness on November 26, 1914 with the loss of 781 crew and in May 1915, also in Sheerness, a former Canadian Pacific Railway ferry converted to a minelayer, HMS Princess Irene, blew up with the loss of 225 crew, 80 petty officers from Chatham on training and 76 dock workers. Later that year in Cromarty Firth, Invergordon, the cruiser, HMS Natal, was destroyed by a huge internal explosion that claimed all her crew of 390 plus 13 visitors to the ship.

A little less than a year before I joined Agincourt, the St Vincent class battleship HMS Vanguard exploded at anchor in Scapa Flow with only 2 survivors from her complement of 843.

Among my responsibilities was checking the state of the priming and main charges for our gun as well as monitoring temperatures in the magazines – a more rigourous set of inspections being another aftermath of all those previous explosions as well as the Battle of Jutland.

At "Action Stations" my position was in the little armoured hood at the top of the turret, between the two guns. I was also a gun-control watchkeeper on the bridge for the secondary armament (the 6in guns). Everyone of course slept at or near their action stations so I slung a hammock in the gun house between the guns.

I will never forget the first time the Grand Fleet went to sea after I joined the ship. Rumour had it that the German High Seas Fleet had been ordered out and we all thought that the time it would be another, and more decisive, Jutland.

It was a most impressive sight when the British Grand Fleet steamed south from Scapa Flow, truly the biggest display of Naval might and power the world has ever seen.

We, in the Agincourt were more or less in the middle of the long line of battleships which stretched from horizon to horizon. Out of sight ahead were the battlecruisers, on our flanks from skyline to skyline and beyond were light cruisers and destroyers providing an anti submarine screen. Although the station of all the ships in the fleet was specified in relation to the flagship (carrying the Admiral of the Fleet) the size and presence of Agincourt was such that in reality all those in view marked their position relative to us.

We in our stately battleship, proceeding at the Fleet's economical speed of 14 knots, merely curtsied gently to the seas whereas the destroyers and light cruisers looked anything but comfortable. The German Fleet was not at sea and did not come out to meet us, in spite of the fact that we were obviously "trailing the tail of our coat." It was more than a little disappointing, we were itching for the order "battle speed" that would have been the first signal of a possible engagement.

After the sweep south, the fleet returned and Agincourt anchored at Invergordon from where we carried out a series of battle practice shoots, going to sea and firing our guns at a battle practice target towed by the King Orray, a requisitioned Isle of Man ferry. (The King Orray had been converted to an armed boarding vessel and had been involved in the capture of several ships carrying supplies to and from Germany in the North Sea. She was one of the first ships built with geared steam turbines and was very economical even when steaming at 20 knots. After returning to ferry duties after the First War she was again requisitioned by the navy in World War II and saved some 1100 troops from Dunkirk before being torpedoed on her second trip to that beleaguered port.)

After having been at sea, it was of course imperative that the whole fleet should be refuelled at once so as to be ready for emergency. The amount of coal that was used by one of those old "battle wagons" in a few days steaming, was terrific – in Agincourt's case it amounted to some 1500 tons.

Coaling ship in those days was therefore quite a performance. All hands took part, and what an evolution it was.

First of all "Hands shift into coaling rig" would be piped by the bos'n's mates. This meant that all hands would get into their oldest overalls, shorts, football jerseys any old clothes in fact the whole ship's company looked like a lot of pirates so diverse was the garb that appeared.

A collier would come alongside, sometimes two, one to each side of our ship. Parties of our ship's company already detailed would swarm down into the holds of the colliers and start filling hundredweight (112lbs or about 50kg) sacks with coal ready to be transferred in slings by the collier's derricks to our own ship's upper deck. There, the sacks of coal were transferred to porters' barrows, usually handled by the Marine detachment and then trundled at a smart double to the various coal chutes that fed our bunkers. Down in the bunkers were our stokers whose job it was to trim the coal as it arrived down the chutes. The band, also dressed up like pirates, encouraged our efforts by playing marches in double time. This must have been the origin of "music while you work," that became such a feature of the BBC programmes in the Second World War. We had of course one song that started off with "30 thousand sacks of coal lying in a hole."

Every hour, each ship of the Fleet hoisted a signal at the yard arm, indicating the number of tons of coal embarked, and it was a race to see which ship could hoist the "Coaling completed" signal first. The prize was the signal that followed from the admiral to the ship concerned, "coaling well executed."

I think the Navy, more than any other Service, knows how to obtain efficiency by turning every exercise, manoeuvre or evolution into a friendly competition. This rivalry started first of all between the "Parts of the Ship" Focslemen, Foretopmen, Main Topmen, quarter deckmen, Royal Marines, stokers and engine room ratings all competed against each other in boat pulling, sailing and games all the turret and gun crews vied with each other in loading competitions, target shooting or stowing ammunition.

Finally, all parts of the ship joined together enthusiastically for the honour of the ship when it came to fleet exercises or evolutions, from fleet regattas to collision stations, from coaling to abandon ship exercises. The end result was (and still is, I hope and believe) a state of efficiency that can never be equalled in the other services and one with which no form of commercial organisation can ever compete.

Agincourt was a proud and "tiddly" (the naval slang for tidy and neat) ship. Possibly as a combined result of the royal yacht origin of the crew and the ambitions of her original owners, our crew seemed to spend more time than many other ships in the fleet keeping everything clean and shiny. It was a matter of almost bitter rivalry that HMS Erin (the renamed battleship Reshadieh which had also been built for Turkey) was moored near to us and their crew were often seen as having a much more relaxed routine than Agincourt's. And the reason? Erin kept winning the coaling races and having won that contest were beyond any other reproach.

I suppose by modern standards those old ships would be considered uncomfortable, over-crowded and lacking in civilised amenities and yet, I for one (and I know there are many like me) used to come back to the Ship from leave with a sense of home coming. Back to the familiar faces and machinery noises, the pleasant warmth and ship smells, the comradeship, the responsibility and all that goes with life in a happy, disciplined and efficient ship.

Leave, that much prized privilege, was extremely well organised by the Navy in those days. The Grand Fleet, being based at Scapa Flow, had to have well-organised channels of communication for mails and personnel from London. The Naval Express (known to all in the services as Jellicoe's Express) which ran daily each way between Euston and Thurso in the far north of Scotland was the main channel for mails and leave and was a model of efficiency and punctuality. From Thurso to Scapa Flow the old ferry St Ninian, which in peacetime carried mails and passengers to the Orkneys, took the Fleet mails and passengers to and from HMS Imperieuse, the Fleet Depot Ship in Scapa Flow.

Each battleship and group of smaller ships had a drifter attached which collected mails and stores from the Depot ship.

The Imperieuse was an old wooden line of Battle Ship captured from the French in Nelson's day, and was serving the last years of her long and honourable life as a Fleet Depot Ship.

It was quite an experience to travel on the Naval Express, the only stops as far as I remember between Thurso and London were at Inverness, Edinburgh and Crewe.

I remember we arrived at Euston about 7.30am after the 24-hour journey and I would first of all soak in a bath at the Euston Hotel, then go and sit in a barber's chair and say "yes" to every suggestion the barber made. Feeling a new man after a shave, haircut, vibro massage, hot towels and what have you, I ate an enormous hotel breakfast (we didn't seem to do too badly on those ration cards in the First War, specially when in uniform), and then took a much slower and less comfortable train to Manchester in order to reach my parents' home in Cheshire.

On the return journey, the Naval Express left Euston at 6pm and to me, it was much more exciting to be returning to the Ship. Leave probably meant less to me than to most youngsters, because all my contemporary friends were in the Services and apart from my parents, my elder brother and my younger sisters (the latter in their teens then), I knew no one in Cheshire, so I really looked forward to the full life that awaited me back in the Agincourt. I had made no female attachments and I felt more relieved than otherwise that I had no one to say goodbye to me in London - my farewells had been made with my family at home.

Once on the train, I quickly found a shipmate and I seem to remember that our chief subjects of discussion on the journey north were to do with the Ship, her movements, whether we'd missed any excitement and so on. On re-joining the ship, life was more full than ever, what with Officer of the Watch duty in harbour, 2nd Officer of the Watch at sea, Marine detachment duties, turret drill, seamanship classes with midshipmen, and boat work which included running a picket boat and handling all the boats in the ship in turn.

For a period around September 1918, Agincourt, with several units of the Fleet in addition to our own Battle Squadron, came down to the Firth of Forth where we anchored above the bridge. From there we had occasional leave in Edinburgh, but for the afternoon only. We would catch the 1.30pm liberty boat ashore to Queensferry, take the train to Edinburgh, shop, go to a tea dance and return to Queensferry in time to catch the 6.30 liberty boat to the ship.

I remember one night in the Forth vividly. I had the Middle Watch, and it was blowing really hard and increasing to gale force. At about 2am the Yeoman of the Watch on the signal bridge reported that the cruiser anchored ahead of us appeared to be dragging her anchor and was drifting towards us with a danger of collision. I gave orders to the quartermaster and Corporal of the Watch to muster the cable party on the fo'c'sle, called the Commander and the Captain, ordered steam on the main engines and went on the fo'c'sle myself to take charge of operations.

As soon as I got there I saw that the cruiser, one of the County class, was less than half her normal distance from our bows and was still dragging her anchor towards us. It was blowing so hard that it was impossible to make myself heard so I placed myself under a yard arm group of electric lights that had been switched on and by means of hand signals to the cable party veered our own cable so that our ship eased downwind at about the same speed as the cruiser was dragging. I saw that the Captain had arrived on the focsle, and was apparently trying to shout orders against the wind. No one could hear him, so I carried on veering cable until a few minutes later the cruiser, having raised sufficient steam, started to move ahead and the danger was over.

I then reported to the Captain who put me under open arrest for not obeying orders and ordered me to my cabin after instructing the Commander to carry on. Next morning at 1100, in great trepidation, I was taken to the Captain's cabin by the Commander.

"I was on the focsle givng orders," the Captain barked. 'Why the devil did you persist in carrying on as if I wasn't there?"

I explained that neither I nor any of the seamen could hear anything in the wind blowing at the time. " So I felt I ought to carry on to the best of my ability for the sake of the safety of the ship. Sir."

The Captain's face cracked slightly and he said, with a twinkle in his eye "Quite right, boy, quite right" then he rang the bell, and when the steward came said "bring some gin." Over drinks, the Captain waxed reminiscent about his younger days as Officer of the Watch, and was a very pleasant host.

We were kept very busy with evolutions, battle practice shoots, and the hundred and one exercises necessary to keep a ship and a fleet efficient in war, until on the 11th November 1918 we were at sea, carrying out battle practice firing at a target once again towed by the King Orray. We returned to harbour just before dark, and anchored below the Forth Bridge in the next berth to HMS Argus, then the first "flat top" aircraft carrier in the Navy. At 6pm we received a signal from the Admiral informing us that the Armistice had been declared at 11am that day. The signal concluded "Splice the Main Brace." The Wardroom Officers promptly invited the Captain, the Warrant Officers and the Gunroom Officers to dine. It was a most successful dinner although it was rather spoilt for me because after it I had to kccp the Middle Watch from midnight to 4.

As we were find out later, we very nearly had that great naval battle we thought we wanted. On October 30, with the German army in retreat and civilian population starving and demoralised, Admiral Scheer had ordered the German fleet to put to sea and make a last-ditch attack on our Grand Fleet. In Kiel, many crews either refused to sail or deserted and this lead fairly quickly to revolution in Germany with Bavaria declaring a republic and Kaiser Wilhelm abdicating, thus speeding up the Armistice.

My next memory and one of the most impressive is of the surrender of the German High Seas Fleet on November 21, 1918. Our Grand Fleet steamed east in two columns of battleships and battle cruisers in line ahead. The battleships and battle cruisers, even in two columns, stretched from horizon to horizon, with the cruisers and destroyer screens on our flanks. HMS Agincourt was roughly in the middle of the southern column, and we had on board with us, Oscar Parkes, as one of the official artists. Oscar, as assistant editor of "Jane's Fighting Ships" not only had an encyclopaedic knowledge of the warships of all nations but he was also a first class marine artist. He was also a doctor, and during his visit to the ship he wore the uniform of a Surgeon Lieutenant Commander RNVR. He and I spent most of that day in the foretop, and we had a wonderful view from there. When we met the German Fleet, 50 miles from port, our leading ships turned 180deg in succession, so that the Germans in single line ahead, were escorted back to Scapa Flow by a line of British battleships on each side with three miles between the columns. It was a marvellous spectacle, three lines of mighty ships steaming west at a stately 12 knots, the centre line of monsters with the White ensign flying above the German Imperial ensign, and the British ships on either flank proudly wearing the White Ensign alone. To honour the merchant navy contribution to the war, Admiral Jellicoe had the King Orray lead the line of German light cruisers in behind the battleships and battle cruisers, which many of us suspected would have been a further humiliation of our recent enemy.

We had weighed anchor at about 0200 that morning and went to closed battle stations as soon as we sighted the Germans fleet at 0400. Beatty had ordered that we have all our turrets and guns in the securing positions (i.e. the main turrets were trained fore and aft) but free. The guns were all empty but ammunition cages were up and reading for instant loading. The gunnery directors, however, were to be trained on the nearest German target once the fleets were joined up and correct range and deflection maintained. There was still some thought that the Germans might try a last-ditch action or that even an individual ship might decide to fire upon us and thus go out in a blaze of glory. Later investigations showed we need not have worried, all charges and ammunition had been removed from the ships as well as rangefinders, sights, gun controls and even breech blocks. (Perhaps after the Kiel Mutiny, no-one was taking any chances.)

There were many photographs taken (some aerial) of that surrender and for weeks after there were numerous illustrated publications on sale. The photographs were all black and white of course but I don't think they would have looked much different in colour. It was a monochrome occasion, long lines of grey ships on a grey day. Although we were all aware of the moment and grandeur of the occasion, the overwhelming feeling was of pity and disappointment.

At the entrance to the Firth of Forth, Beatty signalled one of the German squadrons to increase speed and close up formation. He received a reply stating that they could make no more than 12 knots due to a lack of lubricating oil which underlined the state of the High Seas Fleet. They obviously had been run down in equipment and maintenance and even food seemed in short supply because it was noticeable that the ships had only just anchored when many of the crew dropped fishing lines over the side. We guessed they were trying to catch their supper.

I still feel proud to think that I was one of the vast number who witnessed that famous surrender. One seldom hears it referred to now, although at the time the surrender of a complete fleet in being was world news. I was lucky enough to be given Christmas leave after the end of the war in 1918, and returned to the Agincourt just in time to pay off the ship in the dockyard in the Forth. That was the last I saw of the good old "Gin Palace". She was regarded with affection by all who served on her. She was placed in reserve shortly after I left her and an unsuccessful attempt was made to sell her back to Brazil. She then went back to Armstrongs and work was started to convert her to fuel oil but was halted by the post-war economies. She was used for gunnery training for a while but was finally scrapped in 1922.

Early in January 1919 I went marching into Forton Barracks again, behind the Divisional Band which had met us at the Gosport Ferry, with the RMLI portion of HMS Agincourt's detachment behind me. After handing the men over to the Divisional Headquarters staff, I was once again greeted warmly by First Drill Gibbs. I have pleasant memories of a quiet session over a bottle with him in my quarters that evening while we exchanged yarns. Unfortunately I had to part with my old friend and marine servant, Private Stevens, he to retire from the Corps he had served so long and faithfully and I to discover what peace-time service meant.

Chapter 3

China Station

Early in 1919, while serving as Assistant Musketry Instructor at Browndown Camp where the R M Musketry ranges were on the shores of the Solent, I went down with flu in the dreadful epidemic that broke out at that time. Flu turned to pneumonia and I was very ill for about six weeks in Haslar Hospital.

When I was in the convalescent stage and was allowed out of hospital for an hour or two in the afternoon, Freddy Garnett, who had been a staunch visitor suggested that I should have a few drinks and a meal with him in the Mess at Forton Barracks before he sailed back to South Africa. The trouble was that leave after 6pm for patients was not allowed. However, Freddy sent a telegram purporting to come from my mother asking permission for me to see her off to London on the 9.30pm train, so I was given leave until 10pm. At 10pm I arrived back in hospital feeling rather happy after a lot of good food and a certain amount of alcohol and I took back with me a large bottle of a special cocktail mixed by the Mess corporal. The Night Sister was a friend of mine, so after lights out, I collected another patient, a Surgeon Lieutenant and we took the bottle of cocktail to the Sister's little office. Around midnight we were caught by the Matron, two patients in our dressing gowns and two Sisters on duty, drinking cocktails out of tea cups. There was quite a fuss and the upshot was that we two patients were "expelled" to the convalescent hospital at Peebles Hydro and the two Sisters were reprimanded. Peebles was a delightful spot, and what with the excellent food, and physiotherapy treatment we were given, I was soon back to duty.

My next job was with the Field Training detachment at Browndown Camp when I served under an unforgettable character, a most delightful Scottish Major whose nickname was "Skintight." "Skintight" was a very gallant and efficient officer who on Gallipoli had earned the praise of all who served with him and should have been highly decorated. Unfortunately, in peacetime he had such a propensity for putting up "blacks" that he was never decorated and never rose beyond the rank of Major.

I remember on the first route march he took us he arranged that for our second "stand easy" when on one hour we halted for 10 minutes rest, we were close to a little country inn. Just before he fell us out he told the detachment they could go into the pub for a beer but he put them on their honour to have no more than a pint each. All but five of the Marines went in so he said "What's the matter, boys, aren't you thirsty?"

"No money, sir," they dolefully answered. "Well, go and order it on me," said "Skintight."

We all loved him, and he taught us a lot. He was a born raconteur, a delightful messmate, a generous host, a fine soldier and leader and I missed him tremendously when he retired from the Corps. On June 21 we heard the news that the Germans had scuttled most of their ships at Scapa Flow with disbelief and sadness. To us it seemed an ignominious end and such a waste of fine ships. It also seemed very stupid, a waste of money and lives for no gain.

My next appointment was to HMS Hawkins, the flagship of the China Station. In July 1919, I was sent to R M Barracks, Chatham to take over the detachment of RMLI and commission the new cruiser in Chatham Dockyard.

At Chatham Barracks I found Lt Colonel B G Weller, DSO, the Fleet Marine Officer, China Station, awaiting me. "Sammy" Weller, as he was affectionately known throughout the service, was a most distinguished officer who had been awarded his DSO for gallantry at Zeebrugge. "Sammy" was a charming personality with a great sense of humour who knew how to delegate authority, but was always available with kindly advice and backed his subordinates up to the hilt. He did a lot to make that first peacetime commission on a foreign station a happy and rewarding experience for me.

HMS Hawkins was a new cruiser armed with 7.5 inch guns, and the whole ship's company felt honoured to serve in her, the new flagship in China.

Our Captain (who was also Chief of Staff to the Commander in Chief) was Reggie Henderson (later to be Admiral Sir Reginald Henderson), a gunnery expert, a most efficient staff officer and a fine seaman who was formerly commander of HMS Erin referred to previously. "Wiggy" Bennett was our commander, then I think, the youngest "brass hat" in the Navy.

Other names that come to mind are Lt Commander "Donkey" Drew, our First Lieutenant, Lieut Jeans, our "Guns," Lieut J D Chapple, a divisional officer and a particular friend of mine, Commander Norman Wodehouse, the Staff Commander. All fine shipmates, and good officers who did so much to earn for the ship the name of "Appy Awkins."

Norman Wodehouse was about ten years older than me. He joined the Royal Navy as a midshipman in 1904 and played Rugby for England from 1910 to 1913 - he captained the team on six occasions and lead his country to its first "grand slam" (unbeaten season). He was a big, strong, man and was still a formidable forward when playing Rugby for the ship. He was gunnery officer on the battleship, HMS Revenge, at the Battle of Jutland. He was later aide-de-camp to the newly-crowned King George VI (in 1937) and retired as a Rear Admiral just before World War II but was almost immediately recalled to active service as a Vice Admiral. He was commodore of convoy OB-337 from Liverpool to South Africa aboard the armed merchantman Robert S Holt in July 1941 and his ship was never seen again after he had ordered his charges to scatter near the Canary Islands when they were attacked by submarines. We later learned that the Robert S. Holt had been sunk in a gun battle with U-69. The German commander (Jost Metzler) had kept the Holt's gun crew at bay with machine-gun fire until he could ready and fire his 88mm main armament. Norman, the ship's master John Kendall, 41 crew members and six naval staff were all lost.

After commissioning in Chatham dockyard, Hawkins went round to Portsmouth for final "working up" trials and evolutions and we sailed for the Far East in September 1919, resplendent in our tropical colours of white hull with light grey funnels and upper-works.

We called briefly at Gibraltar, Malta and Alexandria before going through the Suez Canal, then had a very hot passage through the Red Sea to Aden. All these ports were new to me and most interesting. We remained a few days in Aden where I had my first ride on a camel and played my first game of polo ("'Orse 'ockey" our sailors called it!)

Our paymaster was unfortunately persuaded to exchange most of our frozen beef for frozen mutton with the Aden commissariat people. The Army in Aden had been living on mutton for months and were tired of it. I'm afraid we had such a surfeit of mutton in Hawkins after this exchange that to this day I cannot bear to eat even lamb unless there is nothing else! (Such a predilection almost made me persona non grata when I came to New Zealand.)

At Colombo we really felt we were approaching our new station. We were entertained royally there, visited tea estates, dined at the Galle Face, bathed at Mount Lavinia, and were quite glad to be at sea again for a comparative rest.

Our first port on the China Station was Penang. Here, as the first big British warship to be seen in peacetime, we were given a terrific welcome by the British community.

I went with a party of four or five up to a rubber plantation on the mainland of Malaya. Our hosts met us with cars just after day break and drove us about 30 miles inland to the plantation where we ate a quick breakfast and were taken to shoot snipe. Our perfect hosts came with us, but carried no guns so that we had all the sport.

Our bag was excellent but by noon, after wading for about three or four hours through paddy fields, we were glad when our hosts called a halt for refreshments.

The refreshments were ice-cold gin slings and after two or three of these we were driven to the manager's bungalow for baths and a change. Our hosts had even sent a special truck with ice to put in our baths and in that tropical heat the ice was most welcome. After more gin slings we were given a delicious curry tiffin before being driven back to our ship in a rather somnolent condition. We persuaded our planter hosts to dine in the wardroom that night, and we managed to return their hospitality so well that "where they dined they slept"; in fact some of them were still on board for lunch the following day!

Our next call was Singapore, where we remained for some time. In those days, Singapore was at the peak of its prosperity and was a very bright and lively city indeed. (I would have called it a "gay" place in those days but oh how our language and perceptions have changed). We were entertained almost to exhaustion, picnics and excursions were arranged for the ships' company who even in that heat played soccer against the Army.

With golf, tennis, sailing and cricket by day, dinners and dancing at night (when our duties would allow) and entertaining our new friends on board when possible, we were again glad to get to sea for a rest.

Shortly after leaving Singapore en route for Hong Kong, our Captain took the ship over the equator in order to give Father Neptune a chance to come aboard. Although I had "crossed the line" twice before, I had to go through the traditional ceremony again in order to be baptised real "Navy fashion."

The Chief Bosun's Mate was an excellent Father Neptune and I remember the ship's butcher (one of my detachment of Marines) acting as the Barber, made me take a large soap pill before he shaved me, and there were two large Marines in Neptune's entourage who saw to it that I was well and truly baptised.

Hawkins duly arrived in Hong Kong, where she officially hoisted the flag of C-in-C China Station. We there met the other ships of the China Squadron. HMS Alacrity, the C-in-C's yacht, HMS Cairo, Curlew and Colombo (C-class cruisers), HMS Medway, the submarine depot ship and her flotilla of submarines, two sloops and several river gunboats, and also the old wooden troopship, HMS Talmar, then used as Depot Ship, Hong Kong.

There followed rather a hectic round of parties between ships and of course I met my "opposite numbers" in the other cruisers, Captain "Bobbie" Sturgess on Cairo, Captain Bashall on Colombo, and E J Woodington, the only other subaltern, on Curlew.

Bobbie Sturges was to become Major General Sir Robert Sturges in the next war. He is an outstanding soldier and one of the nicest men I've met. In addition he was an all round sportsman, a very fine horseman and deservedly attained high rank in the Corps.

Hawkins did not remain long in Hong Kong. We were next sent up the Yangtze River. This was a most memorable cruise, particularly because Hawkins was the largest British ship to steam as far up river as Hangkow, some 600 miles or more inland from Shanghai.

We called first at Shanghai, which was then in it's heyday of prosperity, and was known as the Paris of the Far East. It too was a bright, lively and happy city and we were entertained lavishly and again we did our best to return hospitality with parties on board.

When we steamed up the Yangtze, the river was at a high level and flowing very fast so that Hawkins, steaming at a mere 12 knots, moved very slowly past the river banks. If she had used more speed, her wash in the confined waters would have created havoc in the low lying villages and farms along the banks. We took it in easy stages, anchoring at night and calling at river ports on the way, including Nanking, until we finally reached Hankow. At each of the ports we stayed a day or two and were made much of by the European community and in return had parties on board.

At Wuhu we were invited to witness the execution of some criminals by the Chinese authorities. I did not go as seeing someone killed in cold blood certainly did not appeal to me, but some of my messmates did and someone took photographs which I saw afterwards. They were horrible. The poor wretches were beheaded. I gather the whole affair was most gruesome yet thousands of Chinese and quite a few Europeans turned out to watch.

The victims were apparently quite stoical I was told. Their crimes were generally described as piracy. In those days piracy was a thriving "industry" in China, both in the rivers and on the coasts.

There was a tremendous amount of traffic on the Yangtze river, sampans, trading junks of all sizes and river steamers. I was amazed to see several beam-engine paddle steamers; shallow draught, broad-beamed, tall-funnelled craft, with the enormous beam slowly rocking up and down above the upper works as the large crank turned the paddles. The Chinese called them "Walkee Walkee Topsides."

At Hankow we stayed about 10 days. We had to anchor in mid river as there was no wharf large enough to take Hawkins. The river was flowing so fast that our power boats, when going to and from the ship or the landing stage ashore, had to steer about 45deg to the current. When returning to the ship one night by sampan, although the sampan started from shore a mile up river from the ship, we were swept past the ship, and eventually reached the bank a mile down river, took a rickshaw up the river road, and took another sampan from a mile and a half above the ship. That time we made it.

We were given a great welcome at Hankow, particularly as times were troublesome with a number of power-seeking Chinese War Lords and their private armies in the offing. The presence of a large British cruiser so far up the Yangtze was very welcome to the local authorities, as well as the European community and at least for the time being, the British Navy kept the peace.

I must pay tribute to the wonderful service carried out by the little river gunboats in China in those days. These were small craft commanded by a Lieutenant R N, with a doctor and a Sub Lieutenant as the only officers, and a ship's company of about 25 to 30 all told.

They kept down piracy, backed up the Chinese Customs and generally acted as a very efficient police force on the tremendous inland waterway of the Yangtze. The phrase "send a gunboat" has become a bit of a joke and is often used mockingly these days but those craft were an excellent safeguard to water-borne trade in those troublesome times.

After our cruise up the Yangtze, Hawkins went to Wei Hai Wei, the summer base for the China Squadron. Wei Hai Wei is an island which was British in those days and had an excellent sheltered anchorage. There was a small dockyard, a naval hospital, a canteen, a hotel and a nine-hole golf course.

It was a wonderful summer holiday resort for the fleet. There we held the Fleet Regatta and when we were not at sea doing gunnery exercises, evolutions or torpedo exercises, we were training our various crews in boat pulling or sailing. Whenever there was a "make and mend" afternoon there would be a sailing race. On Sundays, after the midday meal, I usually got the Commander's permission to take a ship's boat on a sailing picnic with as many of the Marine detachment as the boat would accommodate. These picnics were very popular, and there was never a lack of volunteers from the detachment. After a couple of hours sailing we would make for a secluded beach where all hands could bathe, then build a fire, boil a billy for tea, fry eggs and bacon and tinned sausages, then sail back to the ship feeling pleasantly relaxed and rather full of food!

As a result of these sailing picnics, I had no difficulty in selecting an efficient crew of Royal Marines to man the cutter which I was lucky enough to draw in the ballot for the Fleet regatta. We won the all comers sailing race and were very pleased with ourselves because the real seaman tended to look disparagingly at Royal Marines as sailors. Norman Wodehouse took me aside at the celebrations that evening and warned me with mock seriousness that my career could suffer if I repeated such a feat too often. "It's not good form to have the Captain's cutter beaten into second place. Particularly by a subaltern of Marines."

From Wei Hai Wei, Hawkins went back to Hong Kong for a short re fit and during this time the R M Detachment disembarked for the annual musketry course. This was held on Stonecutters Island, where the Naval rifle range and camp was established and was a very pleasant break from shipboard routine.

We went to Java (now Indonesia) next and anchored at Batavia (now Jakarta). The Dutch were very hospitable, and they impressed us as being very good colonists. In particular, the Javanese of those days appeared to be happy and contented. Everywhere we went showed evidence of a benevolent, efficient administration.

When we left Java, we certainly needed to rest our digestive organs because our Dutch hosts had given us such a round of curry tiffins and dinner parties with unaccustomed rich foods. Every meal was preceded by "Rijstaffel" a delicious selection of hors d'oeuvres in such quantities that we never really enjoyed the main courses that followed. Our next call was in Singapore again, where, as before, we anchored in the Roadstead about a mile from the shore. The Naval Base was not in existence then, nor was there an aerodrome, broadcasting did not exist, mails could only come by sea, and the long-range radio telegraph was in its infancy. Even the famous Raffles Hotel still had manually operated punkahs (fans), as did many private houses. Rickshaws were the most common transport, although taxis had become popular for the wealthier travellers. Life in general seemed to proceed at a slower and less noisy speed than the rest of the world we were used to.

All this sounds as though Hawkins did nothing but cruise and pay social visits. In fact, we were kept very busy at gunnery and torpedo exercises, "evolutions" which covered every emergency from collision stations to abandon ship so that our two years' commission passed rapidly.

About May 1921, Hawkins paid off and recommissioned in Hong Kong and we returned to England in the old P. and O. liner, Devenha which also brought out our reliefs to China.

After handing over the Royal Marine Detachment at Chatham Barracks, I reported back to my own division at Forton Barracks, Gosport, to find that my leave had been curtailed as the 11th Battalion had gone into training for service in Ireland where fighting was still going on.

Our training was carried out from Fort Borstal, Rochester, another of the old forts built during the Napoleonic wars.

We were under canvas and during that hot summer of 1921 we became very fit by hard training. A 25-mile march with full battle order meant nothing to us and instruction in unarmed combat, assault practice, night exercises and the like were the basis of what is now known as commando training which the Royal Marines initiated in the last war.

Just as the battalion was ready to go to Ireland, a sort of truce was declared, so that the battalion was disbanded and we were all returned to our respective divisions at Chatham, Gosport and Plymouth.

Chapter 4

Revolution and Mutiny

After leave I found myself appointed to the 8th R M Battalion which was already in Ireland.

The Battalion which had been in Ireland for some time was doing a rather specialised job of peace-keeping. A platoon was stationed at each of the major coastguard stations round the coast of Ireland and battalion headquarters was in HMS Cumberland in the dockyard at Queenstown (now known as Cobh). Cumberland, an old three-funnelled County class cruiser was out of commission and merely served as a barracks for the Headquarters Company.

Colonel Chichester, an old friend who was mentioned earlier, was the Battalion Commander, and St Clair Morford, my old Company Commander in France in 1916 was Adjutant. Morford had recently returned to the Corps after being seconded to the RFC where he had gained further honours. I was assistant Adjutant, and eventually relieved Morford as Adjutant.

Although there was a truce in being it was an uneasy one because there were many of the imported American gangsters (most of whom had Italian names) still "on the run" and wanted for murder. Although the Marines were on good terms with the local people, most of whom were completely uninterested in the rebellion, we always had to carry arms because there were still odd attempts by the IRA and their imported thugs to shoot anyone in British uniform.

On one occasion I had to deliver some despatches to Army headquarters in Cork. Captain Bath who was the fortunate owner of a motorcycle and sidecar offered to drive me up. We were warned that there was likely to be an IRA ambush between Queenstown and Cork so we travelled as fast as possible. Sure enough, on a lonely stretch of road between hawthorne hedges, we were fired on. Luckily both shots missed. I had a Mills bomb ready and as Bath accelerated, I withdrew the pin, and dropped the bomb in the road. By the time it exploded we were out of range but the sniper evidently wasn't, because the police stated later that a rifle and some bloodstains were found behind the hedge in the vicinity where we reported the shots had been fired. In the spring of 1922 we were withdrawn from Ireland and I was posted to Deal for the Military Courses. This was a sort of "pressure cooker" course for the benefit of the junior Marine officers who owing to war had missed the normal instruction they would have had in peacetime. What with military law, imperial military history and geography, field surveying and sketching, tactical exercises without troops etc, we were kept very busy, and then at the end of the course we all took (and passed) the Army promotion exams.

After leave I was appointed to HMS Constance, then commissioning in Devonport Dockyard to go to the West Indies Station.

Constance was an early C-class Light Cruiser, with a main armament of six-inch guns. The Royal Marine detachment was 30 strong with the addition of 14 Bandsmen. Constance seemed very small after the Hawkins, but she was a lovely old ship and a very happy one. Our Captain was Douglas Campbell, brother of the famous Gordon Campbell, the Q-Boat VC. We sailed from Plymouth in the spring of 1923 and had a very rough crossing, calling first at the Azores, and after 14 days were very glad to reach Bermuda, which was to be our base for the next two years.

Bermuda was a lovely place where everything moved at a gentle speed in those days. Motor cars were not allowed on the island, so bicycles and horse drawn buggies were the only means of road transport. Unfortunately, it was also the loading base for a lot of "boot leggers" and every tourist ship from America brought a horde of thirsty Americans, who seemed to remain in a haze of alcohol for the whole of their stay.

The naval dockyard, on Ireland Island, however, was a long way from the capital, Hamilton. As there were adequate sports grounds, and a canteen for the ship's company, with plenty of bathing, sailing and picnic facilities, we were not worried or concerned much with the high life in Hamilton.

One Sunday afternoon, we were at anchor in Grassy Bay, and I was officer of the day when a speed boat came alongside, and a pleasant American couple asked if they could look round the ship. I invited them on board, showed them round, then gave them tea. They were Caldwell Walker and his charming wife. Caldy Walker turned out to be a son of Hiram Walker and Sons, the distillers of Detroit and was of course a very wealthy man. They were a delightful couple and we had a lot of fun together, in which the speed boat played no small part.

One night, I and a brother officer were guests of the Walkers to dinner, and Caldy Walker had said "I do want you to meet Mrs , she's so delightfully English and such an aristocrat." I was seated next to her at dinner, and found that the "delightfully English" woman was a complete phoney. She tried, unsuccessfully to disguise her original Cockney accent by an exaggerated overlay of what she fondly hoped was a "refeened" accent, and of course her American hosts lapped this up. She was shooting a colossal line about grouse shooting with Sir this, and parties with Lady So and so, and eventually asked me "Tell mah, wheah is yoah peepulls place?" I couldn't stand it any longer, and I replied in a Cockney accent "Dahn the Mile End Road, me farver's a dustman, and I'm prahd of 'im." Inexcusable I know, but it made me cross to see our kind host and hostess being taken in by a phoney who was so blatantly "putting on the dog." Needless to say, no lasting friendship developed between the "aristocratic" one and me!

Constance was soon off on her first cruise. We called first at Jamaica, where we had the usual round of parties. We then found that we were required to take the Inspector General of the West Indian Local Forces on a tour of inspection. Being only a light cruiser, in fact only a little larger than a destroyer, we had no spare accommodation, so a special temporary cabin was built of timber by the shipwrights (an unheard of thing in a steel ship, but after all, it was peacetime) in the Captain's cabin flat. It was impossible, however, to find any accommodation for the Inspector General's Staff Officer, so being a soldier, I was detailed to act as Staff Officer, aide-de-camp, secretary and what have you for the cruise. And damned hard work it was. On arrival at St Kitt's (full title St Christopher's) the IG with his ADC (me) went ashore, and were accommodated in state at Government House as guests of the Governor.

The hospitality was wonderful, my master the Inspector General was a grand chap but he forgot that I was carrying out (or trying to) the jobs that were done in Jamaica by three - a Major (Staff Officer), a Captain (ADC) and a civil secretary.

I will only describe the routine at St Kitts, but at all our other islands of inspection, it was of the same pattern.

We were called at 6.30am with a cup of tea, and fruit. 7am I had to bestride a polo pony, and endeavour to knock a polo ball around the Savannah with the IG, who was a magnificent horseman and a polo enthusiast. (Remember that old saying "the horse is the friend of man, but the enemy of the Marine Officer?)

9am after a bathe, change into uniform, inspection (usually mounted on a rather unmanageable "charger").

11.30am breakfast (or should I call it "brunch") after a flock of "swizzles." The "swizzle" habit in the West Indies is a pleasant, but a pernicious one. The basic ingredient of the "swizzle" is fresh lime, after that one can have infinite variety of spiriits - rum (most popular), gin, whiskey or brandy. Into the alcohol base go the lime juice, Angostura or other bitters, crushed ice then mixed by means of a three or four pronged stick twirled between the palms of the hands. You can buy a "swizzle stick" in silver from a jeweller at a high price but in those days the best ones were just picked off the trees.

After "breakfast" which ran into several courses, everyone had a siesta from about 2pm to 4pm when, dammit, my boss would drag me on to the tennis court (and he was good) then a bathe, more "swizzles" an official dinner, followed by a ball, where of course I did my duty (and liked it) and then about 1.30 to 2am I hopefully thought of sleep when my Inspector General said "Come to my room for a nightcap, and we'll go over today's inspection! Over a final drink I had to give him a précis of my notes, which he corrected and altered as I went on, then, at about 3am he said "Right, I'll sign them at 9 in the morning see you on the Savannah at 7 must keep fit, my boy." My trouble was that although I had a portable typewriter, I was only a one finger typist. I was too poor a horseman to make anything but mental notes when mounted and so my draft reports must have been terrible at 9 the next morning, however, somehow, I was approved of. The reports were agreed and signed in draft form by the IG but oh how I wanted to sleep!

We had about three or four days at each island. We went to Antigua, Barbados, Trinidad, Barbuda, Montserrat, St Lucia, St Vincent, Grenada, where the procedure was the same and just as tiring. Most of the Local Forces were the armed police who were trained as soldiers as well as police. The remainder were a sort of territorial or volunteer force very keen with no equipment or arms other than short Lee Enfield rifles.

I think it was St Kitts that the IG told me to go by myself and inspect some outlying police posts in the Island. I was given a native constable driver, and a Model T Ford. Off we went, and as I am an awful back seat driver (and anyhow I think one sees more from the front seat than from the back) I sat talking with the driver as we went into the interior on dreadful dirt roads, with hairpin bends, cliffs on one side, precipices on the other. Meantime, my chatty native driver, pleased that a white man should talk to him, informed me very proudly that he had been three months in the local mental hospital because he'd had the "vapours" but he was now allowed out on probation. My nerves had been shattered already by his driving, but when I heard his life story, I wondered how I'd save my life and his.

I had a brainwave, told him that the last time I had driven a Model T Ford had been in the Orkneys during the First War, and asked if I could possibly try my skill and I felt that on these roads I wouldn't dare unless he sat beside me to instruct. Thank goodness he agreed and so it was we finished our tour of inspection of the outlying posts. I gathered that he got a certain amount of kudos because he told all his friends at the stations we inspected that he had taught me to drive and in any case it was an honour to be driven by a white officer!

At the end of our inspection cruise of the islands, we returned to Jamaica, and there the IG insisted that I should stay at his house for a few days rest.

It was a very pleasant holiday. My host and hostess were kindness itself and, inspections over, the only work I had to do was a little revision of the inspector's reports with the aid of a competent secretary. The rest of my time was chiefly spent at the beck and call of two delightful teenage girls, daughters of my host. I found this quite painless!

From Jamaica, Constance went north to Newfoundland and our first port was St Johns. Newfoundland in those days was a tough country and the inhabitants were still pioneers. Lumber and fish were the chief industries and sealing was a major attraction for the hardy fisherman in the winter.

It intrigued us to note that the Newfoundland accent had a strong Irish brogue mixed with a Canadian accent. A result of the early Irish colonists, of course.

The two weeks in Newfoundland hold mixed memories. We arrived on a Saturday early in September 1924 and the larger ships of the squadron, HMS Hood, HMS Repulse and HMS Adelaide anchored in Conception Bay while we went into St Johns Harbour. On Tuesday of that week we staged a full naval ceremonial parade with detachments from all our ships and it appeared that all of Newfoundland turned out for the occasion.

The St John's Telegram reported: "Five hundred Blue Jackets and Marines from the Special Service Squadron paraded in the city yesterday morning, His Excellency the Governor taking the salute and through a principal officer laid a wreath on the National Memorial. Water Street was decorated with flags in honor of the occasion and the parade was a most impressive event."

At St Johns we played rugby against the local team who were very keen and beat us handsomely. We, the Constance Rugby team were invited to dinner by our victorious hosts. We were driven about 10 or 12 miles out to a road house because there was a form of prohibition in St Johns. The dinner was excellent, but I remember that we only had a glass of sherry before the meal, and a glass of beer with our food and a port to drink the loyal toast afterwards. This was by mutual agreement because we were due to play a return match against our hosts the following day.

The captain of the St Johns team and our chief host, was a young lawyer, son of Sir William Duff Reid, the man who built the Newfoundland railway. Young Leonard, was a fine chap, who had insisted on making his own way through college and obtained his law degree without any help from his distinguished and wealthy father or his estate.

The father, when he built and financed the railway was given in payment every alternate square mile of land on each side of the railway. The Government of the day thought this a cunning way of discharging a considerable debt at no apparent cost. When, however, the interior was opened up by the railway and townships and settlements sprang up, Sir William's investments in land paid off handsomely.

Although Sir William had been hailed as a benefactor in his day and was knighted for his services, after he died it was realised that the original government while thinking it was obtaining a cheap railway had committed the taxpayers to considerable payments as the country developed. Of course, politics being what they are, Sir William was held entirely to blame and by 1924, although he was dead, the name Reid was reviled. I mention this hearsay story because it appears to account for the shabby treatment meted out to our friend, young Leonard, in the story I now have to tell.

At about 11.30pm our party broke up and we piled into several cars provided by our hosts. As it happened, I went in the first car. Our route back to St Johns, the Topsail Road, ran part of the way along an embankment on either side of which and several feet below, was swampy ground. There was a road house set back from the road at one portion of this embankment at a place called Donovans and just as we approached this, a bus from the opposite direction pulled up on the far side of the road. We slowed down to pass, sounded our horn and even so narrowly missed two or three staggering figures who came round from behind the bus to cross to the road house. The car a few minutes behind us was driven by Len Reid with our "Guns" (Lieutenant William Slayter) sitting beside him, and our Sub (Lieutenant Edmund Burrows) and our Senior Watchkeeper (Lieutenant Denys O'Callaghan) in the back seat together with with two of Len's friends and colleagues, George Harrison and Clinton Duder.

Apparently, as Len was abreast of the bus, another group of figures staggered across from behind it. Len swerved in an unsuccessful attempt to avoid them and in doing so the car went over the bank and overturned into the swamp. Len and Guns managed to crawl out because the windscreen pillars held and gave them some room, but the four in the back were smothered in the bog before the car could be lifted off them. Two of the men on the road, Gerald Whitty and William King, both prominent Newfoundland war veterans were killed and Chief Petty Officer Lovett from Constance was injured.

Whitty was secretary-general of the Newfoundland Great War Veterans' Association and had been awarded both the OBE and Military Cross during the war.

We others in the leading car knew nothing of this at the time, and it was not until an hour or so after I had returned to the ship that I got news of the tragedy. We heard later from Guns that Len, who was naturally in a state of shock, was bullied unmercifully by the Chief of Police who came out to the scene himself. The day after the accident poor Len was charged initially with murder but this was reduced to manslaughter. Although Guns was sent up from Bermuda as an eye witness for the defence such was the political bias against any relative of Sir William Reid that Len was convicted and sentenced to a year's imprisonment. It was a grievous affair and the loss of our mess-mates in the accident was made all the worse by the vicious treatment we felt Len had received.

And so it was that only a week and a day after our triumphant and celebratory St Johns parade we held a sombre but even bigger ceremony when Burrows and O'Callaghan were buried with full naval honours in the morning and we attended the military funeral of Whitty and King in the afternoon. The same day, Harrison and Duder were also laid to rest at less public funerals.

The St John's Telegram (Sept 19, 1924) reported: "Funeral obsequies of victims of Monday night's motor accident were marked by an unusual display of public sympathy. Large concourses of citizens followed the bodies to the grave side while the streets were lined by thousands of people who stood in sympathetic silence. The naval funeral in the morning was particularly impressing, the bodies being carried on gun carriages and followed by large numbers of sailors from the ship bearing arms.

Bill Slayter ("Guns") was an almost legendary survivor. As a midshipman he was one of only nine survivors from HMS Queen Mary at Jutland and as a Sub Lieutenant he was awarded the DSC for action on one of the Coastal Motor Boats in the raid on Ostend. He later gained the DSO for his involvement on HMS Duke of York in the sinking of the German battlecruiser Scharnhorst in 1944 and he was knighted and became Admiral Sir William Slayter shortly before his retirement as Commander in Chief, East Indies Station in 1954.

One hot day after Constance's return to Bermuda we found ourselves suddenly ordered to sea. A revolution had begun in Mexico. The Captain informed us that we had been ordered to proceed with all dispatch to a place in Mexico called Minatitlan to safeguard British interests there, namely the British-owned oil refinery and the British staff who operated it. So we left Bermuda at much more than economical speed. We were rather fed up at being sent away so soon, we'd only just come back from a cruise on which we spent a lot of energy, shall we say, on being entertained and entertaining and we had been looking forward to being five or six weeks in Bermuda where we would have a certain amount of football, cricket, tennis, sailing and "poodle faking" as we called it in the Navy, and so forth, but we were suddenly uprooted from all this, and off we went.

However, eventually we arrived off the Mexican coast. Now, Minatitlan is on the Coatzacoalcos River and is rather an oasis in what I would have called a desert. There was a considerable township housing about 300 families in the British-owned refinery surrounded by drab green scrub and sunbaked earth. About two miles away was a very primitive Mexican village which had nothing but a few wattle huts, I believe, a post office and I seem to remember it had a mayor, although I never met him. This village provided the local labour required in the refinery.

We steamed for several hours up a sluggish river with nothing on either side but endless shallows and mud flats. When we arrived at the refinery there was a wharf which had been built to accommodate ocean-going tankers and the river was wide enough to turn around.

We had to drop an anchor and steam round on the anchor so as to be facing down stream when we tied up alongside the wharf. Everything appeared quiet and it wasn't until we made a reconnaissance that we realised that the village about two miles away was in the process of being occupied by a force of the Mexican Army. Now this Mexican Army, as I saw it, was very funny. Their uniforms (if you could call them that) were weird and wonderful - no two alike - and very few complete. Some men had rifles, some revolvers, one or two mules or donkeys in each company carried ancient old Maxim guns and any soldier who was lucky enough to own a mule, a donkey or an old screw of a horse was riding it.

The next day there was considerable activity and when we looked through our field-glasses we discovered that the Army was digging in along the bank of the river.

The trenches eventually ended about a hundred yards from our quarterdeck and came right up to the refinery boundary fence, so we gathered that the Army was expecting an attack from the river. We were told that the Army were on the Federal or Government side, and the Navy they were expecting to repel were on the revolutionary side and in fact at that moment the Navy were steaming up river and would reach Minatitlan before dark.

Without any ostentation, HMS Constance went to action stations. In other words, all guns were manned, but the gun crews kept out of sight as far as possible. I had to post a couple of Lewis gun crews at strategic points in case they were required. (I am not sure whether that was to repel boarders or what.) However, so there was no mistake, we were flying our largest white Ensign and Union Jack because we had strict orders not to "start anything."

In due course, the rebel Navy came in sight, and a wonderful sight it was! First came an ancient gunboat that I imagine the British navy had discarded about 1885 and this nice old ship had probably done at least 30 years yeoman service before that. Then came an armed trawler which had probably done good service as a minesweeper in WWI and lastly came two ex American motor craft, sub chasers also from the first war.

The bulwarks of each ship were piled with sand bags behind which we could see quite a number of men armed mostly with rifles. As they passed our quarter deck, barely a hundred yards out in the main deep water channel, we saw a black bottle being passed from hand to hand (or should I say from mouth to mouth) amongst the sailors and we gathered that some form of Dutch courage was being absorbed. Or should I call it, Mexican courage? Nothing happened until the rebel ships anchored abreast of the village and the gunboat fired two rounds from her one 3-inch gun and we saw the dust and the smoke of the explosions rising beyond the village. This was the signal for ragged and quite uncontrolled small-arms fire from the entrenched army on the river bank. Then darkness fell. There was desultory firing from small arms on both sides during the night and at dawn "battle was really commenced."

At about 6.30 in the grey steamy first light, the gunboat and the trawler fired about five rounds each into the village and the army replied with rifles, machine guns and even revolvers. We noticed some very good shooting being done by one man who was established at the end of a trench nearest to our quarter deck. Through my binoculars I saw that he was an officer wearing highly-polished field boots and "Sam Browne" belt. He was by any standards very well dressed and I noticed that he had a telescopic sight on his rifle. This turned out to be the General commanding the Government forces and he seemed to us to be the only one who knew how to aim his rifle. In any case he was the only one who seemed to score any hits.

About noon, the Rebel Navy had enough of the battle, so they weighed anchor, steamed down river past us again and this was the signal for a yelling cheering mob to chase down the track that ran along the river bank. They broke through the refinery gates and streamed past the ship firing any weapons they possessed wildly and without any aim at all.

As I have said our Captain was Captain J D Campbell and our 1st Lieutenant Commander Massey Goulden, a very fine, efficient and likeable officer, about six feet three or four, normally quiet, but a man who when he bit, bit very hard. We were still on the quarterdeck, when one of our signalmen fell at our feet with a bullet through his head just after handing a signal to the Captain. The bullet, which had obviously been fired into the air from some considerable distance away was nearly spent when it came down through the quarterdeck awning and hit the poor boy who unfortunately died soon afterwards.

The Captain said to Massey Goulden "Number One stop this ruddy nonsense and bring whoever is in charge of that rabble on board to report to me."

"Aye, aye, Sir," replied Number One.

Well, it was quite amazing. Number One stalked over the gangway, past our Royal Marine sentry who was posted at the foot of the gangway. Number One was unarmed of course and stood with upheld hand in the way of the passing rabble and just shouted "Halt! who's in charge of this party, bring him here." They stopped and gaped, because although they couldn't understand a word he said they recognised authority in this tall Naval officer who immaculate as he was and cool as he was, was very obviously angry. The Mexican Army stopped in its tracks, gathered round Massey Goulden, and stared. Very shortly, the officer who had been sniping rode up on the only decent horse we had seen and smartly saluting our First Lieutenant, said in reasonable English "Have my men do something wrong?"

"Like hell they have," replied Number One, "Tell those men of yours to unload their rifles while they are on British property and come on board yourself, the Captain wants to see you."

General Beltrand (as we later discovered his name to be) gave an order to his gaping troops who unloaded their rifles and proceeded to squat around the wharf still gaping. The General then attempted to follow Massey Goulden up the gangway, but was shocked to find that Marine Jackson, the Marine sentry, had his bayonet at his chest. Jackson growled, "Can't go on board with that armoury," and held the General up until I had relieved him of two automatics and two vicious looking sheath knives, then allowed him to pass.

What our Captain said to the General I don't know, but later on a very chastened officer was conducted down to the ward room for a drink to help him to recover and he told us that he considered that he had achieved a victory over the rebels and had called the battle off. After a couple of stiff ones General Beltrand waxed eloquent, and told us the story of his life. He was very proud of the fact that he had been trained at the French Military College at St Cyr, and was a professional soldier who had always fought on the Government side. This meant that more than once when the Government had been defeated in a revolution, he had been in exile until the new Government had realised his worth. He wound up by saying disgustedly, "In Mexican army most General are politicians, we call them "Finger General" because in revolution, politician who wants to be President points his finger to all his friends and says, "You General, you Colonel, you General" and so on. Pah! all General and Colonels no soldiers in Mexican Army except Beltrand!" With that he went rather unsteadily ashore, retrieved his armoury and led his straggling but mystified troops back to the village.

Two days later Minatitlan was empty of troops and three days later HMS Constance was recalled to Bermuda. The revolution was over, and we could only conclude that Lieutenant Commander (now Captain) Massey Goulden was responsible for the stopping of "all this nonsense."

After our return from Mexico to Bermuda, HMS Constance was anchored in Grassy Bay. We had been enjoying a break when we were given sailing orders to proceed next day on a cruise to Newfoundland and Canada. The watch off duty was having a last run ashore, two or three of us were chatting and smoking on the quarter deck, and then we spotted a large merchant ship approaching assisted by the dockyard tug.

She was flying the Spanish flag and had the "out of control" signals from the yard arm. It transpired that she was a Spanish emigrant ship on her way from Spain to South America. She had lost one of her propellers and had come into Bermuda for repairs.

In the naval dockyard there was a floating dock which the Spaniard would have to occupy for at least 14 days. This raised complications because, in dry dock, the ship's boilers would have to be let out and there would be no machinery or lights working on board. Accommodation would have to be found ashore for the passengers, of which she carried about 20 or 30 in the first class and nearly 1000 in the steerage.

The first class passengers could be accommodated in the hotels, but only just, because it was the height of the tourist season, and rooms were very scarce.

The only quarters the authorities ashore could find for the 1000 steerage emigrants was on two small islands in the old First War prisoner of war huts, so it was arranged that the male immigrants should go to one island and the females to the other.

Shortly after dark (we were still at dinner in the ward room) the Yeoman of Signals reported that SOS was being signalled from the bridge of the Spanish ship. This was followed by a message in broken English of which the chief words he could decipher were "Mutiny" and "Armed Guard."

The Captain sent for me and ordered me to take a Sergeant and 12 Marines and act as I considered necessary. In 10 minutes we were on our way in the motorboat each man with a rifle and bayonet and with five rounds of ammunition in his pouch. I gave orders that no one was to load or fire except on direct orders from me. When we came alongside we saw that the ship's officers and the first class passengers were clustered on the boat deck and that the after well-deck was crowded by the emigrants listening to someone haranguing them from the top of the after hatch.

We climbed on board and after posting sentries with fixed bayonets at the top of the four ladders leading to the first class and officer's accommodation, I got the story in broken English from the Captain.

Amongst the emigrants was a so called cabaret troupe of about 20 girls and a man who called himself the manager of the troupe. He was the cause of the trouble.

When this fellow heard that men and women were to stay on separate islands he had produced a revolver and at that moment was haranguing the immigrants with a view to rushing the officer's quarters and taking over the first-class quarters. This apparently was because he objected to being separated from his "artistes".

The officers had panicked and the first class passengers were terrified all because a nasty little under-sized rat of a man was waving a revolver and shouting.

I selected the biggest man in my little detachment, Marine Jackson, a first class soldier of about six feet two and told him to follow me with his rifle and fixed bayonet at the "high port" and said, "We'll arrest this little blighter. If he tries any funny business hit him on the jaw with the butt of your rifle, Jackson." "Don't worry, I'll fix him, sir."

So off we went down to the after well-deck. As we got to the crowd, Jackson merely shouted "Gangway." Faces turned, and when they saw a smallish officer followed by an enormous marine with a fixed bayonet towering above and behind him an avenue opened up like magic.

We went straight up to the hatch where the man was still addressing the crowd. He saw us and stopped mid sentence. We stepped on to the hatch and while Jackson presented the bayonet at his chest, I gently relieved him of the revolver, took him by the ear (not so gently), placed him in the charthouse and put him in handcuffs under the charge of one of our sentries.

I signalled HMS Constance asking for civil police escort to take the prisoner to cells in Hamilton, then through an interpreter told the still staring and murmuring crowd to go to bed and to stay there until morning. Then came the instruction by signal to remain on board with the guard until 8am next day when civil police would take over.

By this time, it was quiet and peaceful, all the emigrants were below decks and Captain, officers and first class passengers were embarrassingly grateful.

Reliefs for the sentries were arranged two hours on and four off – and the off duty guard were given cabins to sleep in. I was offered a suite, champagne, brandy and goodness knows what. However, as I intended to stay awake all night I asked for black coffee so the Purser detailed a steward to be at our orders all night. Each relief of sentries had coffee and as much as they could eat in the way of sandwiches and cakes before they went on watch and I arranged to inspect the emigrants' accommodation with my Sergeant every hour to make sure all was quiet. When we made our first inspection we were horrified at the conditions of the steerage passengers. They were all sleeping on palliases in the cargo space around the hatches in the hold. On three levels. Men, women and children all mixed indiscriminately. Each with their poor little bundle of personal belongings beside him. The smell was frightful there was no ventilation that we could see and goodness knows how they washed, (most of them looked as though they didn't). No wonder they were ripe for mutiny.

Just after daybreak at 6am I asked for breakfast and what a breakfast they gave us. Tropical fruit, an enormous dish of kidney, bacon and eggs, toast, hot rolls and marmalade. Our hosts were quite hurt because we refused to have liqueur in our coffee. The Sergeant and I ate together at a table brought out on deck (after our night of inspections we felt we needed all the fresh air we could get).

It was most embarrassing; most of the first class passengers (and there were some very pretty girls amongst them) came and stood round watching us eat. From what little I could understand of their remarks, they promoted my Sergeant to Captain and me to Colonel!

At about 7.30 the Civil Police arrived and took over and our own motor boat came to take us back to our ship.

Just before HMS Constance sailed we saw launches coming alongside the Spaniard to take the men and women to their respective islands. We heard later that the chief mutineer was sentenced to prison, but was allowed to sail in the ship with his troupe of women.

I suppose that was what Kipling referred to as a "Board School Mutiny." (The phrase comes from Kipling's "Soldier An' Sailor Too," referring to the occasion when a detachment of Royal marines was posted to Bermuda after riotous behaviour in barracks. The "Onion Guards" are the Welsh Guards.)

Our cruise to Canada had the main object of meeting HMS Repulse with the Prince of Wales on board. She had been to Australia, New Zealand and round the world and the British Empire. Canada and Newfoundland were the last calls of a long and exacting cruise.

Our most important job was to take libertymen from Repulse from Quebec up the St Lawrence to Montreal and back. Officers and ship's company of Repulse were weary with a surfeit of hospitality and entertainment, both as hosts and guests and we gathered that they were very glad to be nearing the end of the cruise.

When Constance was returning from Newfoundland to Bermuda she ran into a dense fog such as are frequent off that coast. We were creeping along with barely steerage way, sounding our siren when an SOS was picked up on our W/T.

An oil tanker was on fire some 200 miles to the south of us. Our Captain ordered revolutions for 20 knots, and with our siren blazing we charged through the fog. It was a frightening experience. Visibility was about 100 yards and we narrowly missed several fishing schooners. After some two hours of this we intercepted another signal from a merchant ship to the effect that she was within sight of the burning tanker so the Captain was able to reduce to a safer speed. We heard later that the survivors had been picked up in their lifeboats.

On our arrival in Bermuda we received Admiralty Orders announcing the introduction of the Fleet Air Arm. Up to then, the RAF had provided the pilots and the Navy the Observers, and Airborne Telegraphists for carrier-borne aircraft.

Volunteers were now called for from junior officers of the Royal Navy and Royal Marines to be trained as pilots. Not surprisingly, I quickly volunteered and after a medical examination at the Naval Hospital, I was passed fit, except for enlarged tonsils. After a certain amount of waiting, I got impatient and asked to have my tonsils removed. The Surgeon Commander at the hospital was instructed to arrange this and I think he must have resented being ordered to do the operation. On our own doctor's instructions I took gear to the hospital in readiness for about 10 days in bed. To my horror, with no preparation at all, the hospital doctor seated me in a hard-backed chair, produced an instrument like a large cigar cutter and snipped off the offending tonsils without any anaesthetic. Most unpleasant, particularly the second one because by the time he got round to that I knew what was coming.

I remained for an hour or so, rinsing my mouth, then walked back to the ship which was in the floating dock at the time. I couldn't speak, and my throat hurt damnably and of course I was unable to swallow any food for a time.

Our own doctor, Surgeon Commander Sprague was ashore when I returned to the ship. When he returned he was amazed to find me back so soon, looked at my gory throat, and promptly put me to bed. He was very angry with the hospital people and I believe he complained to higher authority. However, I survived and in due course found myself on board the Royal Mail Steam Packet Ship, Orca, which called in at Bermuda on her return from a West Indies cruise.

Chapter 5

A Flying Marine

Back in England, I eventually passed the full medical tests at Air Ministry and in January 1925 I reported to No 1 Flying Training School at Netheravon, which as the birthplace of British military aviation had a tremendous tradition even then.

There were some distinguished men there. Our CO was Group Captain "Ginger" Mitchell an accomplished and famous World War I pilot, who was commanding 12 Wing RAF at the end of the war. The Chief Flying Instructor was Squadron Leader "Bill" Sowrey, another distinguished RFC fighter pilot who later came to further fame during the Abyssinian "crisis" in 1934-35. We were taught to fly in the good old Avro 504K, with the Gnome Monosoupape rotary engine. One of its unique and identifying features was a long skid or "toothpick" between the under carriage wheels which had shock absorbers composed of thick rubber in a fabric casing. The skid was to prevent the aircraft nosing over and it also protected the propeller. There was another skid instead of a tail wheel and there were also rudimentary skids near the lower wing tips to minimise any danger from touching a wing on landing.

It was a wonderful old aircraft, with no vices except that the engine was tricky to handle because it had no carburettor. The hollow crankshaft was fixed and the cylinders to which the propeller was attached revolved around it. The most vital control was the air lever on the throttle quadrant. After starting the engine by swinging the propeller, the maximum revolutions were obtained by adjusting the air lever then the engine was controlled by what we called a "blip switch", a small press button on the top of the "stick" or control column. This cut out the current from the magneto to the spark plugs and effectively turned the engine off for a moment. So we taxied using short bursts of full power by "blipping" the engine off rather than on and reduced speed for landing in the same manner. There were a few tricks to the procedure – if you held the blip too long there was a danger of the engine stopping altogether. There were also cases of the engine exploding from being re-fired with too much fuel in the system.

The gyroscopic effect of the rotating engine, as well as the inertial effect were other factors which did not affect the Avro too much because it was such a stable aircraft. The same type of engine made the Sopwith Camel turn to port almost immediately but it went to starboard with reluctance. In a dogfight, the sudden turn could be used to advantage, but the Camel was notoriously difficult to control. In order to achieve maximum tactical manoeuvrability it was designed to be inherently unstable and more pilots died in that machine while learning to master it than in combat.

The Gnome engine of the Avro 504k was lubricated with almost pure castor oil and breathing those castor oil fumes had a magnificent purgative effect until we got used to them! Some pilots carried a flask of blackberry brandy which was reputed to stop the laxative effect. My first instructor on the 504k was a terrific character called "Dicky" Bain, a young Flying Officer who was a first-class pilot and an excellent instructor. As I was wise enough to keep dark the fact that I had already gained a little flying experience during the war, I was first of our course to go solo in Avros and also later in DH9A's, the service type on which we trained. My first solo in the Avro was on Friday February 13, 1925 after 9 hours and 5 minutes dual and it was only when writing up my logbook I realised what Dicky meant when he said "I hope you're not superstitious – you are on your own!" That first solo was a mere 10 minutes but of course represented a real milestone and the true start of a career as a pilot.

My logbook notes: "Found machine much more comfortable solo."

I had again found that flying was really something to be enthusiastic about and primitive as those aircraft were by modern standards, they were never dull.

Our technical instruction was very thorough, covering theory of flight, navigation (mostly map reading in those days), engine maintenance, rigging, aerial gunnery and bombing, plus air force law and administration.

Most of us had forced landings during the course, due largely to engine failure of one sort or another and even the occasional bowel emergency due to the castor oil mentioned above. We were trained to be always ready for an emergency landing. When on a cross country flight, we kept an eye open for suitable fields within gliding distance of the flight path. This was long before blind flying instruments were invented so we were discouraged from flying in cloud. Our only instruments were petrol and oil pressure gauges, air speed indicator, altimeter, cross level and magnetic compass.

We literally flew by the "seat of our pants" sitting in draughty open cockpits – and we loved it. (Although the terminology was second-nature to us, it probably needs explanation for the uninitiated. All our piloting skills and judgements were dependant on being able to feel the attitude, the rate of climb or descent and any turning motion through our seat – it was as simple – and sometimes not so simple – as that.)

When we had finished our Avro course, I was sent to the DH9A flight commanded by Flight Lieutenant "Tommy" Thomson, a Scot and a most efficient instructor. On my first flight in the DH9A I noted "Found the machine wonderfully nice to handle" and after three hours instruction was allowed to solo. That was on April 29, 1925 by which time I had logged a total of 19 hours dual flying and 36 hours solo. "Tommy" Thomson (his real name was George) later left the RAF and became one of the aviation pioneers in New Guinea, flying heavy mining equipment up country to the gold mines there; flying over impassable jungle and high mountains which up to then had made the interior almost unknown to white men.

One of the talking points among us all at the time of starting our flying training was what became known as "The Great Race of Mercy" in February of that year when 20 mushers and about 150 sled dogs relayed urgently-needed diphtheria serum across Alaska to save the occupants of Nome from a growing epidemic. The relay was in sub-zero and often blizzard conditions but the dogs covered 675 miles in a record-breaking five and a half days. Our initial response was to wonder why they had not used aircraft but once we heard about the conditions (particularly the whiteout visibility) we realised that aviation then was still not able to compete with dogs when it came to Arctic travel.

The DH9A deserves some description. It was designed towards the end of the war by de Havillands as a single-engined bomber to be capable of bombing Berlin from our airfields in France. It was a two-seater, with one forward Vickers gun firing through the propeller, using the Constantinesco interrupter gear and a Lewis gun mounted on a Scarff ring in the rear cockpit. The engine was an American-designed Liberty engine, mass-produced and reputedly supposed to be scrapped after a hundred hours running. As this was seven years after the war, the hundred hours must have been stretched somewhat!

The Liberty engine was much more reliable than the old "Mono" of the Avro 504k and I do not remember any engine failures in my DH9A flying time. The DH9A saw a lot of service in the 1920's and 1930's particularly in the Middle East and the North West Frontier of India where it was used in an aerial policing role, effectively reducing the need for large numbers of ground troops. As this type of flying required time over hostile territory and sometimes involved forced landings in some fairly interesting terrain, it was quite usual to carry spare wheels, an extensive tool kit, emergency food and water and even bedding. I was eventually to get first-hand experience of just this type of situation in Palestine.

On July 2 I reached my 100 hours by making a 10-minute flight in a DH9A. I passed my "B" certificate on July 21 with 86 hours solo logged and a total of 107 hours 35 minutes. By then the totals showed 50 hours solo in the DH9A and 37 hours in the Avro 504k. I had also made short flights in a Fairey Fawn and an Avro Aldershot and flown on a 2 hour 20 minute flight in a Vickers Virginia with a visiting bomber flight.

It was customary for the pupils to invite the instructors to dinner after being awarded our wings at the end of the course. (I received my wings on August 8, 1925.) Our flight decided to dine our instructors in the Mess, the other flight took their instructors into Salisbury. After dinner, I unwisely told Dicky Bain about my flying experience during the war at Gosport. That cost me a lot of drinks! About 11.30 the other flight returned with their instructors and staged a friendly raid on our party. The resulting battle damaged a certain amount of mess furniture for which we all cheerfully paid out of our next pay.

The next morning we were given our flying log books by the Chief Flying Instructor, "Bill" Sowrey, and I was delighted to find that mine had been endorsed with "Exceptional" as a pilot. As the categories awarded in those days consisted of "below the average," "average," "above the average" and "exceptional" I felt I was justified in being pleased. Bill Sowrey, in his wisdom then pointed out that I was approaching the most dangerous period of a pilot's life, when with about 200 flying hours in his log book, a pilot began to think he knew it all. His final remarks were "beware of over confidence, never be tempted to show off and remember in flying there is always something to learn."

Sound advice from an exceptionally sound instructor and pilot.

Later that August, I was appointed to Gosport for deck landing and torpedo-dropping training. The torpedo bomber in use then was the Blackburn Dart, a great lumbering single-seater biplane with a maximum speed of about 65 knots. The Dart carried a 2500lb, 18-inch torpedo and was powered by a Napier Lion engine. Our preliminary deck-landing training consisted of approaches and landings on a dummy deck laid out on the aerodrome. We did our torpedo dropping in Stokes Bay in the nearby Solent. I had expected to be given some detailed instruction before going solo in the Dart but all that happened was a preliminary cockpit check by an experienced pilot and I was waved off. "Right lad, give it a shot. But mind, she's a bit heavier on landing than the DH9A." And she was even heavier the first time I went up with a torpedo slung underneath.

The officers mess and quarters at Gosport were still in the old fort I remembered from 1917, but modern barrack accommodation had been built for the NCO's and airmen. It was sad however to find that the old RMLI Barracks at Forton had been handed over to the Navy. The RMLI and the RMA had been amalgamated and were just known as Royal Marines. Forton Barracks had become HMS St Vincent.

My first practice torpedo attack on a ship was disappointing. I was supposed to make a run and drop a torpedo in an attack on the cruiser HMS Champion but heavy mist meant we had to abandon the sortie. However, two days later, I made the perfect drop, the torpedo ran straight without breaking the surface and hit Champion amidships.

On November 11, 1925 I was taken to Haslar Hospital at about two hours notice to have my appendix removed. This proved lucky for me because I was scheduled to go out with the submarine M1 for the experience the following day. When I came out of the anaesthetic the next evening, a depressed sick berth steward informed me that M1 had gone down with all hands. But for the appendix I would have gone too. I decided after that not to be tempted again to have submarine experience. There were three M-Class submarines built. With a length of nearly 300ft and a displacement of 1950 tons, they were huge compared with conventional subs, but it was the armament that was particularly unusual. They were fitted with one 12-inch gun (almost identical to a gun off the Agincourt, that was why I was keen to go out on M1) which was intended for use against merchant ships in preference to torpedoes. The Royal Navy spent a week of intensive effort trying to locate the missing vessel and the reason for the sinking remained a mystery until shortly after that when the Swedish collier SS Vidal reported striking an underwater object the morning of the disappearance. Subsequent examination showed a bent stem and sprung plates on the Vidal and scrapings of the experimental antifouling from the M1. To this day, even with modern equipment, the location of M1 and her crew of 69 remains a mystery. (The wreck was possibly located in 84 fathoms about 35 miles from Portsmouth by the survey ship HMS Bulldog in 1991 and the position finally confirmed by a diving team lead by Innes MCartney in 1999. The wreckage has the gun torn off its mounting which supports the collision theory).

Towards the end of the year we did our first deck landings on HMS Furious. At that time, Furious was equipped with a type of arrester gear which was soon abandoned. This gear consisted of fore and aft wires, supported about a foot above the deck by hinged plates every 15 feet or so along their length. On the axle of the deck-landing aircraft were half a dozen clip hooks. The theory was that on touching the deck one or more of the hooks caught a wire and the wheels knocked the plates flat as they came to them. The tension could be increased on the wire by hydraulic pressure, thus having a braking effect as the hook ran along it. (Aircraft were not fitted with wheel brakes then).

The trouble was that if a pilot landed too far up the deck, at best the aircraft went on its nose when it reached the forward end of the wire. At worst, if he opened his engine to go round again (there was no means of knowing if a hook had caught a wire) the undercarriage would break with the extra strain or the aircraft would nose over and a much worse crash would occur.

I think we did our six training landings using these wires and then it was decided to remove them leaving a bare deck so that a safe landing depended on the pilot's skill and the agility of the deck-handling party.

The deck-handling party was stationed in the nettings on each side of the landing deck and as the aircraft touched down they would dash out and seize the wings. (The nickname for this team was "the scrum"). All this sounds much more dangerous than it really was, because although the aircraft had no brakes, the carrier always steamed into wind in order to produce a steady air speed over the deck of about 30 knots. For instance, if the wind speed was 10 knots, the carrier would steam at 20 knots into it and there was a steam jet as the forward end of the deck which showed at once if the ship was the slightest bit out of wind.

The old Dart had a landing speed of about 50 knots, so the touch-down speed on the deck was only 20 knots and there was then the braking power of a steady 30 knots wind over the deck. Later, palisades were fitted on each side of the deck for about two thirds of the length of the deck and set on an angle of about 40deg sloping outwards. The purpose of these was to prevent an aircraft going over the side in case of a bad landing. They certainly saved a few aircraft from anything but minor damage.

We always had an attendant destroyer, sometimes two, steaming on the quarter of the carrier whenever aircraft were operating. Their job was to pick up any aircrew who went over the side (the aircraft was usually a write off anyway). Although a relatively large aircraft (the wing span was 45 ft 6in and the length was 35 ft) the Dart had a stalling speed of only 38 knots and it had a responsiveness to control yet docility that made it one of the "pilot's aeroplanes."

In October 1925 (this time after an hour and a half of dual instruction) I flew the Fairey IIID seaplane and qualified in this machine at the Calshot Seaplane Course. There was a moment or two of initial apprehension but by the time I'd finished the course it was a real pleasure to take off and land on the water.

Early in 1926 I was appointed to No 461 Flight, Fleet Air Arm, in HMS Furious. The Flight Commander was Flight Lieutenant "Jimmy" Riddle, a very experienced deck-landing pilot and a delightful character.

We did a lot of flying, carrying out runner torpedo attacks using Furious as target and later when Fleet Exercises were held, attacking a battleship on the "opposing" side. These attacks were carried out with proper torpedoes but fitted with a "collision head." This was a dummy head which was fitted with a calcium flare so at the end of the run the torpedo floated to the surface, the flare ignited and it could be spotted easily by the destroyer detailed to pick up the torpedoes. The torpedo was set to float on completing its run, whether it hit the target or not. Torpedoes were too valuable to be lost in peacetime and we used the same ones over and over again.

To aim the torpedo the pilot had to estimate the target's speed and course relative to the intended track of the torpedo. The only assistance we had was a rather primitive aiming device composed of blobs on a wire stretched across the centre section at the pilot's eye level. It was rather like trying to shoot a large hare with a rifle from a range of a thousand yards, but all in slow motion. Experience and practice and a good eye were our main assets.

The maximum height we could safely drop the torpedo was about 30 feet, otherwise the shock of impact was apt to upset the gyro which kept the torpedo on a straight course after it was dropped. The ideal height was considered to be 15 feet above the wave tops – quite an exciting place to be, particularly in rough weather (and obviously it would be even more "exciting" in wartime with your target shooting back, the ideal range was within 1000 yards). Many years later, developments such as circling and homing devices were invented and incorporated in the design of the torpedo. The aircraft designers in the 20s were greatly hampered by the requirements laid down by the Royal Navy for their aircraft with the result that the Fleet Spotter Reconnaisance aircraft of those early days were unnecessarily slow, ungainly and cumbersome. The navy insisted that the navigator's portion of the aircraft was like a ship's charthouse, hence aircraft like the Avro Bison and the Blackburn R1 Blackburn or Fleet Spotter. However these old aircraft were strong, amazingly reliable for their time and provided valuable training for pilots, navigators and telegraphists. Such aircraft also began to teach the more conservative senior officers in the Navy to be air minded. My flying log book for this period brings back memories of some of the pioneering flying experiences that would soon be commonplace. I made my first night flights in May and June, 1926. We then made night ADDL (aerodrome dummy deck landings) in July and I was on Furious when Flt Lieutenant Gerald Boyce made the historic first night deck touch-and-go landing on an aircraft carrier on July 1, 1926. It wasn't until November 26, 1929 that the first full night deck landing was made on HMS Courageous by a Fairey Flycatcher flown from Hal Far, Malta by Flight Lieutenant Owen Cathcart-Jones. I made two dummy runs over the deck that night and two days later made three night landings in "my" Dart on Courageous.

With two-way radio-telephony in its infancy, its use was generally noted in the logbook with entries such as "Formation R/T", "R/T practice with ground", "Torpedo attack on fleet controlled by R/T" and "Slow landing by R/T."

As a bit of light relief from the Dart, I made my first solo in a Fairey Flycatcher on September 14, 1926. What a delightful little aircraft! It was the first purpose-built single-seater fighter for carrier work and it was light and responsive to fly. I was so carried away with its manoeuvrability that I did two loops and two three-point landings on my first short flight. (As I sit in the garden in my home in New Zealand, I am reminded of that aircraft whenever I watch the antics of the little native fantail, the Piwakwaka, which is of course an original flycatcher.)

As a result of my Calshot float plane qualification, to my joy, I was allowed to fly the one experimental Fairey III D float plane that Furious carried, in addition to my Dart. This meant that I managed to put in quite a bit of flying when the ship was in harbour as well as normal exercises with the Dart flight when at sea.

My observer was Lieutenant "Cam" Camidge RN, a very good friend of mine. Unfortunately Cam weighed over 18 stone so the Fairey III D, which was supposed to be a three-seater, just would not get off the water with Cam and a telegraphist on board.

Another factor was that the aircraft was experimental because it was fitted with the first all-metal floats. We had successfully carried out some trial landings on the deck to prove that landing and taking a float plane off the deck was possible in an emergency, but as a result, the floats were leaking badly owing to loosened rivets. We had no means of repairing them on board, so that after being hoisted into the water I had to waste no time before taking off otherwise the weight of the water in the floats plus "Cam's" 18 stone was too much for the Napier Lion engine. When I think back on it, that was probably my first experience as a test pilot in the real sense, we were often sent on flights to test and report on an aircraft after minor repairs or an engine change but in this case I was breaking new ground and we were venturing into the unknown.

While Furious was anchored at Ullapool, in the north west coast of Scotland, for a week or so, Cam and I flew across daily in the III D to deliver and collect mails for HMS Hood, the flagship, anchored in Gairloch Firth. We landed astern of Hood, she streamed a lifebuoy on a grass line for us to make fast to, I turned the engine off and a boat was then sent across to exchange the bags of mail. Cam then wound furiously on the starting handle and we took off hurriedly before too much water seeped into the floats. On several occasions we had great difficulty in getting airborne. Once in the air, the water took about an hour to drain out of the floats. On one occasion, when the sea-plane crane in Furious developed some defect we nearly sank before we were hooked on.

At the end of November, Furious went into Portsmouth dockyard for a refit after we in her aircraft had flown off and landed at Gosport. I was then attached to the Torpedo Development Flight at Gosport for a few months and gained a lot of experience in more types of aircraft including the Hawker Horseley, a land based torpedo bomber which later, piloted by Flight Lieutenant Roderick Carr, a New Zealander (now Air Marshal Sir Roderick Carr) made an attempt on the long-distance record. They flew over 3400 miles from Cranwell to the Persian Gulf before being forced to land.

During this period I was detached with a drogue towing Fairey III D sea plane for about a month to Weymouth, where we towed a target for HMS Tiger to practise anti aircraft gunnery. Captain Gordon Campbell VC was then Captain of HMS Tiger. I found him to be a most impressive and charming man who was so convinced of the importance of the Fleet Air Arm that he instructed me to give as many of his officers as possible flying experience as passengers. As a result, I put in a lot of flying time.

The drogue target was like a wind sock, which after being released by the observer was towed on a wire about 1000 feet behind the aircraft. The wire was wound on a drum in the back cockpit and could be unwound or brought in by a geared winch driven by a small four-bladed propeller turned into the slipstream. I was not very impressed by the accuracy of the AA fire, because although the drogue was never hit, on one occasion a burst severed the towing wire only about 20 feet behind my tail. I think the gun layer must have aimed at the towing aircraft instead of at the drogue target! The naval officer I was carrying as a passenger at the time was quite shaken, because he saw the burst and I didn't, although I certainly heard it and felt the concussion.

By the middle of 1927 the types of aircraft flown had expanded – the Avro Bison, Blackburn Blackburn, Fairey IIIF, Hawker Hawfinch and Blackburn Ripon were added to my logbook. Among the more interesting flights was one from Gosport to Worthy Down to pick up parts and an engineer to repair an Avro 504k that had force landed in a paddock some 20 minutes away from base. After a new magneto had been fitted, I flew the Avro back home as a way of air testing it – then I was given a ride back to bring back my Dart.

In August 1927 I spent an excellent leave helping to bring a motor cruiser from Cette, in the Rhone estuary, up the Rivers Rhone and Saone, then through the French canals to Calais. About this time, I was promoted to Captain RM and to celebrate I bought my first car, a new baby Austin (Austin 7) which only cost 125 pounds then.

Shortly after taking delivery of the car, I was posted to No 460 Flight in HMS Eagle (July 27, 1927) and ordered to join the ship in Malta. I obtained permission to go by car and drove from Calais, across France, Switzerland, over the Simplon Pass into Italy, then via Milan, Rome, Naples and Salerno to the toe of Italy, across in the ferry to Messina, then by ship from Catania to Malta. The Italian roads, except for the Autostrade at Milan were shocking, particularly from Naples south and I was quite pleased to complete the journey in 13 days. Between Naples and Catania I repaired 35 punctures, all caused by picking up shoe nails like large drawing pins which the peasants seemed to cast from their boots deliberately. The little car stood up to the bad roads amazingly well and I subsequently wrote up an article on the journey for the Austin Magazine. (see appendix)

Chapter 6

The Perch Club

Two months after I joined HMS Eagle, we sailed for Venice where the Schneider Cup race was being flown. On board we carried some spare engines and parts for the British aircraft competing in the race. That year, the Royal Air Force had entered with two Supermarine S5 aircraft and a Gloster IV, all powered by Napier racing engines (direct-drive, high compression derivatives of the Napier Lion engine already in service in such aircraft as the Fairey 111D). A Short Crusader, powered by a Bristol Mercury engine was also in the British line-up but crashed during its first flight in Venice, several days before the race. The pilot, Harry Schofield, escaped with concussion and facial cuts. This crash was found to be due to the aileron control cables being spliced back to front. Schofield went on to co-author a book called The Pictorial Flying Course with "Captain" W.E. Johns, the author of the classic Biggles books, which appeared in 1932. Schofield also became a director and test pilot of the General Aviation Company which produced Britain's first purpose-built aerial ambulance (a modified Monospar ST 11) in 1936.

We carried out flying exercises on the way up the Adriatic Sea and anchored off Venice. This Schneider Cup race was memorable, not only because the British won, but because the winning aircraft, the Supermarine S5, was the design from which the Spitfire was developed.

The names I remember are Flight Lieutenants Sidney Webster (the winner), Owen Worsley and Sam Kinkhead in the British team and Count Mario de Bernardi, Arturo Ferrarin and Frederico Guazetti on the Italian side. The defending Italian team were all flying Macchi M52 aircraft, painted a bright scarlet.

I watched the race on September 26, 1927 from the bridge of HMS Worcester (our attendant destroyer for the cruise) as a guest of her Captain, Lieutenant Commander Patrick Fell, a fine seaman and a very good friend. Worcester was stationed off Chioggia, at the turning point furthest from the Lido finishing line. The race, scheduled for Sunday, September 25, was postponed due to rough weather but the well-publicised event still drew an estimated crowd of over 200,000 Italians the next day. The race had become very much a showpiece for Mussolini's fascist Italy and there was a great deal of propaganda on radio, leaflets and posters throughout the country. Special trains were run from many major cities and half-price fares were offered over the entire rail network.

Visibility was poor because of haze at the start and rain during the latter stages so the presence of a destroyer close to the turning-point marker buoy was a great help to the competing pilots. It was interesting to see the different piloting tactics as well as the competing designs. Our pilots flew wide at the turns, banking gently and holding level flight while the Italians went high in a deep vertical bank and dived back to the course.

The race was over seven 50km laps of the elongated triangular course with very sharp turns at each end and a fairly gentle apex turn off Alberoni. Kinkhead started the race for Britain in the Gloster IV and recorded an opening lap of 266.5mph but when Bernardi recorded an opening lap of 275mph it became obvious that our hopes rested with the two S5 entries. Ferrarin had a spectacular engine failure on his first lap and crash landed in a cloud of smoke, almost hitting the Excelsior Palace where many dignitaries and team officials were watching. Bernardi also had engine failure and force landed about half a mile from HMS Worcester after only two laps. He made a good landing and Worcester sent her motor boat to his assistance. The officer in charge of the motor boat took Bernardi aboard and invited him back to watch the rest of the race from Worcester and to have a drink or two. Bernhardi was in a foul temper and refused, rudely asking to be taken ashore. When asked what he wanted done with the aircraft he indicated that he couldn't care less, so he was taken to the beach and landed. Later, the aircraft was towed ashore and handed over to the Italians.

Guazetti completed six laps and then force landed with engine trouble, leaving Webster to win the race with Worsley second, a triumph for the British aircraft and pilots. The third British entry, Kinkhead (in a Gloster IV biplane) had dropped out on the fifth lap with damaged propeller due to a loose engine cowling.

The Napier Racing engine was a 12-cyclinder arranged in three banks of four ("broad arrowhead" configuration) and had the distinction that year of also powering Sir Henry Seagrave to win the World Motor Boat Speed Championship and Malcolm Campbell to setting a new land speed record (which he took from Seagrave).

Before the race, a celebration dinner for both teams had been arranged to take place the night after the race was over and this was presided over by Crown Prince Umberto of Italy.

It was an amazing fact that Count Bernardi did not turn up to the dinner and as far as the British team knew, sent no apology.

Just after our arrival in Venice, four of us were dining at the Danielli when a tall distinguished man who was the image of George Grossmith jr (the English actor famous in those days for his role in "No, No Nanette") came in, complete with monocle. As he passed our table, one of our party exclaimed, "Look, I believe that is George Grossmith." The stranger heard him, smiled and pausing at our table said "I have been mistaken for George Grossmith in England before now, so you must be English officers from the aircraft carrier." We apologised and mutual introductions followed. He was the Baron von Behr, but naturally he remained "George" to us. When we had finished our meal, "George" invited us over to his table for liqueurs and introduced us to his lovely English wife, Joy. George told us that he was a former cavalry officer who had been more or less exiled from the post-war Germany of those days. We asked him to the ship for lunch the following day and he asked us to dinner at his palazzo. We found him and his wife to be charming and most hospitable. He was so kind to us that we eventually invited him to take passage with us when we sailed to Brioni and he witnessed our flying exercises on the way. Subsequently, "George" made a point of calling on HMS Courageous when the following year I had been transferred to her and pretended astonishment at finding me on board. On that occasion, in spite of broad hints from him he did not get invited to witness flying exercises. On looking back I could not help feeling that he was a very clever and charming intelligence officer for our former (and future) enemy.

Some years after the Second World War, far more sinister revelations about this "charming and most hospitable" man came to light. "George" was none other than the notorious Baron Kurt von Behr who helped Goering in the systematic looting of art and furniture from France, mostly from the private collections of dispossessed or murdered Jews. Von Behr was appointed Paris Chief of the Einsatzstab Reichsleiter Rosenberg (ERR) when Goering started to use the ERR for his own ends early in March of 1940. In November 1940 he ordered von Behr to confiscate art collections owned by Jews in the Occupied Zone of France. There is no doubt that von Behr's motives were greed for power and status in the Nazi hierarchy as well as personal profit from sale of art and bribery on all sides. In many cases he was known to betray Jews and wealthy French families to the Gestapo or Vichy police to gain access to either paintings or valuable (usually antique) furniture. An American intelligence report from the Office of Strategic Services (OSS) in 1946 stated that he had "no special occupation" between the wars but became an ardent Nazi and went frequently to Italy on "some kind of liaison duty with the Fascist Government". He had fought briefly in the Great War, as an NCO and served time as a British prisoner of war. When American forces were approaching Schloss Banz in 1945, Baron von Behr and his aristocratic English-born wife committed suicide by drinking the very best of confiscated Champagne laced with prussic acid. It was also reported that during the war years, von Behr was intensely vain and wore many uniforms (eventually claiming the rank of Lieutenant Colonel) although he remained no more than a civilian officer of the German Red Cross. He was said to have a table reserved at Maxims in Paris every evening for two years and lavishly entertained generals, diplomats and artists, as well showing a particular hospitality to naval (usually U-boat) officers and Luftwaffe pilots on leave in Paris. James S. Plaut, the director of the OSS Art Looting Investigation

Unit published a revealing two-part article on the activities of von Behr and Goering in The Atlantic Monthly in September and October 1946.

In 1927, Brioni was a very fashionable and most expensive island in the Adriatic, mainly populated by wealthy German tourists and film stars. It was so high-priced that we were glad our stay was brief. My birthday in 1928 was a celebration I nearly missed as at about 10 am I crashed at Hal Far. We were practising formation landings and take offs, when my engine failed just after take off at about 40 feet above the ground. I had no height to turn so the only thing for it was to try to land in one of the little fields bordering the landing area. These were very small and surrounded by stone walls. I nearly made it, but unfortunately, in trying to lift the old Dart over the nearest wall, the wheels just touched and we finished up on our nose. Luckily, I was only winded by the impact, my safety belt had saved me from further damage.

Before I could climb out I saw an officer vault a stone wall and run across the field to me with a sort of hop, skip and a jump. It was Squadron Leader Reggie Marix who, in spite of his artificial leg, was the first to get to me. A great character was Reggie, famous in the first war as the first pilot to successfully drop bombs in anger. He flew a little Sopwith Tabloid (one of two machines adapted from Schneider Cup racers of April 1914)from Antwerp to Dusseldorf where he destroyed the new Zeppelin Z-9 (airship) with two 20lb bombs dropped from a height of only 500ft on October 8, 1914. His machine received some 30 bullet holes in the attack and he had to make the flight back with a locked rudder. He abandoned the aircraft after force-landing some 50 miles short of home when he ran out of fuel and the next day he and his RNAS squadron had to evacuate Antwerp – he was dissuaded from going back to pick up the Sopwith. At the time, the Germans were horrified at being attacked so deep in their homeland and in one published report, criticised the British for flying over "neutral territory" to make the raid. "I thought they had a bloody nerve," Reggie told me. "On the journey to and from Dusseldorf I was flying over half their damned army while it invaded neutral Belgium."

(He lost his leg in July 1916, when as squadron commander he volunteered to test a Nieuport fresh from the factory in Paris but he was back with the RFC before the war ended and was a founder member of the RAF when it was formed in April 1918. Shortly after I met him, he returned to England and regained his "wings", requalifying with Harry Day as instructor).

Reggie took me in his car to sick quarters, where the doctor gave me a thorough checkover, then said "You are okay, but in case there's any delayed shock, my advice is to take a fair amount of alcohol." I found that my friends were only too willing to subscribe to this idea when I arrived at the mess, but the amazing thing was that the large amount of gin that I had pressed on me had no effect whatsoever, except that I slept for about six hours after lunch. However, I suffered no shock and the birthday is one I always remember.

When my aircraft was examined, it was discovered that the engine failure was due to water in the petrol. This meant that all aircraft fuel tanks had to be drained and the source of the water was found to be in an almost empty bulk-storage tank. After this, all our petrol was very carefully filtered through chamois leathers when the aircraft were refuelled, which made refuelling a very slow job for some time to come. The main workshops were at Kalafrana, so when an aircraft had been stripped down and repaired it had to be towed up a narrow road minus its wings and re-assembled at the aerodrome. However, there was a concrete wharf about the same length as the deck of an aircraft carrier at the workshops, with the sea on one side and hangars on the other side. I was asked if I would try to fly an Avro Bison off from this when we had a suitable wind. I did so and had no trouble at all with the first one. A little time later I repeated the performance, but owing to the wind being from the opposite direction, I had to fly between a large crane and the hangar just after take off. Although I just made it, this frightened me and the onlookers so much that I did not try it again.

The AOC in Malta then was Air Commodore (later Air Chief Marshal) Sir Robert Clark Hall, a New Zealander who as a Captain R N had commanded HMS Ark Royal, the first British sea-plane carrier, in the first war. He was a fine and able man, who after retiring from the RAF as an Air Marshal in 1934, joined the RNZAF as a Wing Commander in 1940 and eventually commanded the RNZAF in the Pacific Islands in the last war as an Air Commodore RNZAF. As a midshipman in the Royal Navy he had been detached to the Naval Brigade sent to Tongshan to deal with the Boxer Rebellion in 1900. He had also been a wing commander in the Royal Naval Air Service (RNAS) in 1917 and was Grand Fleet Aviation Officer as a Wing Captain in 1918 when I was on HMS Agincourt.

All who were in Malta on March 11, 1928 remember it as the day the fleet did not sail. For some months, we had been preparing for the Royal Navy Combined Spring Exercises in which the Mediterranean Fleet would take part in training manoeuvres with and against the Atlantic Fleet which had sailed from England. It was the major and most expensive evolution in the RN calendar but at 1600 that day, the time decreed as sailing time by Admiral Sir Roger Keyes, not a ship moved. Most had steam up and were ready but instead of the usual noisy and hectic bustle of activity that accompanied the fleet's sailing, there was, as many noted, a "dreadful 'ush" over Malta. Those who needed to know were told that sailing had been postponed to midnight and we first thought that it was merely done to exercise the fleet with a night departure. We did not however, sail until 0700 on Monday, March 12. By then a mixture of scuttlebutt and gossip had circulated regarding the cause of the delay and many were aware that there had been some sort of trouble on HMS Royal Oak, but most of that was forgotten with duties and the more immediate problems of our own part in the combined fleet exercises. Our aircraft made torpedo attacks on the "Red" (Atlantic) battle fleet and my flight was credited with "sinking" HMS Furious and the battleship Nelson. By the time we returned to Malta after the exercises, we had all but forgotten the speculation of a few days previously but we were to be soon both enlightened and perhaps disillusioned by the facts that unfolded. At the end of the month, Eagle was ordered to Gibraltar to provide the venue for the famous Royal Oak Courts Martial. By then "this regrettable incident" had been so widely publicised that it became a public spectacle. Fittingly, the trial began on April 1, 1928 and ran for five days. An aircraft carrier was the only ship that could accommodate the large numbers of the press, as well as the many officers attending from the Fleet and the Garrison, so our aircraft were stowed on deck and the hangar became the courtroom.

The trouble arose out of a clash of personalities, with Admiral Bernard St George Collard on the one side and Captain Kenneth Dewar and Commander Henry Daniel on the other. The miserable and unwitting cause of it all was a bandmaster who had the improbable name of Percy Barnacle. The Admiral was well known for being a relic of the days when Admirals could do no wrong and at a party, when the band was playing on the quarterdeck, the admiral called the bandmaster a bugger in front of the " lady guests". The Captain and Commander protested in writing and Collard had them brought before a court of enquiry and subsequently dismissed from their ship. I forget the actual charge but one can be sure that on both sides the accusation of "Conduct to the prejudice of Royal Naval discipline" appeared somewhere. Admiral Collard was himself ordered to strike his flag and remain at Malta. The Captain and Commander then requested a Courts Martial in the hope of reinstatement when the facts were brought out.

The Daily Mail did much to fan the publicity flames and briefed counsel for Dewar and Daniel. The newspaper lost a libel action brought by Collard before the war when the admiral had been concerned in putting down what he saw as a semi mutiny at Portsmouth. (Interestingly enough, the author of the article concerned, Edgar Wallace, was sacked by the Daily Mail but not apparently harmed by the experience – the publicity gained helped set him up as a novelist and playwright).

During the evidence, we heard in detail how the admiral had first become agitated at the shipboard dance because he felt that some of the ladies were "without partners." He then walked across to the band and called to the bandmaster "Come here you! Stand here! You call yourself a flagship band? I never heard such a bloody awful noise in my life. Your playing is like a dirge and everyone is complaining". After suggesting to the commander that they get a jazz band from somewhere he said very loudly "I won't have a bugger like that on my ship." The Major of Marines and the ship's chaplain also complained to the admiral about the incident but had the sense not to put anything in writing. As a further example of the indignation caused, a senior wardroom officer of Royal Oak said in evidence "He might just as well have called my wife a tart."

It was quite a spectacle, which was made the most of by the press. The Captain and Commander were convicted and dismissed their ship, but of course, all three officers' naval careers were ruined – Daniel left the navy shortly after the Court Martial. Dewar obviously had some friends left at the Admiralty as he was appointed CO of HMS Tiger on November 5 that year but Admiral Collard was placed on the retired list and "sank without trace". Captain Dewar's appointment was to allow him to retire within a year with the rank of Rear-Admiral (and thus a better pension) and during the war he was recalled to active service but only in a training role in what was considered the backwater of the Royal Navy, the Historical Section. For a short time Daniel became a journalist writing for the Daily Mail and eventually published a book entitled *"The Navy From Within"*.

As far as most of us were concerned, the worst aspect of the proceedings was the damage to the standing of the Royal Navy. All the evidence confirmed that the commander and captain were absolutely right in their reasons for complaint against the admiral, but the finding was effectively that no complaint should be made in writing against a senior officer.

A wag at the time said "He may have called the bandmaster a bugger, but who was the bugger in the first who place made the bugger a bandmaster?" Long after that, during a wartime concert in Malta, I was to hear another twist on this. "Who called the Bandmaster Barnacle a bugger – or more to the point, who called that bugger Barnacle a Bandmaster?" Poor Bandmaster Barnacle, he reportedly suffered a nervous breakdown at the time but he stayed on the ship for about a year after the affair and he was quietly respected for that and even became a minor celebrity. His name was too good to be true and portrayals of him appeared in comedic sketches on stages all over Britain. In modern times, a good publicity agent could have netted him a fortune. He was also to outlive all the major players in the Courts Martial.

The day after the Court Martial when we had reclaimed our hangar, there was a general feeling of relief to be rid of "that lot" and it took several days before shipboard routine and conversation returned to normality. There was a general feeling that the Admiralty had seen fit to wash its dirty linen in public but there had certainly been no gain in the exercise.

On our return to Malta, we flew the aircraft off at Hal Far (then the only aerodrome on the island). Our aircraft were housed in Bessoneau hangars, composed of canvas over a wood and steel framework. Our flight offices, stores etc, were temporary affairs made out of aircraft packing cases. In addition, there was the flying boat base in Kalafrana Bay which had the only air force living accommodation.

In June 1928, HMS Courageous came out to Malta and I was given command of No 464 Flight (also Blackburn Darts) in Courageous when Eagle went home to refit and recommission.

On Courageous, I met Lieutenant-commander Glen Kidston, who had been commander of the submarine H48 but who was more famous as one of the "Bentley Boys" racing 6-litre Bentley cars in the Le Mans events of the late 1920's. Glen was very much a larger-than-life character and by this time had become an enthusiastic airman with a growing reputation in adventurous flying exploits. He was the scion of a wealthy English family with estates in England and South Africa. Although regarded through the newspapers as a playboy, he was in fact very serious about the future of aviation and was very much at home amongst air force and naval pilots. He was also a very generous (and trusting) man – when I happened to mention that I had a lady friend who had never been flying and who was unable to understand my love of aircraft, he insisted on me taking her flying over two days in his DH60 Moth. (G-EBVK). My logbook records 60 minutes "aerobatics and 6 landings" on the first day and she obviously enjoyed the experience as the next day it was 85 minutes of aerobatics and 9 landings.

HMS Courageous was then the most modern British aircraft carrier. Like her sister ship, Furious, she was designed originally as a fast cruiser armed with 15-inch guns. Unlike Furious, which had no superstructure, Courageous had a funnel and superstructure on the starboard side of the flight deck, which was of course much larger than that of the Eagle. She had no arrester wires but was fitted with palisades.

We had three "clubs" in those early days of the Fleet Air Arm; the Bathing Club, the Palisade Club and the Perch Club. The names of the first two clubs are self explanatory; the "Perch" Club however was not so easy to join.

To qualify as a "Perch" member, pilots had to complete a hundred deck landings without joining either of the two other clubs. We had a badge awarded on qualifying. It was a little enamelled brooch in the form of a perch (the fish) fitted with landing wheels and a tail skid and the motto was "Perchance!"

I had just qualified as a "Perch" (in June 1929) when Courageous from the Mediterranean Fleet, met Eagle and Furious from the Atlantic Fleet at Gibraltar. I think there were eight of us who had qualified for the Perch Club amongst the three carriers, so we celebrated by dining ashore.

After dinner we went to La Linea over the Spanish border and on our return after midnight found ourselves locked out of the fortress. We all got into a certain amount of trouble on our belated return to our ships. At least one of that party was an Admiral a little later in his career.

(During that meeting of the three aircraft carriers there was one period where in the space of 45 minutes, 464 flight took of from Courageous, made two successive landings on each of the other carriers and then landed back on Courageous. Aircraft from Eagle and Furious were making similar sorties, so for a brief period there were aircraft coming and going in all directions. The exhausted deck-landing party was very glad when we finally stopped.)

HMS Courageous returned to Malta where she carried out a short refit in the dockyard. During this time we pilots were ashore with our aircraft at Hal Far aerodrome.

On the evening of August 26, 1929 most of us were at dinner in the Mess or at the Club when we were ordered to stand by to fly onboard the carrier at first light and a battalion of infantry, the South Staffordshire Regiment, were to embark during the night. We were told that our destination was Palestine, trouble between the Arabs and the Jews had broken out again. Apparently the trouble had started at the famous Wailing Wall in Jerusalem and Jews and Arabs all over the country were in a state bordering on civil war. This of course was before the creation of the state of Israel, when Palestine was under the British Mandate.

We landed all our aircraft on board Courageous early the next day. The Staffordshires with all their equipment formed a considerable clutter on the forward end of the lower flying off deck. Captain then set course at high speed for Haifa, a distance of 1034 nautical miles. Luckily the weather was fine for the two day journey because most of the army equipment was merely parked on the flight deck right up to the bow and to our nautical eyes was not properly secured.

The aircraft HMS Courageous carried in those days were two flights of Fairey IIIF Spotter Reconaissance aircraft, two flights of Fairey Flycatcher fighters and two flights of Blackburn Dart Torpedo Bombers.

I commanded one of the Torpedo Bomber Flights. These aircraft were single-seat torpedo or bomb carriers which had no guns and to our dismay the Wing Commander told us that we would not be flying ashore because of our lack of guns. He thought bombs would be too drastic, if anything, machine guns were required, although we hoped that the threat itself would be enough to keep the peace.

With the aid of the rigger and armourer sergeants, I got busy and converted my own Dart into a two-seater, by moving the radio set back into the tool locker and slinging a canvas seat from the top longerons for the rear gunner and fixing a peg at each side for mounting a Lewis gun.

Then Wings agreed that the Dart flights should fly ashore,and could all be converted to two- seaters if necessary.

In the meantime, our job was to be showing the flag and leaflet dropping to persuade the people to keep calm.

We flew from the ship early in the morning before the midsummer heat was up and followed the coastline south to Gaza, leaving behind the fertile irrigated land and the cool green orange groves of Haifa and flying over parched brown desert, with a few white mud villages dotted here and there.

Gaza itself was just a larger collection of white, flat-topped houses and a railway station which did not even have a platform. The landing ground was distinguished from the surrounding country only by a wind sock, a landing T, a large canvas hangar, and a small group of buildings in one corner. In those days it was merely a staging-post for one of the British airlines. The sole Englishman in charge of the refuelling arrangements led a very lonely life. His only excitements were occasional landings by the old Handley Page Hannibal aircraft that were used in those days. Not surprisingly, he enthusiastically welcomed all seven of us and revived us with food and cold beer. Our first job was to decide how to organise a hot meal for the ground troops, about 50 of them, who were to arrive that evening by train with tents and tool kits and so on. This proved easy. We bought a couple of rather skinny sheep on the hoof, had them killed, skinned and cleaned by the Arab vendor, then the Arabs roasted them for us, native fashion. They dug a trench, lit a fire and the two sheep were roasted whole.

When the troops arrived just before dark, we took them to their roast mutton and it was delicious. Everyone carved his own portion off the still roasting sheep and with the aid of clasp knives and tin plates, had a real blow out. We pitched our tents in the dark and slept soundly after posting a skeleton guard. Next day we were ordered to fly up to Kalundia, the airstrip just outside Jerusalem, for briefing.

We were each given bundles of leaflets, some in Arabic, some in Hebrew, to drop on towns and villages, telling the people "to be good"! The Army staff had prepared the bundles and each bundle had the name of a designated town or village. Our job was simply to do some accurate map reading and heave our leaflet bundles over the side at their proper target. We went off in pairs, in case one aircraft had to force land with engine or other trouble (aircraft were still not too reliable in those days).

Phillips in his normal Dart and I with my home-made two-seater Dart, dropped leaflets over our allotted towns and villages. Our last target was Nablus, a considerable town lying deep in a valley between high hills where we were badly shaken by the turbulence because of the high wind blowing down the valley. We had to fly below the hill tops to try and drop accurately and the "bumps" were so bad that we nearly lost control. We dropped our leaflets and saw the local inhabitants running to collect them, then flew to Amman to re fuel.

After tea I told Phillips to go ahead back to Gaza independently. The CO of 41 Squadron at Amman, Squadron Leader Stan Vincent, later Air Vice Marshal Vincent, had a conference which I had to attend so I was to fly back to Gaza next morning.

Just before dark, a garbled message came through to Amman that Phillips had force landed in the desert with oil-pressure trouble. Vincent immediately organised affairs, he gave me a six-wheeler truck fitted with a scarf ring behind the driver's cab, on which was mounted a Lewis Gun, and four airmen. Off we went in the dark and after about 60 miles on a very shaky compass bearing across the desert we arrived in the neighbourhood of the crash. We fired a white Verey light and sure enough, from about two miles away, saw an answering green Verey light.

Eventually, after a rough cross-country passage, we sighted the grounded aircraft lying in a shallow valley. It was obviously immobile, with one wing almost on the ground and the starboard leg of the under carriage collapsed. But that was not all. In the distance, on one side of the valley was an Arab village, on the other side was a Jewish village and as we guessed, they weren't friends. In fact, there had been a serious skirmish between them a few days before.

On the top of a hill, about a mile away, was a monastery which we could just see against the moonlight sky. When we arrived in our six-wheeler, clattering over the rough ground and dodging boulders with the aid of our headlights, we found an unhurt but rather worried Phillips. There were 40 or 50 Arabs from the village about, all in their flowing Arab dress; some were examining the aircraft, others were standing around in truculent groups. They did not attempt to do anything but it all made us feel rather uneasy. Phillips had a revolver in his holster, but the Arabs were armed with a variety of weapons, from knives to rifles.

I asked Phillips to lead me to the headman. In the meantime our gunner in the truck remained at his post. In the moonlight a tall strong shadowy figure held out his hand to me. We shook hands and then, to my amazement although we had no common language, this Sheikh and I discovered that we were brothers. We were members of the same Masonic craft as our use of the "secret" handshake had shown.

After that, everything was a piece of cake. The headman said a few words to his tribesmen and a fire was lighted and a sheep killed and set roasting. Phillips and I, feeling much more relaxed, sat before the blaze and began talking about the crash and ways of repairing the aircraft. There was an oil leak to mend and the under carriage, one leg of which had been wiped off by one of the sand-coloured boulders scattered about. We were immersed in this when we became aware of new figures coming into the circle of firelight. They were clearly not Arabs. They wore long black robes and their heads were bare and shaven. In a few moments we realised they were a party of monks from the monastery on the hill.

They were all very sunburnt; it was noticeable even in the firelight. One or two addressed me in Italian and then another came forward, shook me warmly by the hand and said to my utter astonishment "Eh, lad Ah am right glad to see tha' wheer does tha' cum fro?" After a stunned silence I replied, "By gum I cum fra' Lancashire and so does thou!"

"By gum I do an' all," he said. This was my second surprise in a very short time. How on earth did a Lancashire man come to be in a Palestine monastery? He told me that he had left England many years before to study with his church in Rome and after many travels had been sent to this monastery in Palestine.

Well, what with the Arab Sheikh belonging to a similar lodge to mine and one of the monks being practically a townie of mine, young Phillips, the pilot of the crashed aircraft had a marvellous time.

With a clear conscience, I left him with two airmen as guard until next morning and I arranged through the good offices of my Lancashire friend as interpreter, that under Phillips' instruction, boulders should be cleared by the Arabs to make a runway. The next day I would fly in a spare undercarriage leg, mend the oil leak and we would then fly both aircraft out. Sure enough, next day, in my converted two seater Dart I landed on the improvised runway, 400 yards long but clear of boulders thanks to our Arab friends. In the back seat I carried a very able Sergeant-Rigger Cottrell with his tool kit and there was a spare undercarriage slung on the torpedo rack. How we blessed that unofficial conversion because no other contemporary aircraft could have done the job with that load.

When it came to jacking up the aircraft, there were no worries. The Arab Sheikh detailed about 20 of his villagers who held two six-inch planks on their backs under the main plane, taking the weight, while Phillips, the Cottrell and I replaced the broken undercarriage leg in under an hour. We checked up on the engine trouble in Phillip's aircraft and fixed it thanks to the good old RAF NCO who although he was only a rigger knew his engine stuff and before noon we took off from the improvised airstrip and returned to Gaza.

When we landed I thought young Phillips was looking a little pale and wan and I asked him if he was feeling shaky. "No," he said, "but what with hot roast mutton from the Arabs, cold roast chicken from the monks topped off with Benedictine and coffee and six eggs for breakfast this morning with warm milk straight from the cow, how do you expect me not to be air sick as we flew through all that turbulence?"

Shortly after the Palestine troubles were over, Courageous carried out another flag showing operation, this time over the Dardanelles. The Italians had been trespassing by taking a flight of seaplanes over the Dardanelles, so at the request of Turkey, we staged a flying display over Constantinople. As a compliment to our hosts, we did a formation flight in the form of a star and crescent (October 18, 1929).

All 36 aircraft from the ship took part and everyone told us it was a very creditable show, particularly in view of the short time available for rehearsal. It certainly went down well with the Turks. When the aircraft had landed on again, Courageous steamed through the Dardanelles and anchored off Constantinople, where we remained for about a week and were extremely well entertained and shown all the sights. There were quite a number of Royal Marines and some seaman who had memories of the Dardanelles and the Turks in the not-too-distant war and we could not but reflect on the fickleness (and idiocy) of some aspects of national politics.

During this time I made several flights in an Avro Lynx, which was a slightly-modified Avro 504k with an Armstrong Siddeley Lynx engine. The Lynx was a 7-cylinder radial engine, considerably more powerful than the old Gnome rotary and much more flexible. The aircraft had much the same airframe as its sire but slightly shortened wings and was faster with a higher operating ceiling– in the RAF it became known as the Avro 504N but the RCAF among others knew it as the Avro Lynx.

We returned to Malta and when we flew off the deck we were ordered to carry out dummy attacks on HMS Royal Oak, the flagship, just returning to the station after recommissioning in England. The two Dart flights duly carried out attacks (without torpedoes) while the two Flycatcher flights made dummy machine-gun attacks with the supposed object of distracting the flagship's Anti-Aircraft guns. In fact, they had a glorious "beat up" which did their fighter-pilot's hearts good. Unfortunately, Lieutenant Owen Cathcart Jones, the leader of one of the flights, heaved several packets of brown Service toilet paper as part of his "beat up" with such good effect that squares of service four inch by four inch floated down on the flagship's deck and even desecrated the Admiral's bridge. The Admiral was not amused and the ship's company of the Royal Oak took it as a personal insult. We in the Dart flights knew nothing of this until after we had landed at Hal Far, when we received a signal that all pilots were to repair on board Courageous as soon as she had moored in the harbour. We waited for hours on board, while the Captain of Courageous repaired on board the flagship, in frock coat and sword, to make his apologies we presumed. What action was taken against Cathcart Jones we never knew we guessed that he was "logged".

I must say here that the Fleet Air Arm pilots and crew were highly amused at the Cathcart-Jones toilet-paper bombing and felt that the Navy and in particular the Royal Oak "brass", were being somewhat precious, possibly as a result of the recent Courts Martial. Only 10 years later, the once-mighty and proud ship suffered a final and sad end, when after being relegated to anti-aircraft duty at Scapa Flow, she was an early victim of World War 2. She was sunk by U-boat 47 (Kapitan Gunther Prien) on the night of Friday 13 October, 1939 with the loss of 833 men. Many British commentators seized on the 13th as "sailors' unlucky day" but to my mind that was the same as claiming God was on one side or the other – it was obviously a "lucky" date for the German Kriegsmarine.

Cathcart Jones who was then a subaltern of Marines, retired some 18 months later after serving on HMS Glorious and became famous in several long distance flights, including England to the Cape with Glen Kidston and in the MacRobertson race to Australia in 1934.

It was shortly after setting the London-Capetown record of 6 days 9 hours on April 6, 1931 with Cathcart-Jones in his Lockheed Vega that Kidston and another co-pilot, Captain T.A.Gladstone, were killed trying to cross the Drakensburg Mountains in South Africa. They were by then flying a DH Puss Moth which had been borrowed for the trip as the Vega was considered unsuitable to land on the rough airstrips of the area. The tragedy saddened all of us who had known Glen and I believe that the course of civil aviation was set back by his loss. He was making many of his flights with a view to setting up a South African airline.

Cathcart-Jones flew the Vega at various air pageants in Britain in 1932 and (on behalf of the Kidston family trust) demonstrated the machine to the Maharaja of Jodhpur as well as the director of Imperial Chemical Industries in hopes of selling the aircraft. It was eventually bought by Australian Horrie Miller and also took part in the 1934 MacRobertson air race but was unable to finish after flipping on landing in Aleppo. Cathcart Jones, flying one of the three DH88 Comets in the race finished fourth overall and then set a new record of 13 and a half days for the Sydney –London flight when he made a much-publicised return trip with film from the race. Owen again came to fame in July 1936 touring much of Europe with Spanish millionaire industrialist Victor Urrutia Usaula and the Marquis Luca de Tena, drumming up support for the Nationalist side in the Spanish Civil War. He was flying a then very modern and fast Beechcraft "Staggerwing" and after visiting ex-King Alonso of Spain, his whole party of was interned in Czechoslovakia but Cathcart-Jones made a cheeky escape by flying away from his police guard only to be interned again in Austria after making a forced landing. I believe Cathcart-Jones simply charmed himself out of custody because he was in Cannes within a few days. Slightly later, he was involved in the Spanish Civil War, officially as a 'Ferry pilot'. When next I heard of Owen, he was a squadron leader in the RCAF in World War 2 and he appeared in two American films with a flying theme in 1942 - *Captains of the Clouds* starred James Cagney and *Desperate Journey* had none other than Errol Flynn in the leading role. Owen was also technical director of both films and aptly played the part of chief flying instructor in Captains which had the RFC fighter ace Billy Bishop playing himself as an Air Marshal.

We who remained in the services were somewhat jealous of the machines flown by the adventurous pair of Cathcart-Jones and Kidston – the Lockheed Vega was billed as the most expensive and fastest aeroplane ever to be bought by a private individual when Kidston took delivery of it in September 1930. The de Havilland DH 88 Comet was a private-venture, twin-engined, all-wooden monoplane that was only surpassed in performance by its successor from the same stable, the Mosquito.

But back to the days of biplanes! Late in 1929 we started night flying in earnest and it was only then that I made the discovery that darkness doesn't fall – it rises. (I think it was Glen Kidston who pointed out that this "secret" was one shared only with mountaineers.) When flying at sunset, I could see the shadows growing into darkness, first in the valleys and gullies and then rising higher until only the top of a mountain or sometimes the spire of a church on a hilltop was the one place still in light and almost before noticed, it too was extinguished by the rising shadows.

(When I was getting those first unofficial lessons at Gosport in 1918, one of the instructors told us that only three years previously it was believed that damp air or clouds lacked sufficient lift for safe flying and night air being "black" had no lift at all!)

It was at about the same time that we logged our first "rough weather" landings on the carrier. We had done most of our flying in moderate seas and did not often takeoff in winds of over about 20 knots but obviously in wartime could expect to be called into action in more extreme conditions. (The Swordfish attack on Bismarck in 1941 took place in a Force 9 gale – a wind of up to 48 knots or 87km/hour.) Taking of from a carrier in rough conditions was largely a matter of timing, with the deck rising and falling and rolling by up to 50-60 feet, the idea was to make sure you reached takeoff speed while the runway was still rising. A good deck officer (always known as "Bats") needed a knowledge of the motion of the ship and the capabilities of the aircraft and he also had to have a good sense of anticipation. When he waved, we went. Landing too was exciting, but the Dart was one of the better aircraft in its ability to roll and pitch in time with the ship combined with a stability in strong winds. (It was eventually well-surpassed by the Fairey Swordfish in these regards.) The biggest danger in those early days was the risk to the deck-landing party and it was usually a slippery deck that kept us from flying in winds of over 30 knots. We did have one occasion when the carrier had to be turned off the wind as with our landing speed of only 50 knots Courageous kept steaming away from us as we made the approach. Turbulence close to the ship was another factor, it was often sudden and unpredictable and each carrier had different danger areas according to conditions – particularly as we went over the bow. On Courageous there was an often tricky area of air aft of the superstructure.

Malta in the late 1920's was very much a British naval base. When the ships were in, we used to have a saying. "You can't see the fleet for the funnels." It was not unusual to see seven battleships in Grand Harbour (HMS Queen Elizabeth, Barham, Ramillies, Resolution, Royal Oak, Royal Sovereign, Valiant and Warspite) and as many as 20 light cruisers on moorings in the triple inlets around the harbour. Then there would also be 30 or so destroyers and a dozen submarines. As far as we were concerned, the carriers Eagle and Courageous were the centrepieces of that armada, but to be truthful, the conservative navy tended to class us with submarines as "other vessels". There was also flotilla of ancillary craft such as minesweepers, minelayers, supply ships, corvettes and launches. Added to the naval presence was a steady stream of maritime traffic such as ferries, tramp steamers and mail packets. Regular sailings of "Grey Funnel Line" steamers (troopships) and passenger liners brought not only sailors and other service personnel but also wives and families, sightseers and holidaymakers.

Malta then was in many ways an exotic and lively island and with that almost totally male service population was regarded as a desirable trawling ground for young women looking for a husband. We called the numbers of young and not-so-young women from Britain who were in Malta's social arena the "Fishing Fleet" and the Ladies' lounge of the Union Club in Valetta was the "Snakepit."

It was a period of constant and intense activity for all the Royal Navy vessels. There was always some form of exercise or manoeuvre going on at sea. Ashore, life seemed even more hectic with an endlessly organised round of sport and recreation (deemed necessary to keep both ratings and officers fit and out of trouble). Underpinning the whole scene was the social life both ashore and afloat – it was not surprising that the Bandmaster incident took place in Malta, there seemed to be a dance several times a week on most of the battleships and several cruisers and there was many a young woman in Malta who thought ships were merely for the dancing thereaboard. The navy also provided employment and in many cases prosperity for the Maltese – from the little dghaises providing a water-taxi service (many being paid a retainer by individual ships), through all the locals working in laundries, souvenir shops, bars and food provedores. Huge as the naval population was, it did not surpass the Maltese who had a very organised society, if often even more structured than the Brits. There was a Malta Casino that had strict dress and etiquette and nobody sat down to either the gambling or dinner tables unless invited by a member and most importantly, dressed in white tie and tails.

Not surprisingly, the remainder of that commission seemed to pass very quickly and early in 1930 Courageous was ordered home to pay off.

In the Bay of Biscay, we struck really bad weather. The seas were so high that they buckled the massive steel doors on the lower flying off deck and poured into the forward hangar that housed the Flycatchers. The ship had to turn and proceed down wind and sea while the shipwrights shored up the buckled doors. As soon as we turned, the quarterdeck was continually pounded by seas to such an extent that one of the AA guns was torn loose in its mounting and the sea poured into the officers cabin flat below so that three or four feet of water washed around our cabins. We rigged a submersible electric pump in a large canvas bath in the middle of the flat and bailed the water as it rushed from side to side of the flat into the more confined space of the canvas bath so the pump could obtain continuous suction and thus we eventually got the area comparatively dry. But all hands had a very uncomfortable 48 hours until we ran out of the gale and reached the more sheltered waters of the English channel.

That trip was the last time I was on board Courageous, she was one of the first casualties of the Second World War when she was torpedoed by the submarine U29 (Kapitan Otto Schuhart) in the Western Approaches (south-west of Ireland) on September 17, 1939. The ship went down in less than 15 minutes with the loss of 514 navy lives, including her commander Captain W T Makeig-Jones. Also lost were 26 Fleet Air Arm personnel and 36 RAF servicemen - 811 and 822 Squadrons were flying Swordfish from her at the time of the sinking. The Dutch freighter Veendam and the British freighter Collingsworth participated in rescuing survivors from the oily waters. Her escort, the destroyers, made a ferocious counter-attack on U29 but failed to sink the submarine. By the next morning , news of the sinking had been broadcast worldwide, the sinking of Courageous was the first U-boat offensive against the Royal Navy and Schuhart's victory prompted the Admiralty to withdraw all three remaining carriers from the Western Approaches.

Back in England, all the flights flew off to Gosport aerodrome and after a couple of days disembarking flight personnel and stores, we proceeded on foreign service leave. After about three weeks I was bored so I welcomed a suggestion from my brother that I should bear a hand with instructing at the Midland Light Aeroplane Club of which he was a member. With my flying log book to back up my application I was awarded a civil "B" licence after sitting a written examination on airmanship, meteorology and the like and went to Birmingham to stay with my brother. "Dolly" Hutchinson was the only instructor at Castle Bromwich then and for a month I assisted him in the flying instruction. My logbook records a busy two weeks during March 12 to 27, 1930, flying in two DH60 Moths and a DH80A Puss Moth. (G-AABH, G-AADB and G-AAXT for the sake of the aircraft spotters!). I flew just under 26 hours with some 15 pupils and interestingly enough, among these was the one and only "dud" recorded in my career. In three flights, I was unable to get one aspiring pilot to show any idea of co-ordination with the aircraft.` I handed the pupil over to "Dolly" and he confirmed my finding – keen as he was, this particular man could simply not get the hang of flying.

During this period the film Wings was to be shown in Coventry and I was asked to put up an aerobatic display over Coventry to publicise the film. I borrowed an old SE 5A which had been fitted with a new Airdisco engine.

On the day there was a very high wind and although I had never flown the type before I found that it was a sweet little aircraft, very light on the controls, but with a very narrow undercarriage. I landed safely after the show but found it impossible to taxi across wind owing to the high wind so I had to wait until a couple of helpers came out and grabbed the wing tips. I then learned to my horror that the aircraft had only been given a Certificate of Airworthiness for one day.

The clubhouse library had a copy of "The Air Annual of the British Empire 1929" which was good reading "when the birds were walking" due to low cloud. Among the items from that annual worth noting were statements on the future of British aircraft. One article noted "a tendency at present for the British aircraft industry to flirt with the monoplane although the great bulk of development still remains true to biplane types." While conceding the monoplane had advantages of increased visibility and reduced maintenance, it went on to say that for military purposes, the biplane with its more compact shape and strongly-braced structure would "hold the field."

It was also noted that the Air Ministry had been forced to rethink it's policy with the advent of the Fairey Fox day bomber which had burst onto the scene and could outperform any fighter then in existence. Its capabilities literally made the authorities sit up and think and as a result British designers could concentrate first on high performance and then fit the necessary military equipment into and not merely on the aircraft.

Chapter 7

Too Old to Fly?

At the end of my leave I returned to Gosport and obtained permission to take 464 Flight on a cross-country tour of RAF aerodromes for training purposes. It was rather amusing to see the astonished looks when we peeled off our overalls after landing, folding the wings and pegging down the aircraft (a routine that I insisted on all pilots carrying out without assistance except from each other). The RAF had never seen such a mixture of uniforms. I wore the blue uniform of Captain Royal Marines, there were two Lieutenants and a Sub Lieutenant RN in naval uniform, an RAAF Flying Officer in dark blue uniform and an RAF Flying Officer in light blue. I think they were quite surprised to hear that we spoke English.

It was an instructive tour because we each carried out our own daily inspections on our own aircraft, we landed at a lot of aerodromes and we saw a lot of England.

Shortly after our return to Gosport, 464 Flight was ordered to land on HMS Furious for a brief cruise down to Plymouth. One of the objects of the exercise was to demonstrate a dummy torpedo attack for the benefit of the senior term of naval cadets who were picked up off Dartmouth.

The weather was very poor with horizontal visibility of only a mile, although the cloud base was about 3000 feet. When being briefed I pointed out that we could easily lose sight of the ship in those weather conditions, but the Captain ordered us to carry on. After take off, the flight formed up on me and we climbed to about 2000 feet when visibility became rapidly worse and we lost sight of the ship altogether.

Our radio telephone sets were so poor that although we could communicate with each other we could not hear Furious, so when I realised our petrol was getting low, I led the flight north until we sighted the coast near Lyme Regis.

Here the clouds were barely 100 feet above the cliff tops, so sighting a suitable field near Rousdon which was just large enough I ordered the chaps to follow me in and to land as nearly as possible in my wheel tracks. All six of us landed safely and we had no sooner switched off our engines than the local vicar appeared and asked if he could help.

I asked to be guided to a telephone and he promptly invited us to tea at the vicarage which was close by. We were regaled with "splits and cream", saffron cake and tea after I had telephoned Dartmouth College and sent a signal to Furious, reporting our position, stating that we had only half an hours petrol left and asking the ship for her bearing and distance from Start Point (our nearest prominent landmark).

Within half an hour, Dartmouth telephoned orders from Furious for us to return to Gosport. As Gosport was 80 miles away (roughly one hours flying), I decided to land at Chickerell near Weymouth where there was a forced landing field. We duly landed and found that fuel would have to be brought to the field by truck and could not be arranged until the following morning. So we pegged down our aircraft, organised a guard for the night and found very hospitable accommodation for ourselves in HMS Vulcan, the submarine depot ship at Weymouth.

Early next morning, we re-fuelled the aircraft and flew back to Gosport where I found a signal ordering me to report on board Furious at Plymouth as soon as possible. I drove down in my Austin 7 and reported on board to Wing Commander Pulford (afterwards Air Vice Marshal Pulford who was killed at the fall of Singapore). "Wings" told me I was due for a "raspberry" from the Captain for failing to find the ship and this made me angry. I pointed out that I had protested on being briefed that the weather was impossible at the time and that in my opinion the Captain was responsible for endangering the pilots and aircraft by ordering us off against his (Pulford's) and my advice.

On being taken before the Captain, I got the same statement in first and Wings backed me up, so the Captain apologised handsomely. I was handed a couple of gins instead of a "raspberry."

I did, however, learn a lasting lesson in that incident - the importance of an accurate "homing" direction. The feeling of being lost and having a flight of young airman under my command at risk with no certainty of finding a safe landing stayed with me the rest of my service life and and in my later years as a fighter (and bomber) controller gave me an empathy with the pilots depending on guidance. I could always place myself in their position.

On my return to Gosport I found a letter awaiting from the Royal Marine Office, informing me that I had to return to Corps duty permanently in June as they considered that I was too old (I was then 33!) to continue flying

I went up to the RMO and tried to get them to change their decision, pointing out that the Admiralty would lose valuable specialist aviation experience, but they were adamant. I then asked permission to ask for transfer to the RAF. This was given, with the rather unkind comment that I would probably be offered a short service commission. However, I went straight across to Air Ministry and after an interview with an Air Commodore finished up in the office of a fairly junior civil servant, who in my presence rang a pal of his in the Treasury. The conversation I heard was something like this: "You see he has been taught to fly at Admiralty expense, he's presumably broken all the aircraft he is likely to break now that he has so much experience, again at the Admiralty's expense and the Navy will have to pay at least half his pension when he retires I think he's a good buy, don't you?" Apparently the answer was in the affirmative from the Treasury end, because I was told to put in an official application for transfer to the RAF with a permanent commission as a Flight Lieutenant.

While awaiting results of my written application I was ordered up to Brough to ferry some Blackburn Baffins from there to the RAF stations at Sealand, where they were to be crated to go overseas. (To New Zealand as it transpired.)

Brough, on the Humber near Hull, was the aerodrome of the Blackburn Aircraft Company and there I met Bob Blackburn, the managing director and his brothers.

Bob was one of the pioneer designers of aircraft in England before the first war and has done wonderful service for British aviation ever since.

The Baffin was a two-seater torpedo bomber, rather like an enlarged Dart. My job was simple, as a Baffin was completed I flew it across to Sealand and then came back by train to collect the next one. Unfortunately, the weather was poor so that I had only ferried five aircraft in three weeks due to delays awaiting visual flight conditions. I then got a signal ordering me to ferry the sixth Baffin to Gosport, closely followed by another stating that my transfer to the RAF had come through.

On arrival back at Gosport I was informed that I had been transferred to the RAF as a Flight Lieutenant and given orders to report at once to No 111 Squadron, Hornchurch.

I made my last flight as a Captain R.M. on August 29, 1930 in a Blackburn Ripon and my first flight as a Flight Lieutenant R.A..F. just 10 days later.

I had no time to get my new uniform so I reported in my old uniform as a Captain of Marines. The Station Commander, Wing Commander ER Manning asked me why I was reporting in "fancy dress" so I, rather acidly, asked whether he preferred me to wear plain clothes until I could get my new uniform made and suggested that he could give me leave until the uniform was ready. As an Australian (and a former Cavalry officer who transferred to the RFC in 1915 to avoid the horrors of static trench warfare) he did not mind my dirty crack but he did not give me leave.

My new squadron was armed with Armstrong Siddeley Siskins and the CO was Squadron Leader "Copper" Openshaw who served for some time as an RAF pilot in the Fleet Air Arm.

After only a few months with 111 Squadron I was transferred to No 54 Squadron on the same station, then just re formed and armed with the new Bristol Bulldog fighters. These were much superior to the old Siskins, faster, with a better climb and a much higher "ceiling." The Bulldog did have one particular vice which made low-level aerobatics forbidden – it easily lost up to 400ft in a roll except in the hands of a really skilled pilot.

54 Squadron which was disbanded after the First World War had a great record and to celebrate the resurrection of the squadron we invited as many of the original

members as possible to dine. Two famous fighter pilots from the Great War were among the guests, the original CO, Major K K Horn, MC and "Oxo" Oxspring. They presented the squadron with a wonderful silver model of the Sopwith Pup, the aircraft they first flew in France.

I little knew then that I was to serve with K K Horn in the next war and that "Oxo's" son, Bob, would serve with me at Duxford.

The first CO of the re-formed 54 Squadron was Squadron Leader W E G Bryant, but he was relieved on promotion by Squadron Leader "Poppy" Pope DFC early in 1931. "Poppy" was a terrific character, a wild Irishman, 6ft 7in tall. I could tell a few tales about him, but most of them are rather improper.

I had first met him in Venice in 1927, when with little more than 10/ in his pocket he attached himself to the Schneider Cup team, all of whom were personal friends of his. By some means he was included in the party as one of the officials and was the guest of the Italian Government throughout the race period.

At a wild celebration after the race he swung off on a priceless cut-glass chandelier in the sedate Danielli restaurant. When the Carabiniri were called he escaped by diving into the Grand Canal, complete with dinner jacket.

"Poppy" had a fine record in the First World War. When "Grid" Caldwell, the New Zealander, was shot down and force landed behind the enemy lines "Poppy" landed alongside and took off again with "Grid" on the wing root of his Sopwith Camel and reached safety on his own aerodrome. He also had been an RAF Test Pilot at Martlesham Heath, was a magnificent pilot and a grand friend and comrade to serve with.

We were kept busy training in the new type of aircraft and once familiar with it we practised formation flying ready for the RAF display at Hendon. We also did a lot of night flying, searchlight training, air firing (at Sutton Bridge) and cooperation with the Auxiliary Squadrons from Hendon as well as affording training for the Observer Corps which was then in its infancy.

About this time I first met Douglas Bader who was at Kenley with No 23 Squadron, then armed with Gloster Gamecocks.

23 Squadron had a magnificent aerobatics team led by Flight Lieutenant HMA Day, with Douglas and Geoffrey Stephenson being the other two members. Douglas and Geoffrey were at Cranwell together and strangely enough "Happy" Day was an old friend of mine in the Royal Marines. Unknown to each other we had both applied for transfer to the RAF about the same time.

It was shortly after 23 Squadron had been re equipped with Bristol Bulldogs that Douglas lost his legs in the unfortunate crash at Reading. We were all shocked when we heard, because young as he was, Douglas had already established quite a reputation, not only as a fine pilot but in almost all branches of sport. Rugby, cricket, boxing, squash rackets, he was first class in them all. All his air force friends were delighted to know that he would live but none of us in those days imagined that he would ever fly again. Little did I know at that time what a close and happy association Douglas and I were to have in the war to come.

Jack Satchell joined B Flight 54 Squadron at this time as a Pilot Officer. He was never really happy unless he was flying. He was to have a distinguished war career later, commanding a Polish Fighter Squadron in the Battle of Britain, then serving in Malta and North Africa, eventually retiring as a Group Captain with a well earned DSO.

Flying with the RAF was in a number of ways quite different to the Fleet Air Arm. In addition to the obvious change from carrier work and fleet reconnaissance, there was more emphasis on close formation flying and display aerobatics. In 54 Squadron we also put a lot of flying hours into "battle formation" work and air-to-air attacks and interceptions, the primary roles of a fighter squadron. In addition we did some bombing with our Bulldogs, including several night attacks on the range at Sutton Bridge. Looking over my flying logbook I also note the amount of time spent in testing new machines or those with repairs and modifications such as a newly "slotted" Bristol Bulldog. On one occasion I was asked to test the visibility of the Hawker Fury against the Bulldog. We also made quite a few night patrols and tried interceptions where ground searchlights illuminated an "enemy" for us to attack.

In October 1931 the squadron flew to Farnborough where we had camera guns fitted to the Bulldogs and we also put in some time with the camera guns in dual Siskin Mk 3 aircraft.

In February 1932 I was sent on the first Blind Flying Course at Wittering. An instructor there was Basil Embry (then a Flight Lieutenant) and Squadron Leader Basil "Jackie" Noakes and I were pupils.

Embry who had already been awarded his first DSO for service on the NW frontier (India), became one of the most famous war leaders in the air force. As an Air Vice Marshal in 1943 he often put in "off-duty" hours with his squadrons flying as "Wing Commander Smith". He was a warm and generous comrade but often too openly critical of high command. It was no surprise to many of us when Embry was later forced to retire as C-in-C of Allied Air Forces, Central Europe, for his criticisms of NATO. "Jacky" Noakes, a famous first-war pilot was the man who first demonstrated "crazy flying" at the Hendon Display.

Our blind-flying instruction was carried out in an Avro 504N which had been rigged with no dihedral angle on the main planes. The object of this was to make the aircraft unstable laterally. A hood was fitted over the pupils' cockpit and the blind-flying instruments consisted of a Reid and Siegrist turn-and-bank indicator and primitive bubble-gauges for-and-aft and lateral-level indicators. These of course were in addition to the normal airspeed and revolution indicators, magnetic compass and oil-pressure and temperature gauges.

Jackie and I were the only pupils on the course whose flying time exceeded a thousand hours, the remainder were youngsters with 500 hours or less.

It was significant that we two who had been flying "by the seat of our pants" for so long found it most difficult to believe our instruments when under the hood. We put the aircraft into a spin and on the orders of the instructor to recover, applied corrective control. It was most disconcerting to be told over the Gosport tube that we were now spinning in the opposite direction. It was extraordinary how difficult it was to believe the instruments and disbelieve one's physical sensation.

The younger pilots found it much easier, presumably because they had not relied on the seats of their pants for so long. This was the beginning of instrument flying and later the invention of more accurate instruments like the Sperry Artificial Horizon and the Gyro Compass and the development of the Link trainer (an early form of flight simulator) revolutionised flying safety.

In addition to the Armstrong Whitworth Siskin and Bristol Bulldog, aircraft flown during 1932 included a Blackburn Ripon, AW Atlas, the new Hawker Audax, Fairey Flycatcher, Gypsy Moth and Hawker Fury.

Chapter 8

Go and Try It Again

After two happy years at Hornchurch, to my joy, I was posted in January 1933 to 22 Squadron as a test pilot to the Aircraft Experimental Establishment at Martlesham Heath. (It was a posting I had applied for.) After six months training, I was put on the Air Ministry list of qualified test pilots and given command of 'C' Flight of the aircraft performance-testing squadron. 'A' flight had the single-seat fighters, 'B' Flight had the multi engine bomber and civil aircraft and 'C' Flight the single-engined multi seater types for testing. (It was written somewhere that I would be responsible for testing naval and "other odd aircraft".)

John Boothman, who later won the Schneider Cup outright for England in the Supermarine S6b commanded 'A' Flight and "Lovely" Parker, a delightfully tough Australian, commanded 'B' Flight. I am not sure why Parker was nicknamed "Lovely" unless it was because of his large moustache, or possibly because he was such a tough character and was anything but lovely!

Later, when John Boothman went to the High Speed Flight at Felixstowe, I was given 'A' Flight and "Andy" Anderson took over 'C' Flight. One of the test pilots in 'A' Flight was Flying Officer Bill Pegg, later famous as the senior test pilot for Bristol who put the giant Bristol Brabazon through its tests in the 1950's.

One day Bill Pegg was carrying out a terminal-velocity dive test over the aerodrome in an Avro Cadet when the aircraft's wings came off and he baled out. He told us an amusing story in the mess afterwards. He said that when the aircraft disintegrated he was thrown out of the cockpit and to make sure that he did not fumble with the parachute release cord he took off his right glove. The glove being lighter appeared to float upwards. He pulled the release cord, the parachute opened and the glove then passed him in mid air, closely followed by bits of the aeroplane.

Pegg was in a formation of three Bristol Bulldogs practising on May 19, 1933 in preparation for the Hendon Air Pageant when two of the aircraft collided at the top of a formation loop. Flight Lieutenant Campbell was killed when he failed to pull out of the ensuing dive and his aircraft exploded on impact while Flight Lieutenant Moir barely escaped his spinning aircraft and parachuted safely. A very shaken Bill Pegg circled the wreckage before landing without further incident. I was watching from the opposite side of the aerodrome along with the wives of both Moir and Campbell. But life in the air force had to continue in spite of such tragedies and two days later, with the wreckage taken away, we were back to our normal routine. Shortly after that, I was in the Bulldog display flight.

I had a major crash at Martlesham on June 30, 1933. This was when testing the Blackburn M1/30 at full load. The M1/30 was a large single-engined torpedo bomber, designed to carry a 2500lb torpedo. It happened about 7am and the load consisted of a dummy torpedo which was wired on to the torpedo rack to prevent accidental release. An RAF fitter, Aircraftsman, Jim Skyrme, volunteered to occupy the back cockpit in order to complete the load. The test was to be a normal full-load take off, followed by a ceiling climb.

Shortly after take off the engine failed when we were at about 60 feet. If I had been able to release the torpedo, I think I could have glided into the adjacent rugger field. However, we were too low to try to turn back to the aerodrome so I had to glide into a belt of fir trees. In the dead silence that followed the engine failure, I yelled to my passenger, "Hang on, we're going birds' nesting, we've got to go for the trees." Although it must have only been a matter of seconds from the time the engine stopped until we hit the trees, I remember turning off all the petrol cocks, switching off the ignition and then just before impact, kicking on full rudder so that the starboard wings took the first shock. Both starboard wings crumpled, then the port wings crumpled and I found myself unhurt, but slightly winded, still sitting in the cockpit about eight feet above the ground. Petrol was pouring out of the centre-section tanks and blue smoke was coming up from the engine. Expecting an explosion and fire, I shouted to Skyrme "Jump and run like hell."

I unfastened my harness and looking behind, I saw the fitter was knocked out and blood was coming from under his leather flying helmet.

The next thing I remember was that I was kneeling over Skyrme, about 50 yards from the crash and unfastening his helmet to see where he was hurt, then the Station MO arrived on a bicycle, with half his face covered in shaving soap. The doctor told me afterwards that he was in the middle of shaving in his married quarters when he heard the engine stop. He dashed out, jumped on his bicycle and saw me lift the fitter on to my shoulder and jump to the ground with him.

I apparently carried him at a smart trot for about 50 yards and the doctor was amazed that I was not even breathing hard. To this day, I cannot remember getting Skyrme and myself out of the aircraft, or of carrying him on my shoulder. Following the old adage taught me by Orde-Lees ("The best way to recover from a fall is get back up on a horse!") I made A 10-minute "Air Log test" in a Hawker Hart later the same morning.

Jim Skyrme went on to quite a varied RAF career, serving in Iraq, Basra and Kurdistan with 203 Squadron servicing flying boats in 1934-35. He was in Aden 1935 to 1936 with 41 Squadron and he then went out to India with a Wapiti squadron. On his return to Britain in 1938 he became a Merlin engine specialist and he was at RAF Peterborough in the Battle of Britain days. He went out to Canada to a training squadron in Toronto and then came back to RAF Waddington where he was with 44 Bomber Squadron. From 1943 to 1945 he was with a bomber training unit at RAF Winthorpe and he left the service as a Flight Sergeant in 1945.

The crashed aircraft was a 50-ft wingspan biplane built by Blackburn to the same specifications as the original Fairey Swordfish but while the pilot and observer-gunner were in tandem cockpits, the second observer was to be in a prone position under the pilot's floor – not a happy nor comfortable position, especially in a crash. The other feature of the aircraft was it was designed around the new Rolls Royce FXII V-12 engine that was to develop into the famous Merlin range. Following the crash, Blackburn built a private-venture successor which they called the M1/30A. Among other advances, this aircraft featured an all-metal monocoque fuselage which was designed to float – not a bad idea in a carrier-borne aircraft – and it also had four ailerons that could all be depressed via a handwheel to act as flaps. It was the first aircraft I flew with pneumatic wheel brakes.

All the test flights we carried out at Martlesham were arranged and checked by a team of civilian scientists who were rather disrespectfully (but often affectionately) known as "Boffins."

Aeronautics to them was just a science and the test pilots were just incidental necessities to the solving and checking of their theories and problems, as the following story will show.

It must be realised that in those comparatively early days, the only automatic recording instrument carried in the aircraft was a recording baragraph which showed the exact height reached and the time taken. All other details were noted by the pilot on a knee pad from the readings of the cockpit instruments and a stop watch clipped on the kneepad.

In this particular case the problem was to find out why the Fairey TSR, the original Swordfish prototype, had failed to recover from a spin, with near-fatal results for Fairey's factory test pilot, Chris Staniland. One theory was that the carrying of four 24lb smoke floats on bomb racks which were placed only a couple of feet from the wing tips, had a sort of gyroscopic effect once the aircraft was in the spin.

I was instructed to carry out spinning tests in the second prototype Swordfish, the Fairey TSR2 (later K4190) with smoke floats attached. (This machine differed from the original in having a slightly longer fuselage, a three-bladed propeller and "anti-spin strakes" fitted in front of the tail-plane). In the standard spinning tests, which all service aircraft had to go through, the pilot climbed to 14,000 or 15,000ft, then deliberately put the aircraft into a spin by closing the throttle, easing back the stick until the aircraft stalled, then kicking on full rudder and holding the controls in this position until six complete revolutions were accomplished. The number of turns was checked by watching some prominent railway line or main road and counting the number of times the wings spun past the landmark. At the end of six revolutions the pilot then tried to recover by easing the stick forward and centralising, or if necessary, putting on opposite rudder. If after taking recovery action, the aircraft did not come out of the spin for a further four turns, the pilot was allowed to bale out.

On this occasion, after going into the spin I noted that for the first two and a half turns the aircraft was in a rapid flat spin, i.e. it was almost horizontal, then the nose dropped and the revolutions were slower for about three turns. When I tried to take recovery action after a complete six turns, the aircraft refused to recover so after five further turns I released my harness and started to climb out of the cockpit. As I was about to go over the side the aircraft came out of the spin and went into a deep dive. Greatly relieved, I hurriedly sat back at the controls, pulled the aircraft out of the dive and landed. I presumed that the cause of recovery was the altered airflow produced when I stood on the seat. I made my report to the head "Boffin" who after a lot of thought and after studying the notes from my knee pad, said "I see that when you tried to recover you were in the flat spin period, I think that if you had waited until the nose dropped and then applied forward stick and opposite rudder you would have had no difficulty in recovering. Go and try it again!" I thought this a bit much, but I did try again and the "Boffin" was proved to be right.

During my time at Martlesham, I met many notable people in the aircraft industry, including Dick Fairey, the Blackburn Brothers, Handley Page, Archie Frazer Nash (who from designing racing cars had just turned to designing power-operated rear gun turrets for aircraft), George Bulman (then Chief Test Pilot at Hawker's), Tom Sopwith and many others.

"Performance testing" at Martlesham covered just about every aspect of flying. When a new aircraft arrived it would typically undergo a series of "stick and unstuck" (takeoff and landing) evaluations, usually by different pilots and with different loads. Then a series of partial climbs and climbs to various heights would culminate in an "absolute ceiling" test. Absolute ceiling was the point at which the air became so thin that engine, propeller and aerofoils could no longer function effectively and the point was generally indicated by the slowly creeping altimeter finally stopping its upward crawl. Sometimes here was a more dramatic curtailment such as when the engine coolant froze or if someone (usually a rigger or observer) passed out due to lack of oxygen at height.

There was always a whole series of tests around engine efficiency and reliability with sub-tests involving cooling, heating, fuel consumption at varying heights and speeds and any ancillary equipment including gauges and instruments.

Each flight had a detailed set of procedures and parameters to follow and there was a fairly exacting de-briefing. Any problems or discrepancies obviously lead to a series of subsequent tests and sometimes aircraft were returned to the manufacturer for modifications. At the end of the sequence of tests and checks we would start serious manoeuvring such as spins and stalls and when all vices and quirks had been at least noted, if not eliminated, the final test was often the terminal velocity dive. In this, we took the aircraft up to 16,000 feet and then came down to 6,000 feet in a straight dive and noted the highest possible speed. Hopefully, this could be achieved without anything falling off or failing. It was in this test that we often discovered "new" problems such as elevator or aileron flutter (and in cases like the Avro Tutor, the latter caused the wings to fall off and many years later this same problem was eventually found to be the culprit in the mysterious cases of several Typhoons losing their entire tailplane with fatal results).

Among the interesting aircraft that came to Martlesham were two Heinkel monoplanes. The He64C (carrying the civilian registration G-ACBS) was of interest because it had very efficient leading-edge slots combined with trailing-edge flaps which gave it a very low stalling speed (32 mph) and excellent overall handling yet with a top speed of 150mph. In 1934 there was a then unknown irony when Rolls Royce used a Heinkel 70 (also called the "Blitz" which later showed perhaps its true purpose as the first of the Luftwaffe "schnellbombers.") at Martlesham Heath to act as a flying test-bed for their Kestrel engine. This engine was their first V-12 monoblock-cast engine which saw service in a number of RAF aircraft such as the Hawker Hart, Fury and Audax biplanes and in the Miles Master monoplane. The Heinkel 70 had attracted the attention of RJ Mitchell at the Paris Aerosalon in 1932 and in correspondence with Ernst Heinkel he was particularly interested in the all-metal fuselage construction, the streamlining and the elliptical wingform. The Heinkel 70, although soon outmoded as a military type, did see service with the Condor Legion in the Spanish Civil War. It was the direct ancestor of the Heinkel He 111 which used the same distinctive oval wings and streamlined fuselage in a twin-engined configuration. A lesser known derivastive was the He 112 which out-performed the Messerschmidt Bf 109 in many ways during trials when competing to be the Luftwaffe's first monoplane fighter. The Heinkel 70 was also sent to Japan for study and inspired the Aichi D3A (or Val as the allies nick-named it) which was the light carrier-borne bomber used with such devastating results at Pearl Harbor.

The Rolls-Royce Kestrel was a 21-litre supercharged motor which when scaled up to 27-litres and much modified became the Merlin. Though many suspected, none of us knew at the time that both these Heinkel aircraft were in fact being used to train the emerging and then "unlawful" German Luftwaffe. In a further irony, Messerschmitt used a Rolls Royce Kestrel engine in the prototype Bf109 fighter and the Junkers Ju87 (Stuka) also originally flew with a Kestrel engine.

I think it was in May 1933 that the designer Nevil Norway turned up at Martlesham with a team to support the debut of the Airspeed Courier which was the first British production aeroplane fitted with a retractable undercarriage. Such a modern contraption was greeted with a fair amount of scepticism by the flying establishment (although the Lockheed Orion was already in service in the United States with retractable main wheels) and the designer along with their own test pilot (George Stainforth) brought a large lorry with a fully-working model of the undercarriage to demonstrate its safety as a concept. While Bill Pegg and I among others were playing with the model and practising wheels up and down, another of our pilots rather thoughtlessly brought the Courier in for a wheels-up landing having defeated the main safety component of the system – a loud warning hooter – by the simple expedient of turning it off. We had just listened to our demonstrator saying "Any pilot with the most limited experience and intelligence could not possibly forget to put the wheels down.." Luckily, despite their brave words, the designers had anticipated some initial problems with learning curves by having the wheels retract to a secure position which left half the wheel exposed. A wheels-up landing only damaged the propeller and some fairings and that little crash cost a mere 20 pounds to repair. The long-lived and famous Douglas DC-3 uses a similar main-wheel retraction system leaving one-third of the tyres exposed as a safety precaution in the event of a wheels-up landing.

Nevil Norway had formed Airspeed Ltd in partnership with Hessel Tiltman (formerly with de Havilland) and the pioneer aviator, Sir Alan Cobham, along with a number of other backers such as solicitor-director A.E.Hewitt and as a major financial backer he had Lord Grimthorpe.

That original Airspeed Courier was quite extraordinary for its time and when it arrived, out-performed many of our supposedly advanced military machines. Powered with a 240hp Armstrong Siddeley Lynx engine it had a speed of over 160mph with pilot and five passengers. It was used by Sir Alan Cobham in the first air-to-air refuelling experiments (and I confess I was relieved not to get roped-in to those tests). In September 1934, having refuelled successfully twice in the air, Cobham and Squadron Leader Helmore were well on their way to a non-stop record-breaking flight from England to India when they had to turn back and land in Malta due to a split-pin falling out of a throttle linkage.

Nevil Norway and I formed quite a close friendship. As well as our shared love of aircraft and flying, he was also a keen yachtsman so we had much in common. He had been on the design team of the R100 airship working initially as chief calculator under Sir Barnes Wallace and had many a fascinating tale about the building of that airship and the ill-fated competitor, the Government-backed R101. It was not until some years later, while reading his autobiographical Slide Rule, and thinking "I've heard some of this before" that I made the connection and realised that the novelist Nevil Shute was my friend Nevil Norway.

After the interest shown in G-ABXN, the Air Ministry took delivery of a second Airspeed Courier for further evaluation and testing and I think because by this time it was obvious that monoplane fighters with retractable undercarriages were about to out-perform the biplanes which hitherto had been the main focus of military development.

Airspeed then brought out their twin-engined Envoy, firstly with Wolseley AR9 200hp radial engines which were compact, quiet and smooth-running and marked a move by the Nuffield organisation into aero-engine manufacture. Thanks to Government red-tape and imposed pricing conditions these excellent engines never went into full production and the Envoy, eventually powered by Armstrong Siddeley Cheetah radial engines, became the Airspeed Oxford on which most of the World War 2 Bomber Command crews were trained. The ultimate endorsement of the Airspeed Envoy came in 1937 when one was ordered for the King's Flight for the personal use of King George VI.

Over three days in early October 1934, I put a special racing variant of the Envoy through its C of A tests. This aircraft was being prepared for the famous airman Capt T. Neville Stack to compete in the 1934 MacRobertson Air Race from Hendon to Melbourne and was powered by supercharged Armstrong Siddelely Cheetah VI engines and had a large petrol tank in the fuselage in place of the normal passenger space. With no windows in the main fuselage area and different cowlings it was given the name Airspeed Viceroy.

The Viceroy was to have a very interesting career that would have made a wonderful story in the Nevil Shute genre. Due largely to financial stress involved from taking part in the race without sufficient backing, Neville Stack failed to perform up to his usual standards. He started the race with a lot of positive publicity as the official airmail aircraft carrying newsreel film to Australia of race preparations and the start. But he withdrew from the contest at Athens after citing weather, engine and brake problems which many of us thought would not normally have deterred a pilot of his experience and repute. He then started legal action against Airspeed for alleged defects in the machine (on which he had in fact only paid a 1000 pound deposit) but he lost the lengthy court case and the Viceroy eventually came back to Airspeed in Portsmouth. It sat at the back of their hangar waiting another buyer until a man arrived saying he was an agent for a company seeking an aircraft for the rapid distribution of newsreel films around the capitals of Europe. There was, however, a little extra fitting out needed. Could Airspeed fit bomb racks to save carrying the flammable cine-films inside the aeroplane? The request was refused because the Viceroy was built and sold only as a civil machine but after a little wrangling, lugs were fitted under the wings – what the "client" fitted thereafter was of no concern. There was further drama involving the delivery pilot who was recognised as a famous German combat flier and eventually the buyer admitted he was acting on behalf of Emperor Haile Selassie who was fighting the war in Abyssinia against the Italians under Mussolini. The Viceroy was a great deal faster and had a far greater range than anything the Italians were operating on that front and its intended role was to bomb the Italian oil storage tanks at Massawa. Complete secrecy was needed because if warned of the proposed raid with the Viceroy, the Italians would move some faster fighters into the battle. Bombs and racks and guns and other equipment (the same agent had also bought three Gloster Gauntlets) were being supplied by Finland. After getting their money, Airspeed were then asked if they would provide an instructor and pilot to give the delivery pilot some night-flying practice in an Airspeed Envoy around Portsmouth. This was all done and in a scene like something out of a spy movie, the German pilot did a couple of hours of circuits and bumps over a flare path and was whisked away immediately afterwards in a fast car – a "foreign" pilot spending that amount of time flying over our main naval dockyard would have caused a major scandal. Perhaps fortunately, the aircraft never left England as Haile Selassie fled to exile in Cheltenham in May 1936 when the Ethiopian cause became hopeless. And so the Viceroy was for sale again, this time on behalf of an emperor.

The next owners were Ken Waller and Max Findlay who wanted the Viceroy to compete in the London to Johannesburg race in October 1936. Waller had been co-pilot with my old friend Cathcart-Jones in the DH Comet that set the record for the return journey to Australia in 1934. They intended to race the aircraft with a crew of four and were tipped as favourites. But when the Spanish Civil War erupted in July 1936 backers of the Republican side offered them 9500 pounds - a price that would cover the price already paid plus the prize money and the Viceroy left for Spain via France within a few days. Max and Ken bought another modified Airspeed Envoy and did start in the race but crashed at Abercorn in Africa after attempting an uphill take-off. Sadly, Max Findlay and the radio operator were killed. The Viceroy was supposedly never heard of again after appearing against Franco in Republican colours but strangely, years later while serving in Italy, I heard a claim from a Finnish pilot that the aircraft had been in service with the Finns in their war against the Russians in 1940.

In October 1934, Charles Ulm, veteran of many long-distance flights with Charles Kingsford-Smith, chose a Lynx-engined Airspeed Envoy to initiate an airline flying between San Francisco and Sydney. The aircraft was fitted with long-range tanks giving it an estimated range of 3000 nautical miles for the 2,200 nm leg from Oakland to Honolulu but unfortunately the aircraft and crew were lost due to navigation problems.

We were also testing two American machines - the Chance-Vought Corsair V66E (a biplane, not the famous fighter used in World War 2) and the Northrop 2E around this time – both being single-engined American dive-bombers, the latter a monoplane powered by a 750hp Wright Cyclone radial.

It was a very interesting time to be flying. I was in a team still testing several biplane torpedo spotter reconnaissance aircraft under evaluation for the Fleet Air Arm (the

Fairey Swordfish, the Blackburn B-6, the Gloster TSR 38 being among these) yet we were getting a variety of quite different aircraft in as well. A favourite was the Westland Wizard, a lovely "parasol" high-winged monoplane that I was surprised never went into large-scale production.

Quite the most unusual was the Avro Rota which was a licensed version of the Italian Cierva C30 Autogiro which eventually went into service with the Army Co-operation service of the RAF. After some initial apprehension at the concept of trusting my life to what at first look seemed a Heath-Robinson contraption, I found this machine a lot of fun and in a moderate breeze found I could land and takeoff almost vertically. It was the first rotary-wing aircraft to land on a British carrier (and I think on any ship).

Another designer who brought an aircraft in for a C of A was Edgar Percival. He arrived in a Percival Mew Gull (G-ACND) a small civil racing monoplane that was to be flown by a "member of the Royal Family" in the King's Cup Air Race of 1935. He was not terribly amused when we sent him back to a Luton to fit a petrol tap that could be turned off within the cockpit (a fairly standard and basic safety requirement for a C of A).

Another interesting little single-seat monoplane designed and built for racing was the de Havilland TK2, built by the DH Technical School apprentices.

A number of the military prototypes that came to Martlesham in 1934 and 1935 were built to an Air Ministry specification (F7/30) for a day-and-night fighter with a top speed over 250mph and armed with four machine-guns. Preference was given to aircraft using the Rolls Royce Goshawk steam-cooled V-12 engine. Among the contenders I flew was the Westland F7/30 which caused a major stir when we first saw it because it had a mid-engine layout, the propeller being driven by a shaft running in a tube below the pilot. It handled beautifully, but the designers had got their sums wrong somewhere because it never reached its projected speed. Another contender for the fighter contract was of course the Supermarine 224, Mitchell's first monoplane fighter design, which arrived at Martlesham shortly before I left.

The Gloster Gauntlet entered service about this time and their chief designer persuaded the company to build a modified Gauntlet with a covered cockpit, a more powerful radial engine and a number of other enhancements such as wing-mounted Lewis guns. This aircraft arrived at Martlesham as a private-venture machine simply named G37 but when its performance surpassed all the Goshawk-engined fighter contenders it was transferred to RAF ownership as Gloster K5200 and I had the privilege of demonstrating this aeroplane at the 1935 Hendon Air Pageant in June. One month later, it was officially renamed the Gloster Gladiator, the last biplane fighter to enter service with the RAF. It was of course to achieve fame in the hands of skilled pilots fighting in some of the most dramatic battles of the early WW2, in Norway, Malta and France.

Shortly before I left Martlesham we were witness to a very significant test when a prototype Rolls Royce Merlin engine took to the air for the first time in the old Hawker Hart airframe that had been used in many guises as a flying test-bed.

One of the last aircraft I took for performance tests was an Armstrong Whitworth Scimitar which was for export to Norway. We also had what was called a Persian Fury in for delivery tests – it was one of a number of Hawker Furies for delivery to Persia and was I believe one of the last of these very pretty aeroplanes to remain flying. It was still being used for border patrol in 1942.

After three and a half years as a test pilot, I was told that it was my turn for an administrative job. As I had been flying continuously for 10 years I could not grumble at this and found myself posted as Assistant Provost Marshal to Baghdad in September 1935. Whilst I was on embarkation leave, Mussolini started his invasion of Abbysinia, my posting was cancelled and I was ordered to join No 41 (Fighter) Squadron at Northolt.

On arrival at Northolt, I found the Squadron under orders for Aden. The aircraft (Hawker Demons, two-seater versions of the Fury) were already crated and on their way in a freighter. After about a week at Northolt, all the squadron personnel marched at night to a nearby railway siding where a special train was ready for us. After a tedious and boring journey we arrived at our port of embarkation and went onboard the old SS Cameronian, which had been laid up for some time and had been commissioned very hurriedly as a trooper. The Captain, who had also been brought back from retirement, was Captain David Bone, very well known, not only as a seaman but as the author of The Brass Bounder and other books.

Cameronian was very crowded, I think she embarked the personnel of 13 Squadrons, all of whom had been hurriedly put on a war basis and whose aircraft were already on the way by sea.

The CO of 41 Squadron was Squadron Leader Jack Boret, a first class leader and a good friend, who strangely enough, I was to succeed twice during the war. Coincidentally, one of the fitters was Jim Skyrme who had survived that M1/30 crash two years earlier.

The personnel of the various squadrons were disembarked, two squadrons at Malta, several at Alexandria for aerodromes in Egypt and the Canal Zone, then more at Port Sudan and finally, our own squadron at Aden.

The aerodrome was then at Khormaksar and was very primitive. We were all under canvas, as domestic buildings had only just been started. Our aircraft were awaiting us, still in their crates and our first job was to assemble them and test them. When we unpacked the crates we found that the aircraft were those of one of the squadrons disembarked in Malta and presumably the Malta Squadron had our aircraft. Luckily, both squadrons were armed with Hawker Demons, but we were all very cross at this blunder.

However, everyone worked enthusiastically in spite of the terrific heat accentuated by the lack of shade or cover. As a former test pilot, I was given the job of testing each aircraft as it was assembled, which kept me pretty busy for some days.

The AOC Aden at this time was Air Commodore Portal who later became Chief of the Air Staff and later Marshal of the Royal Air Force, Lord Portal.

My first mission was an interesting one. I was told to take two aircraft to an emergency landing ground some 40 miles inland in order to bring out a political officer. The landing ground was on a plateau on the edge of an escarpment 4000 feet high. After landing we were greeted by an Arab radio operator speaking fluent English, but with a pronounced American accent, who introduced me to another Arab who was very travel-stained and dirty and smelt to high heaven. I thought at first that the second Arab was just one of the locals until he climbed into the back seat of my Demon, saying quietly in English, "It's quite all right, I'm your man!"

We flew back to Khormaksar, where my passenger was greeted warmly by the Governor's ADC who brought a car to meet him. The passenger thanked me and said "I'd like you to have a drink with me in the Club this evening. After I have had a bath!" When I arrived in the club that evening I looked around and could see no one I knew until a tall red-haired Captain came over and said "I hope I'm a bit more presentable now." I was astounded, but it was indeed my "Arab" passenger, who turned out to be Captain Robert Hamilton, "Ham" to his friends, the Master of Belhaven, who later succeeded to the title of the Scottish Earldom to which he was then heir. At that stage he was a colonial service administrator in Aden and he stayed there until 1946. I only know that locally he had a fabulous reputation and his achievements in the Aden Protectorate were rumoured to equal those of Lawrence of Arabia.

Towards the end of the year, the cartilage in my left knee (an old football injury) gave trouble and as we were wearing shorts, the doctor soon spotted the swollen knee and promptly sent me to hospital. Thank goodness it was decided not to operate in Aden because of the heat, so my leg was strapped up in a back splint and after three weeks rest in hospital I was sent back to England in the P&O liner Strathmore. She was just returning from her maiden voyage to India and was the most luxurious ship I have ever sailed in.

On arrival in England, I reported to Air Ministry and was given three weeks sick leave after I had signed the usual "blood chit" or indemnity form as I had elected to have the cartilage removed at my own expense. The operation was more complicated than normal owing to some sort of growth that had developed under the knee cap, so after three weeks I was still on crutches. I applied for an extension of sick leave and found that in order to obtain this I had to report to the Medical Board at Air Ministry. After removing the back splint, inspecting the scar and replacing the splint, I was told to go to an ear, nose and throat specialist. In spite of my protests, I was put through a complete medical examination and at the end of it told I must have my top teeth extracted. In the meantime I was given another three weeks sick leave. At the end of this leave, I reported again to the medical board, minus crutches and splint, but plus a brand new set of top "Snappers" and the Board then kindly passed me fit for full flying duties.

I was then appointed as an Instructor to No 1 Flying Training School which had been moved to Leuchars, Fife. The Station Commander was Group Captain Forbes and my old friend "Jackie" Noakes was Chief Flying Instructor.

I was in command of the advanced training flight, responsible for deck landing and catapult instruction, in addition to air-to-ground and air-to-air gunnery training.

My pupils were mainly young naval and army officers. The naval pilots were training for catapulting off convoy escort ships as well as carriers and the army officers were in training as Army co-operation pilots.

Arrester hooks on the aircraft and transverse wires on the aircraft carriers had just come into being. The aircraft-catapult method of launching from cruisers had been recently perfected and in future one or two aircraft were to be carried on each cruiser.

The deck landing training consisted of approaches and landings on a dummy deck marked out on the aerodrome. This was followed by taking each pupil for at least three dual landings on the deck of a carrier. I then acted as "batsman" and controlled him on to the deck for his solo landings.

The catapult training was fun, if rather shattering for a pupil on his first launch. Our training catapult was fired like a gun. The aircraft was hoisted by a crane on to the launching platform which was about eight feet above the aerodrome. Without being too technical, the aircraft was secured to the launching bogey which was attached to the end of a steel wire which went several turns around two multiple blocks. The forward block was attached to the forward end of a powerful ram which looked when extended rather like an enormous telescope. The other block was fixed to the breech end of the "gun." The "gun" was exactly like the breech portion of a 6 1/2 naval gun and a normal cordite cartridge was fitted into the breech with the usual detonator in the touch hole. The charge was fired by pulling a lanyard. The drill for launching was simple, the pilot ran up the engine, opened up to full revs, then raised his left hand from the throttle. On the drop of his hand, the officer on the firing mechanism pulled the lanyard, which exploded the charge, forced out the ram and this launched the bogey with aircraft on it. The acceleration was terrific in the length of the catapult platform (about 35 40 feet) the aircraft reached a speed of about 50 knots. Of course, the engine at full throttle assisted the thrust of the ram so that on leaving the catapult flying speed was reached and the engine then took over. Because of the tremendous acceleration both instructor and pupil were strapped in tightly and braced their heads back on a special air filled cushion fixed behind their heads; if this drill was not carried out one's head and neck could be injured seriously. (It was not until some years later that I heard the term "whiplash injury.")

In January 27, 1937, I was promoted to Squadron Leader and posted to command No 824 FAA Squadron, then forming at Gosport. 824 Squadron was equipped with Fairey Swordfish (the famous old "stringbags") and after a brief working up period we were to embark in HMS Eagle and proceed to the China Station. The old Swordfish was an outstanding aircraft of its day. It was very strong and versatile and the Bristol Pegasus engine was most reliable. I had, of course, test-flown the prototype at Martlesham and if nothing else, I knew all about recovering from a spin in that aircraft. (Much of the work done at Martlesham had in fact been translated into making the Swordfish on of the most docile and pilot-friendly of aeroplanes.)

During the last war Swordfish were used as torpedo bombers, dive bombers, in anti submarine search and attack, as mine layers and when airborne radar was developed they had a further lease of life in spite of their slow speed. Swordfish operated in Norway, dive bombed tanks and bridges at Dunkirk, helped sink the Bismarck, took part in the defeat of the Italians at Matapan, operated very successfully from Malta against Rommel's supply lines, in fact I think they operated in every theatre of the war with good effect. But their single most famous and successful operation was the attack on the Italian Fleet at Taranto which served as a blueprint for the Japanese attack on Pearl Harbour as it proved that aircraft operating alone could sink capital warships. It also outclassed and survived its supposed successor the Fairey Albacore and in many ways had a more illustrious career than more powerful monoplane types such as the Blackburn Skua. One of its outstanding qualities was the capacity to continue flying and return safely with crew in spite of amazing punishment.

We became very fond of our Swordfish in 824 Squadron and I was very pleased with my first command as a Squadron Leader. Owing to the restricted size of HMS Eagle's hangar, the two squadrons she carried had to be limited to nine aircraft each. As Flight Commanders, I had Lieutenant Commander "Alf" Duval RN and Flight Lieutenant "Dusty" Miller RAF. "Alf" was an old friend of mine, we had served together in HMS Constance in 1923 when he was a midshipman. "Dusty" was a typical Cranwell product, I can't say more. (In hindsight, such a statement needs a little elaboration, as does a similar evaluation of Peter Townsend later. As a Cranwell graduate, Dusty was a well-trained, thoughtful and intelligent leader, had excellent values such as integrity, honesty and loyalty and he also had sincerity and discipline. On top of that he had a great sense of humour. I certainly can't say much more than that!) He and I were to be associated later, during the war in Malta.

Lieutenant Henry Gardner RN was my Senior Observer in the squadron and flew with me most of the time, as did Leading Telegraphist Faulkner, who was the wireless operator. They became close friends and we had a loyalty and friendship that was never shaken. From the word go, the whole squadron worked hard and played hard together, so that whether in flying, bombing or torpedo attacks, or sport, 824 was a unit to be proud of.

The other squadron in HMS Eagle was No 813 Squadron, commanded by Lieutenant Commander "Dicky" Pugh R.N.

Naturally there was a considerable amount of friendly rivalry between the two squadrons, which was good for efficiency all round.

Our Wing Commander and OC Flying was Roderick Carr, a New Zealander, who I have mentioned earlier in these pages. He is now Air Chief Marshal Sir Roderick Carr, with a very distinguished career behind him.

When HMS Eagle sailed from Portsmouth, my Swordfish squadron had no official number as HMS Hermes, the carrier we were to relieve on the China Station, already had an 824 Squadron on board. The two carriers were due to meet at Colombo, when Hermes' No 824 Squadron would lose their identity and Eagle's Squadron would assume it.

As can be imagined, the meeting of the two aircraft carriers called for considerable celebration, especially between the old and the new 824 Squadrons. My "opposite number" in Hermes was Squadron Leader "Freddie" Pearce RAF who started the celebrations by sending the time honoured signal "RPC" (request the pleasure of your company) to which I made the equally time honoured reply "WMP" (with much pleasure). We were royally entertained by Freddie Pearce and his boys in Hermes and of course we returned the compliment in Eagle the following day. In the course of the inter-squadron entertainments we gathered much useful information from our "opposite numbers" as well as a considerable hangover. From Freddie Pearce I also acquired a Chinese steward who served as my batman as well as being one of the Chinese stewards in the wardroom.

We were glad to get to sea after our 48 hours of saying "Hello Goodbye" and proceed to our next port of call Singapore, where both squadrons flew ashore to the newly completed aerodrome at Seletar.

The AOC Singapore was Air Commodore Tedder, now Marshal of the Royal Air Force, Lord Tedder, under whom I was to serve again later and who impressed us all with his quiet efficiency. He made a point of knowing all his officers, he had a photographic memory and an encyclopaedic knowledge of his profession, combined with what I can only describe as an unobstrusive charm. As is well known, he served the RAF and his country well and established himself as an outstanding leader in peace and war.

It was at Seletar that I first met Peter Townsend, then a young Flying Officer in one of the Singapore-based squadrons. I was to serve with him later during the war. He was even then, at an early age, obviously an outstanding character, another man with all the qualities that good breeding and the training of Cranwell can produce.

(By the 1960's I was tempted to completely re-write this evaluation but leave it here as it was indicative of the times and attitudes then. Perhaps in more modern terms I should now say that an ordered stable - and yes, comfortable - upbringing combined with the best education and training produced an outstanding and reliable officer and personality.)

During our three weeks or so at Seletar, both squadrons flew hard, practising high level bombing, torpedo dropping and night flying. We also had plenty of relaxation with golf at the Tanglin Club, bathing at the swimming club and dining and dancing at the Cocoanut Grove.

HMS Eagle then sailed for Hong Kong where both Squadrons flew ashore to Kai Tak aerodrome which was then comparatively small and had no sealed landing strips.

Owing to the surrounding hills, night landings were quite hazardous with the wind in certain directions, but in spite of this we did a lot of night-flying training which culminated in the celebrations for the Coronation of King George VI on May 12, 1937. For this our aircraft were outlined by coloured fairy lights and on Coronation night we flew in close formation for about an hour and a half around the island and over the mainland territories. We heard that the local Chinese were quite impressed, particularly as they were celebrating the occasion with their usual firework display and all the ships in harbour were illuminated. (We had started that morning with a Coronation flypast over Happy Valley Racecourse where a ceremonial parade and display was held with a large public audience.) To finish the evening, we changed into mess kit after landing and arrived at the Governor's Coronation Ball just in time for supper.

Before the abdication I had been detailed to lead the RAF Guard of Honour for the planned Coronation of Edward VIII and I had already taken delivery of a ceremonial sword with Edward VIII's crest on it – one of only a few ever struck by Wilkinsons.

Following my disappointment at the cancellation of the ceremony we were planning for Edward VIII, by now the Duke of Windor, I found the Hong Kong flypast and ceremony a reasonable consolation prize.

From Hong Kong, Eagle sailed for Wei Hai Wei. We were due to visit Shanghai on the way, but the Japanese had started their war with China and had occupied the city so the ship was ordered straight to Wei Hai Wei. After a short time there, we were ordered to Tsingtao, the hot weather resort to which all the wives and families of the Shanghai businessmen spent their summer holidays.

The Japanese were rumoured to be advancing on Tsingtao and Eagle was ordered to prepare to evacuate all the European families. We made great preparations to turn our main hangar into a vast dormitory, but were spared that duty when the United States sent a troop transport properly fitted for carrying passengers and evacuated the American families to the Phillipines and the British families to Hong Kong.

We returned to Wei Hai Wei and after a few days sailed at high speed for Tientsin. It was not until we had anchored off Tientsin that we were told we were to pick up a VIP from the British Embassy in Peking and take him to Hong Kong.

The Captain then sent for the Surgeon Commander, "Dickie" Pugh, "Alf" Duval and me. He explained that the VIP who at the time was acting as Charge d'Affaires in the absence of the Ambassador from Peking, was suffering from a nervous breakdown and that he would have to have a senior officer with him for the whole time he was on board. The poor chap was brought off from Tientsin in charge of a British police officer to whom we saw to our horror, he was handcuffed.

He was confined in the Captain's day cabin and Dickie, Alf and I took watches so that one of us was always with him. It was a most distressing experience for us. The poor man never slept and never stopped talking. He had obviously cracked after a lot of over work and mental strain and kept going over his experiences starting with his time at the Embassy in Spain during the Spanish revolution and breaking point had arrived when he was left in charge at Peking on the outbreak of the Chinese Japanese war.

Sedatives appeared to have no effect on him and it was a most nerve-wracking experience to spend hours in the same cabin with him, particularly as he seemed to think he was under arrest. On arrival at Hong Kong he was taken to hospital and we heard later that he committed suicide in a troopship whilst on passage to England for psychiatric treatment. After that experience, I hope I never have to witness the mental breakdown of a man again.

At Hong Kong, the aircraft were again flown ashore to Kai Tak, where we flew hard, practising for the Sassoon Bombing Trophy, which we were to compete for in Singapore.

We duly sailed for Singapore and after competing in the bombing competition from Selatar, our two squadrons landed on Eagle again to take part in the Combined Operations to test the defences of Singapore.

For these exercises, Eagle and her two squadrons of Swordfish represented the enemy. The defending forces consisted of HMS Cumberland (the flagship), a flotilla of destroyers, the Army, with their AA guns and searchlights and the shore-based aircraft of the RAF which consisted of two squadrons of Vickers Vildebeestes, two squadrons of Calcutta flying boats reinforced by three Squadrons of old Westland Wapitis. The latter, which were obsolescent single-engined bombers carried out a magnificent flight from India to Singapore to take part in the exercises.

The object of the combined exercises was primarily to test the efficiency of the defences of the newly-completed fortress of Singapore.

Our role in Eagle was to probe these defences and it was decided that our attacks should take place at night with the aircraft taking off from the carrier at extreme range. As the "enemy", our main object was to avoid the Eagle being spotted by the defending reconnaissance aircraft and by night flying, achieve the maximum surprise with our aircraft. (This was before the days of radar and the defences only had an early form of sound locator).

Eagle and our two squadrons of Swordfish were completely successful. On successive nights we dive-bombed the airfield, the Naval Dockyard and military barracks, using "bombs" composed of flour bags.

It is significant that on each attack we made our final approach from landward side and not from the sea, exactly as the Japanese were to do in 1941.

We were never interfered with by searchlights until after we had dropped our bombs. After each sortie we landed back on Eagle and she steamed at high speed to the east, so that by daylight we were almost out of range of the defending reconnaissance aircraft and HMS Eagle was never attacked throughout the exercises.

After the exercises, there was a full-scale conference which was attended by most of the officers of all three services who took part. An analysis of the exercise was given in turn by each of the Service Commanders. Air Commodore Tedder as AOC of the junior service spoke first and in my opinion made by far the most able and reasoned commentary, which was to the effect that the Singapore defences had been completely penetrated by an inferior but mobile attacking force, owing to lack of inter service co-ordination, inadequate communications and ineffective control between guns, searchlights and aircraft.

He pointed out that there were many obvious deficiencies in modern equipment and sites and bearings of the guns would have to be reconsidered.

The next speaker was the Army Commander, General Sir William Dobbie, who had little to say beyond regretting that AA gun sites and search lights had no communication with each other because of a shortage of telephone lines and instruments.

The last speaker was the Admiral who apologised because his flagship had to return to harbour with an engine defect early in the exercise, but simply stressed that the whole exercise had demonstrated the importance of night flying as demonstrated by HMS Eagle and her squadrons. It was claimed that Eagle's aircraft should have been disqualified from the exercises, however, because we had used our knowledge of the layout of the base and unfairly approached from "the wrong side."

How right Lord Trenchard was when he stated that the big guns of the Singapore fortress were pointing the wrong way and what a pity that he allowed himself to be over ruled in subsequent determinations on the future of Singapore.

During this period in Malaya and Singapore, our two squadrons went to Penang to take part in a flying display at the local aero club there. Our part in the programme consisted of a dive-bombing display with flour bags on a target on the airfield.

The "turn" before ours consisted of a display of aerobatics by Flight Lieutenant Alan Grace, a very good friend of mine, in a Hawker Hart trainer.

We were all in our cockpits waiting for his display to finish when to our horror, Alan failed to recover from a "falling leaf" and crashed in front of our eyes. Luckily, the aircraft did not catch fire and before we took off we were relieved to see him pulled out of the wreckage and taken off in the ambulance. He was very lucky to be alive. Alan and I were to serve together again in the war in which he distinguished himself greatly, but more about his exploits will come later.

During the same period in Malaya, I was instructed to fly Commodore Clark RN from Singapore to Penang for a conference. I took three Swordfish as I thought it a good idea to make an exercise of it by taking two aircraft with me instead of hogging all the flying for myself. The other pilots were Alf Duval and Flying Officer Heriot Hill (the junior pilot in the squadron). Henry Gardner was of course my navigator and the Commodore my passenger. As we had to take off at daylight, I arranged to land at Kuala Lumpur for breakfast, then Taiping and finally Penang. Kuala Lumpur and Taiping were just landing strips hacked out of the jungle and I suppose that a Swordfish was the biggest aircraft that had landed there in those days. On arrival over Kuala Lumpur I landed first and ordered the other two aircraft to follow in turn as soon as the previous aircraft was clear of the runway. I found the runway a little short but landed with a reasonable amount of room to spare. I had just taxied clear of the runway and switched off my engine when Alf Duval came in too fast and too high and to my horror, he overshot and the aircraft disappeared into the jungle at the end of the runway. Henry Gardner and I leaped out of our seats leaving the rather shaken Commodore in the aircraft and ran to the edge of the jungle where Alf's Swordfish had disappeared.

Luckily, the only casualty was Alf who was bleeding from cuts about the face. He was furious with himself and his first words were "Dog bite me! that was bloody clumsy of me."

As far as we could see a broken airscrew was the most serious injury to the aircraft, otherwise it was still serviceable.

We returned to the clubhouse and after putting rough dressings on Alf's face, arranged for him to be sent to Kuala Lumpur Hospital to be fixed up properly by a doctor. In the meantime, Heriot Hill, who was the most inexperienced pilot in the squadron, had made a "copy book" landing.

My VIP passenger was rather silent over breakfast. However, after sending off the necessary signals about the accident and making arrangements for the repair of the damaged aircraft, we took off on our next stage to Taiping and finally landed at the aerodrome at Penang.

Alf Duval remained at Kuala Lumpur with his crew until the aircraft was repaired and eventually flew it back to Singapore.

Two days later, after Commodore Clark's business was completed we returned to Singapore. The Commodore was not keen to land on any more jungle strips so we took off from Penang at first light and made Singapore in one hop. We were flying at 4000 feet and were about an hour out of Singapore when my engine started vibrating very badly and was obviously misfiring on at least one cylinder. There was nowhere to land, nothing but jungle and sea between us and Singapore, so there was nothing to do but ease the throttle back to reduce the vibration as much as possible and try to reach our base. We were losing height gradually but we just made it. It turned out that the central electrode of a spark plug had blown out of one cylinder. The Commodore was very grateful and asked us to a cocktail party at his house that evening and a good time was had by all. He confessed that he was very relieved to arrive back safely. "I had no idea that you chaps had such excitements."

Shortly after this I had a minor crash when landing at night on the deck of Eagle and the doctors suspected my eyesight as being the cause. It was, in my opinion, merely fatigue.

To explain, we were landing on the deck with the use of fairy lights and sector lights only, although the floodlights were in position ready for use in case of necessity which meant the latter were erected along each side of the deck and stood about two feet above it and of course could not be seen.

The fairy lights were a series of dim electric lights let into the deck and outlined the landing area. The sector lights were placed at the after end of the landing area and were rather like traffic lights. These were set to show three coloured beams, red at the bottom, green in the middle and amber at the top. If the approaching pilot saw red it meant that his approach angle was too low, green indicated the correct angle and amber that he was too high. I had already complained that the green light was so pale that at extreme range or in poor visibility conditions it was not easy to distinguish it from the amber.

To be certain that I was approaching "in the green" I made a habit of dipping down into the red at the start of my approach and then climbing gently until I saw the green. On this occasion, I left matters a bit late owing to poor visibility with the result that when I gave a burst of engine to climb over the "round down," the port wing dropped and hit the after-most floodlight.

I am certain that fatigue was the main cause of my crash as I had been without sleep for some time owing to a painful series of boils and we had been carrying out night reconnaissance exercises five nights in a row. However, the next day I was made to do the Ishihara colour-blindness test, which I failed, with the result that I was grounded for six months. A week later, when rested, I did the colour blindness test again successfully for my own satisfaction. At the time, I felt particularly aggrieved that my flying had been curtailed due to a Japanese test – and there seemed a particular barb in the colour-blindness diagnosis. As far as I was concerned I had simply "cocked-up". But the fiat had gone forth and I was "invalided" home at the end of May 1938, taking passage in the troopship Somersetshire. I spent my foreign service leave with my brother and family in Birmingham and at his holiday cottage in Somerset. I was then posted to the staff of the Director of Staff Duties, Air Commodore Willock, at Air Ministry.

Chapter 9

Prelude to War

On arrival at Air Ministry, I had a medical board and found that the restriction on my flying only applied to night flying and to deck landing. I was relieved at this, because when my desk duties allowed, I could go to Hendon and keep my hand in by borrowing an aircraft from No 24 Squadron.

This was the time of Neville Chamberlain's efforts to establish "peace in our time" and the RAF was feverishly trying to expand the forces and train new aircrews.

The Germans had leapt ahead both in numbers of aircraft and crews and they had used the Spanish Civil War as a training and testing ground for both aircraft and crews.

Our aircraft were beginning to come off the line in numbers which exceeded the speed at which aircrew could be trained. This particularly applied to bombers with their more complex crews.

Just before Mr Chamberlain went to Munich to talk to Hitler, I was instructed to find out from Bomber Command the number of operationally-trained crews we had available. I took no notes of my own at the time, but the figure 129 1/2 sticks in my mind as the answer I was given. No wonder Mr Chamberlain played for time!

I was given an interesting job at this time. Lance Sieveking, the BBC producer, playwright and author, was planning a series of broadcasts depicting the activities of the RAF and I was to fly him to any RAF establishment he wished to visit. Lance was a charming, as well as a brilliant man and having been a pilot in the RFC he was delighted to be allowed to handle the controls in the trainer Hart we used. He let me help too, by recording some of the spoken commentaries for him.

My immediate boss in the Directorate of Staff Duties was Group Captain Maynard, the Assistant Director, who was later AOC Malta in 1940 and 1941.

One day as I was returning from lunch, I met a certain character on the steps of Adastral House. I had known this man when he was an accountant officer in the RAF. I remembered that he had been allowed to resign in somewhat doubtful circumstances.

We passed the time of day, he asked me if I was serving in Air Ministry and I told him yes and pleading an appointment, I left. Almost an hour later he telephoned me and asked me if I would meet him for a drink at 6pm. I started to make excuses when he went on to say that he could put me in the way of making some money. Thinking he was trying to sell me some shares, I said I had no money to invest in anything whereupon he became more pressing. He said that if I would do him a small service which he would explain over a drink, I would have no regrets but would be well rewarded. Knowing the man and some of his past record, this sounded very suspicious to me so I told him to ring me back in half an hour. I reported at once to Maynard telling him what I knew of the man and asked what I should do. Maynard told me to go ahead and have a drink with the man, find out what he was after and report the next day.

When this character (who I will call the "Captain" as that was the style he had given himself) rang me again, I agreed to meet him for drinks at a nearby hotel at 6pm.

After a couple of drinks his proposition came out. He claimed to be acting for a large firm of contractors who were tendering for the construction of new airfields and runways. He said his principal would give me 300 pounds if I would arrange to introduce a member of his firm to a certain unnamed person in the Department of Air Ministry Contracts. I asked the name of his principals and the name of the person in Contracts they wanted to meet. He said he would let me have more details when I had agreed and had accepted their cheque. Trying to hide my disgust, I said I wanted time to consider it and told him to ring me the following afternoon. Next morning, I dictated a report of the "Captain's" proposition and handed it to Maynard.

At first, Maynard favoured my going ahead and accepting the bribe in order to get further evidence, but after consideration sent my report to the Director of Public Prosecutions who decided to prosecute the "Captain" on my evidence alone.

When the "Captain" telephoned me, I told him I could not play and rang off. A detective sergeant from Scotland Yard came and took a statement from me and the "Captain" was charged before a Magistrate. He elected to be tried at the Old Bailey by the Recorder.

There he was defended by a KC and he would probably have got away with it if he had not been put in the witness box himself. There he made such a poor showing that he convicted himself by his own conflicting statements. Thus, Frederick John Sharer Short, care of Whitehall Contractors Limited, was fined heavily but as far as I know the names of his principals never came out, nor was the name of the official in the Contracts Department divulged. No doubt Scotland Yard knew more than I did.

Air Vice Marshal Sholto Douglas (now Lord Douglas of Kirtleside) was Assistant Chief of the Air Staff at this time and was our supreme head. He detailed me to be secretary of the Regional Control Committee of which he was a most able chairman.

This committee was set up to establish a system of flying control which would meet the safety requirements of both Civil Aviation and the Services. The increasing volume of air traffic, both service and civilian, combined with higher speeds, new techniques and better communications made it essential for the safety of all that rigid control and safety rules should be laid down.

The committee was composed of the Commanders-in-Chief of Bomber, Fighter, Coastal, Army Co operation and Training Commands together with civil aviation and airline heads plus a host of technical advisors. As far as I remember there were 28 members of the committee, most of whom had decided opinions on their own particular requirements. The resulting discussions developed frequently on the lines of the traditional Naval Officers' argument "starting with a definite statement, followed by a flat contradiction and ending (almost) with personal abuse."

It says much for Sholto Douglas' ability as chairman that eventually amity and agreement and finally positive action resulted. As the poor secretary, although I had two efficient stenographers taking down the proceedings verbatim, I found the preparation of the minutes a positive nightmare until I learnt to gloss over tricky and often libellous passages by substituting that useful portmanteau phrase, "after discussion, it was decided . . ."

In view of the way modern warfare was to develop I think this is worth recording. Major "Tony" Power, Royal Marines, an old friend of mine from 1917 days was in Adastral House on liaison duties and we lunched together frequently. The Russians announced that they had parachute troops in being and the press published photographs showing large numbers of these paratroops floating down at a demonstration. Tony Power and I put our heads together and submitted a joint paper, suggesting that a picked number of fully trained Royal Marines should be trained by the RAF in parachute jumping. Our argument was that fully-trained Royal Marines were the most versatile troops we had. They were trained as infantry, gunners and engineers, in addition to sea training, so that with parachute training they would be quickly available for service as paratroops.In the event of war they would be an elite Corps of Regulars to be expanded and built on to.

We submitted this paper through the official channels and were astonished to have it returned by Sholto Douglas with a brief comment that the dropping of troops by parachute was not considered to be practical or economical and that the Russian experiment was obviously a stunt "carried out for propaganda purposes." I have often wondered at what level our suggestions were turned down and what were the thoughts of the persons who turned it down in May 1940 when we heard the news of German paratroops being dropped in Holland?

Another large part of my job consisted of issuing directives to the various commands. These directives had to go through the "usual channels" which entailed drafting an instruction which was then sent to a civil servant in the department who transformed my letter from a concise page of quarto into at least two pages of what Churchill very aptly called "gobbledegook." Thus, not less than

48 hours later, the directive would be issued over an illegible signature beginning "I am directed to inform (instruct or request) you" and ending "I have the honour to be, Sir, your obedient servant" in the age honoured Civil Service form. In urgent cases I avoided this delay and unnecessary jargon by first telephoning the appropriate Staff Officer at the Command concerned, then confirming the telephone instructions by a "demi official" letter signed by myself, a copy of which would go on the appropriate file together with a minute indicating the resulting action. This achieved speed but caused some resentment amongst certain civil servants - the "usual channels" were being short circuited.

As a result of this, in March 1939, Sholto Douglas sent for me to sign his confidential report on my work. The gist of this was "Woodhall has worked hard and conscientiously and achieved results, but owing to the lack of staff training he is too apt to take short cuts. I think therefore that he will be more suitably employed on an operational station."

Although this was my first adverse report, I was delighted to sign it and I was posted to Duxford Fighter Sector. I handed over my job at Air Ministry to Squadron Leader "Tubby" Grant. I also gave him my Air Ministry "uniform" - a bowler hat and rolled umbrella!

Chapter 10

Duxford and the Big Wing

In my new posting I found myself to be second in command to Wing Commander "Pingo" Lester. My official title was Squadron Leader Flying (Operations) and in addition to being administrative officer, I was made responsible for the development of the Fighter Control system and the training of the operations room crews.

My biggest administrative task was to plan the evacuation from the station of all married families which would take place as soon as mobilisation for war was ordered. As this entailed the arranging of transport by the most economical means for all the wives and children to their chosen destination, it was no mean task.

At this date there were two Squadrons on the station, No 19 and No 66, both armed with the new Mark 1 Spitfires.

Squadron Leader Henry Cozens commanded No 19 Squadron and Squadron Leader Fullergood, an old friend of mine from Netheravon days commanded No 66 Squadron. The Mark 1 Spitfire had a fixed airscrew and therefore a long takeoff because its acceleration was poor until it was airborne, but with the introduction of first the de Havilland two-pitch airscrew and later the Rotol variable-pitch airscrew, it was a magnificent aircraft in every way.

It was at Duxford that I first met Air Vice Marshal Trafford Leigh Mallory, who was then our AOC with his No 12 Group Headquarters at Hucknell in Nottinghamshire.

"LM" was a true gentleman and a most capable and efficient commander who was respected and esteemed by all ranks who served under him. In my opinion he was one of the great leaders who deservedly reached the top in the last war and his death in a flying accident when on the way to India to take over Supreme Command from Mountbatten in 1944 was a great loss to his country and his service. I also lost a good friend. He was the most energetic and selfless of all the Air Vice-Marshals in the RAF and he was always ready to listen to and support the pilots in the front of the air battles. It is a great pity that his memory has been tarnished by the controversies around command and tactics which often seem to come as afterthoughts from those who were not involved.

A notable character at Duxford was Warrant Officer Whiting, the Station Warrant Officer. When I first took over my job I was greeted by Whiting who said, with a beaming smile, "I don't suppose you remember me, Sir." I replied "Your face is familiar and I would say that you were taught to salute in the Royal Marines?"

"That's right, Sir, last time I saw you was in 1917. You were Orderly Officer at Forton Barracks and I was a drummer boy. You had to witness my punishment when I was given half a dozen of the best by the Drum Major for being caught smoking."

Whiting proved to be one of the best disciplinary Warrant Officers I ever served with in the RAF and was a tower of strength to me as the personnel on the station quickly mounted in numbers with the approach of war. The Fighter Control system was rapidly developing, the Observer Corps was already in being for visual and sound reporting and the RDF chain (now known as radar) was developing steadily (and at that stage stealthily).

Joint control of our defences was established so that AA guns and searchlights were co-ordinated with Fighter Control. At the top, Fighter Command and Anti-aircraft Command were closely integrated. At group and sector levels, AA and Searchlight Control officers were established in the same operations rooms as the RAF and worked closely with the Fighter Control Officers.

It was at Sector level (Duxford was a Sector Station) that fighter control became a personal affair. From the Sector Station the Controller was in direct communication with the fighter pilots by RT (radio telephone). With the development and installation of VHF (very high frequency) RT just before the outbreak of war, the distances at which one could communicate increased tremendously.

When I arrived at Duxford there was only a skeleton operations room crew under the charge of the Signals Warrant Officer and controlling was shared between the Station Commander, the two Squadron Commanders and myself. The most important job was to train sufficient personnel to man the operations room on a 24-hour basis.

The RAF Volunteer Reserve, which was in peacetime only on a part-time basis, provided the trainees in the first place When the Women's Auxiliary Air Force (WAAF) came into being in June 1939 we were delighted to get girls as plotters.

One of the first of the RAFVR officers to join was my old friend, K K Horn; I had last seen him in 1930 at Hornchurch when as the first commanding officer of 54 Squadron in the Kaiser's war, he had presented a trophy to the re-formed 54 Squadron. I was astonished and delighted when he walked into my office wearing only a single ring on his sleeve, but with a most impressive display of medal ribbons on his chest.

In May or June, we had another task given to us, the preliminary training of young National Service men. This training was most ably carried out by Warrant Officer Whiting. To accommodate this influx, Nissen huts were hurriedly erected. About this time a Satellite airfield at Fowlmere about three miles away was completed with Nissen huts to accommodate one squadron. The two squadrons were of course training hard on their new Spitfires and even in those pre-war days one flight (known as the Battle Flight) was always at readiness.

By June, night flying training was in full swing and one night when three 66 Squadron pilots were airborne practising night formation with another young pilot on his first night Spitfire solo, what was known in Cambridgeshire as a "hah" materialised.

This "hah" was a kind of thin cloud with a base of about 300 feet which could appear very suddenly and in a few minutes cover the whole of the flat plain. Before I could bring the aircraft in to land, this low cloud had blotted out the flare path so I ordered the pilots by RT to land at Northolt where I knew a flare path was laid out ready. The leader of the formation acknowledged the order but I could not get any reply from Bob Oxspring, who was on his first night solo. All we could do was to fire rockets at intervals to indicate where the aerodrome was.

I went on to the aerodrome and we could hear an aircraft circling overhead. Suddenly Bob appeared below the cloud, obviously sighted the flare path and decided to land. Visibility below the cloud was very poor and Bob hurriedly lowered his flaps and undercarriage, but his speed was so high that he touched down about a hundred yards from the end of the landing T. Still travelling fast, he disappeared through the boundary hedge, bounced over the Royston Newmarket road and through another hedge into a ploughed field. By the time I had jumped into my car and followed by the fire tender and ambulance, reached what I feared would be a rather nasty crash, Bob Oxspring had taxied out of the ploughed field and I met him taxying back along the main road! I sent the fire tender and ambulance back and held up main road traffic until the main gate at the aerodrome was reached. Here we struck a problem. The gate posts were too narrow for the Spitfire to be pushed through and in addition there was a solid cast-iron GPO red pillar box alongside the outer gate post.

I parked my car and arrived back at the gate to find an enthusiastic bunch of pilots trying to push the pillar box over by using an old sports car as a bulldozer. I stopped this and pointed out that by bearing down on the port wing we could lift the starboard wing over the gatepost and the letterbox. The amazing thing was that the only damage to the Spitfire was a dent or two in the aluminium fairing on the legs of the under carriage. Bob Oxspring, who was later a Group Captain and earned high decorations in the war, was the son of an equally distinguished father, affectionately known in the first war as "Oxo", who, with K K Horn, served in the original 54 Squadron RFC.

Shortly before war was declared, mobilisation of reserves and auxiliaries was ordered and Duxford received its quota, including the first of the WAAF. These girls, all volunteers, were grand types and were a very welcome addition to our strength. They were extremely keen to learn their jobs and became efficient as well as decorative in a very short time.

The first detachment of WAAF reported as soon as the wives and families had been evacuated. This evacuation was completed in 48 hours thanks to our earlier planning. The WAAF took over the airmen's married quarters, six girls to a house. I allotted an officers' married quarter to the WAAF officers as a mess and sleeping quarters.

The first girls to report had been issued with a blue burberry and a beret as their only uniform. They were plotters, clerks and MT drivers and had received a little training in their trades. It fell to the unfailing Warrant Officer Whiting to give them their basic disciplinary and parade-ground work.

As soon as their proper uniforms arrived, these girls were a credit to the air force. They were so good looking that an officer from Group Headquarters always referred to them as "Woody's Beauty Chorus!" after seeing the WAAF plotters in the Operations Room.

Shortly after the women took up their quarters, the senior WAAF officer, Flight Officer Margot Robinson, came to see me. "We have a delicate problem," she said.

Expecting a situation involving perhaps one of two of our more enthusiastic pilots, I asked her to sit down and tell me what was wrong.

"There are no baths for the girls," she said. "We have only showers."

"Showers are good enough for the men," I said. "I can't see a problem there."

"Men don't have periods" she replied. "Do you expect the girls to stand on their heads in the shower?"

"How many baths do you think we'll need?" was my somewhat embarrassed response.

Just prior to mobilisation, No 611 Auxiliary Squadron came to Duxford for their annual training and they remained at the station when full mobilisation was ordered. Their CO, Squadron Leader Geoffrey Pilkington was an MP and on the outbreak of war, he handed over command of the Squadron to James McComb, the senior flight commander. James (who retired at the end of the war as a Group Captain) led the Squadron with distinction in the Battle of Britain.

The declaration of war on September 3, 1939 found us reasonably prepared, inasmuch as we had sufficient air raid shelters and we all had gas masks and were familiar with their use. The Fighter Operations room had sufficient trained staff (of both sexes) to provide around-the-clock service. In readiness for bombing attacks, the aircraft were dispersed around the aerodrome perimeter and dispersal huts for ground and aircrews had been built. We only used the hangars for aircraft undergoing inspection or repair.

The Squadrons had very little rest in those early days. From before dawn they were either flying on patrols over the coast-wise convoys passing up and down the east coast, carrying out flying training, or at readiness at their dispersals. Night-flying training was carried on as soon as dusk fell. For forward bases, we used Coltishall and Horsham St. Faith on the Norfolk coast. These aerodromes were completed as far as the landing area was concerned, but the buildings were still under construction so we sent the convoy patrol flight or squadron there daily. This entailed taking off from Duxford before dawn and returning after dark in order to maintain the convoy patrol throughout the daylight hours. The boredom, long hours with insufficient sleep and no action and no leave, soon began to tell on the pilots. This fatigue showed itself rather alarmingly when one of the flight commanders, leading his formation in to land actually fell asleep when on the final approach. I was watching at the time and it seemed as though the flight commander would lead his flight to crash into a hangar. The two pilots in formation realised something was wrong and broke away but the flight commander (who was a tough Australian affectionately nicknamed Granny) only awoke when his wheels hit the ground and he was lucky enough, by use of full throttle, to just clear the hangar and go round again.

When I greeted him as he climbed out of the aircraft he nearly broke down and was almost asleep on his feet.

I felt so strongly about this fatigue that the boys were being subjected to that I immediately wrote a very strong letter to the AOC pointing out that the rigid state of readiness should be relaxed and provisions made for regular leave and recreation, otherwise we were asking for accidents. I got Pingo Lester to sign as station commander and flew up to Group Headquarters at Hucknall to deliver the letter myself. Leigh Mallory saw me at once and I am afraid I rather forgot myself and thumped his table when he said he could not alter orders from Fighter Command. I said something to the effect that we were wearing out the pilots by sheer fatigue. I never admired "L M" more than I did when, ignoring my distressing lack of discipline and manners, he said "Woody, believe me, I have tried already to persuade the C-in-C to relax the boys, but I'll try again now" and with that he picked up the scrambler phone to Fighter Command. The outcome was that the state of readiness was considerably relaxed and pilots were given 48-hours leave at reasonable intervals.

The sad part was that when we landed back at Duxford, (Jimmy Copley the Station Adjutant flew up with me as a passenger) we were greeted by Pingo Lester with the dreadful news that Jimmy Copley's son had been killed in a flying accident in a Spitfire with 41 Squadron that afternoon (September 14, 1939) at Wittering and it was thought that fatigue was the cause.

After war was declared, the numbers at Duxford increased rapidly. Number 222 Squadron, commanded by Squadron Leader HW "Tubby" Mermagen arrived on 5 October 1939 equipped as a shipping protection squadron with Bristol Blenheim fighters, but in March 1940 was re-armed Spitfires as a day fighter unit.

One day in January 1940, Douglas Bader flew over from Central Flying School in a Hurricane, I was delighted and amazed to see him. He was in terrific form (doubtless feeling very pleased to be back in the air again) and as it happened, Leigh-Mallory the AOC, also came to visit us that day. I introduced Douglas to the AOC and over lunch, Douglas used his considerable charm in persuading the AOC to take him into one of his operational squadrons. After lunch, with the AOC watching, Douglas put on a most finished display of aerobatics and this finally decided 'L-M'. Douglas was posted almost at once to 19 Squadron under his old friend and term-mate from Cranwell, Geoffrey Stephenson. Douglas, although only a Flying Officer then, impressed us all with his terrific personality and his amazing keenness and drive. I have never known anyone to equal him. Flying was his supreme passion and his enthusiasm infected us all. As a spectator, I was intrigued to see the impact Douglas had on the AOC – and vice versa. Air Vice Marshal and Flying Officer, rank did not enter into it, they were two of a kind – born leaders. They were both men who were respected by all and affectionately esteemed by most. Their attraction for each other was immediate and their friendship was, I am sure, firmly established at that first meeting.

I had not seen Douglas since his crash in 1930 and now in his maturity (he turned 30 two weeks after his posting to Duxford) he appealed to me very strongly. Such was his zest for living and flying that one completely forgot his artificial legs. He ignored them and so did everyone else. His prowess at golf and squash racquets was such that very few people on the station were a match for him at either game. And of course, as a pilot he was superb.

He had made an intimate study of the fighter tactics developed by famous pilots like McCudden, Ball and Bishop in the first war and was a great believer in the advantages of making the correct use of the sun and first gaining superior height.

Certain stereotyped forms of attack had been laid down in peacetime by Fighter Command, but these were in my opinion, only valuable as a sort of air drill which trained the pilots to react rapidly to their leader's instructions.

As I saw it, my job as Sector Controller was to vector the Fighter Leader on a course and to a height which would place him above and up sun of the enemy and then to keep him informed of the enemy's position, course and speed as accurately as possible from the information we had on the operations table. As soon as our Fighter Leader sighted the enemy it was over to him.

In those early days, the radar information was not very accurate, particularly as regards height and numbers of aircraft. There was also a time lag of several minutes before the information reached the Sector Operations room.

The Sector Controller therefore had to use intelligent guesswork in order to direct his fighters on an intercepting course and to position them up-sun and above the enemy.

To begin with, the operations tables in No 12 Group only extended to the north bank of the Thames and enemy plots were only passed to us when they reached this point. In No 11 Group however, enemy plots were received while the enemy was still over France. The Fighter Command Operations Room, of course had the whole picture, but in my opinion there was not enough liaison between No 11 and 12 Groups. Luckily, Victor Beamish, the Sector Commander at North Weald, was a good friend of mine so I extended our operations table to the south as far into France as

St Omer. As soon as North Weald were informed of enemy activity, we kept the tie line telephone open and plots were passed from North Weald to Duxford. In that way we obtained earlier warning, but in spite of this, we were frequently "scrambled" too late, because we were not allowed to fly over 11 Group territory unless asked for by that Group.

It was frustrating to see an enemy raid plotted on our board, obviously going for a target in 11 Group, then to wait on the ground, with the pilots in their cockpits for 15 or 20 minutes and finally to be "scrambled" too late to get into the fight.

Situated as Duxford was, about 60 miles north of the Thames, our fighters could be over Kent at 25,000 feet 15 minutes after take off. Under Douglas Bader's leadership, first of all three squadrons and later five squadrons, could be airborne and climbing as a wing on an intercepting course in under six minutes from the order "scramble."

On the few occasions when the Duxford wing was called in time, Douglas Bader more than justified his theories, as the Station "scoreboard" showed. This was rather like a cricket scoreboard which I had erected outside the guardroom with the squadrons listed by number and columns for Destroyed Probable and Damaged.

The squadrons were 19 Squadron, 242 Squadron, 310 Squadron, 66 Squadron and 222 Squadron.

In order to maintain a close liaison between aircraft, anti-aircraft guns and searchlights, each Sector Operations room was in direct communication with the appropriate AA Brigade.

The senior Gun Control Officer was Captain Walter Kester, who in civil life was a well-known lawyer in Cambridge. Walter was a great character with an impish sense of humour as the following story will show.

At the time of the arrival of the first WAAF's, we had a certain elderly RAF type who joined as an Ops B officer. I will merely call him 'A'. Now 'A' who was balding with rather prominent bags under his eyes, thought himself rather a devil with the ladies, but unfortunately the ladies did not agree.

He went on short leave and on his return we noticed that he had freshly-healed scars under each eye which he said were the result of flying glass in a car accident. Walter Kester whispered to me "The blighter has had his face lifted!" About a fortnight later, "A" appeared after another visit to London, looking surprisingly youthful. For some time we could not account for it, until about 2am in the Operations Room, when things were very quiet, Walter Kester called across to me "I've discovered the secret of eternal youth, Woody" and leaning forward, plucked a toupee from the wretched "A's" head, to the joy of the whole Ops room crew. "A" got himself posted to another station soon after that. We often wondered if his facelift and toupee had their desired effect elsewhere!

When Christmas 1939 arrived, the increased numbers on the station stretched our cooking facilities to the limit. However, by dint of our WAAF's boiling the Christmas puddings in the coppers in their billets in the old married quarters, augmenting our cook house with field kitchens to which access was only possible through the mud and snow by means of duck boards, everyone agreed that the Christmas dinner was more than adequate.

Duxford was the Fighter Station chosen by the BBC for the Commonwealth-wide broadcast that went round the world just prior to the King's Christmas speech. As luck would have it, we had at least one man or woman from every Commonwealth country on our strength and each in turn gave a brief message to his countrymen at home.

On January 1, 1940, I was promoted to Wing Commander and to my sorrow, was posted as Senior Personnel Staff Officer (SPSO) to No 20 Technical Training Group at Market Drayton. This was, to me, an irksome chair-borne job, so when in the middle of March 1940, I was posted back to Duxford as Station Commander, my joy can be imagined.

Most of my old friends were still there, but Geoffrey Stephenson had taken over command of No 19 Squadron from Cozens and Rupert Leigh had succeeded Larry Fullergood in command of No 66 Squadron. Douglas Bader was still there and he was soon promoted to Flight Commander in No 222 Squadron, then under "Tubby" Mermagen's command and equipped with Spitfires.

The "phoney" war was still in being and our time was fully occupied with convoy patrols, night flying training, battle training and long periods of readiness.

About this time, England was split up in regions, each with its own Regional Commissioner, who was the King's representative and who would act as Governor of his region in the event of dire emergency. Our Regional Commissioner for East Anglia was Sir Will Spens, the Master of Trinity College, Cambridge.

It was conceivable that, with the expected heavy bombing, possible invasion, or any national calamity, that the control normally exercised by Parliament from London would fail through disrupted communications, or even the obliteration of London and the Houses of Parliament. In this event, the plans were laid for each region to carry on the fight, controlling it's own food distribution, civil defence, medical services as well as its armed services. The RAF Liaison Officer was Air Vice-Marshal Norman McEwen, affectionately known to us all as "Uncle Norman."

Although Uncle Norman had retired in the 1930s he was a tower of strength to us at Duxford in particular and to No 12 Group in general. Leigh Mallory had served under him as SASO (Senior Air Staff Officer) and the respect which had resulted from this association was mutual. I shall never forget one of our parties in the mess when both "L M" and "Uncle Norman" were present. Both showed themselves to be "one of the boys" and certainly far from any accusations of being distant or pompous.Someone produced some bagpipes and in no time Uncle Norman's Scottish blood took charge and he did a sword dance on the table with a pair of crossed sticks instead of swords. L M followed him and although he was a Sassenach he performed nearly as well as his old AOC. I think it must be the only time in history that two Air Vice-Marshals have done a sword dance at the same party. It was only when talking to L-M at this party that I realised he was the younger brother of the famed George Mallory who had perished in the attempt to climb Mt Everest in 1924. Leigh-Mallory seemed to thrive on lack of sleep and it was not unusual for him to be working to 3am and back on duty before 7 the next morning. On at least one occasion he was on duty in the Operations Room at Hucknall for over 24 hours but still went out talking to pilots when they returned from a sortie. On many an evening he came into the mess, stood everyone a round of drinks and invited suggestions or complaints from the pilots.

Uncle Norman could fix anything, from supplies of sandbags for defence purposes, angle iron and broomsticks to make pikes, boiler plate to act as armour behind the pilot's seat in our early un armoured fighters, or additional beer for the canteen. If we wanted any essential and it could not be bought, he would requisition it.

He requisitioned Sawston Hall for us when it was vital that the Operations Room should be away from the aerodrome owing to bomb damage. We turned this stately old mansion into an up to date Operations Room with sleeping and feeding accommodation for all our WAAF operations' girls on the premises.

On August 17, 1940 No 310 (Czech) Squadron was formed at Duxford. Most of the pilots reported in French uniform. After the invasion of Czechoslovakia they had joined the French Air Force. When they had no aircraft left they found their way by devious routes to England.

On arrival in England, they spoke little English and had to be converted to our aircraft (Hurricanes in this case), so they were provided with an English Squadron Commander and Flight Commanders and a flying instructor as well as an interpreter.

Squadron Leader Douglas Blackwood was the Squadron Commander and Flight Lieutenants Gordon Sinclair and Jerrard Jefferies were the flight commanders. The Czech CO was Squadron Leader Sacha Hess, who was to become a very good friend of mine. Sacha was quite famous in Czech air circles, amongst other exploits, he had been leader of the Czech aerobatics team at peacetime European air displays. Much older than the rest (he was about 45) he was a first class pilot and a dedicated fighter.

Our first problem was to overcome the language difficulties, so after much thought, I rang Lance Sieveking at the BBC with the result that, together with the Czech interpreter I spent a day at Broadcasting House. There we recorded a series of orders, first in English followed by the Czech translation exactly as would be issued by the Sector Controller from "Scramble" (take off) to "Pancake (land) with every conceivable order in between. The BBC quickly sent us several copies of these records and in a very short time the Czechs were conversant with the orders in English alone.

The Czechs (they were a handsome crowd) very quickly collected girlfriends in the WAAF and it was most amusing to be able to guess from the accent they developed which WAAF taught English to which Czech. Some developed Scottish, some Yorkshire, some Cockney accents. It gave us as onlookers quite a lot of fun at the time. Flight Officer Margot Robinson was the very best at recognising accents, she could generally name the county of origin of anyone with a regional accent and with her WAAF "girls" usually could get the town and village after quite a short conversation.

310 Squadron had a spare Hurricane (needless to say it was the oldest and slowest) which was always at my disposal. On the few occasions when I could spare the time from my other duties as Station Commander and Sector Controller, I flew on operations with the Squadron as rear-end Charlie. It was possibly lucky that we made no interceptions on these flights, but at the time I was confident and itching to prove my ability. Such sorties also gave me first-hand experience of what it was like to be put in the wrong place by Sector Control and gave me even more incentive to get fighters into a good tactical position when there was an incoming raid.

The Czechs were fine men and most of them had survived terrific hardships in their escape from Czechoslovakia after the German invasion. As one instance, Sacha Hess' wife and daughter had been taken to a concentration camp and he had been informed that they were dead. He could only hope that they died quickly, but he vowed that he would never show any mercy to any German and would never take prisoners.

On the first occasion the Czechs got into action, early in the Battle of Britain, they made an excellent showing. I met them on their return to the aerodrome and heard the following story from Sacha Hess. He had disabled a Dornier over Epping Forest and when it made a wheels up landing in a field with both engines stopped, he followed it down with the intention of making certain that no one got out of it alive. He saw three Germans climb out, who held up their hands when they realised that Sacha was diving on them. To quote his own words "I hesitate, then it was too late, so I go round again to make sure I kill them they wave something white again I did not shoot then" (disgustedly) "I think it is no use, I am become too bloody British!"

The Czechs were a very proud and supportive of their own and they seemed to know exactly where all their countrymen were stationed. Sacha particularly, kept in touch with all his old friends and felt any losses deeply. He was most upset on an occasion when two of his NCO pilots, after flying to a neighbouring aerodrome to visit a comrade were refused entry to the only lunch available at the Officers' Mess. As they had both been officers in the Czechoslovakian Air Force, they felt snubbed and decided to do a beat-up as a form of reprisal. Unfortunately, one of them crashed into a hangar and was killed.

Later, Sacha came to discuss an even more troubling problem. There were a number of pilots who believed they had a traitor somewhere among their number. This was never proved during the war but some time after the war, Sacha (by then in the USA) told me that it had been true. A Czech pilot, Augustin Preucil, had flown a Hurricane from No 5 OCU to the Germans in 1941 and betrayed many of his countrymen to the Gestapo. He was eventually unmasked and executed in Prague around 1948.

I always consider that the Battle of Britain began just before the evacuation of Dunkirk and more or less coincided with the over-running of Holland and Belgium.

From Duxford our fighters were certainly heavily committed at that time. In May 1940, we made our first sortie over Holland with six Defiants of No 264 Squadron led by Squadron Leader Philip Hunter and six Spitfires as top cover, led by Squadron Leader Rupert Leigh.

Because of the long sea crossing, they landed at Martlesham Heath, the night before, refuelled and took off early the following morning. This was the first time the Defiant had been in action. The Boulton and Paul Defiant was an unusual fighter in that it was a two-seater with a four-gun Frazer Nash turret in the back seat and no forward guns.

At a distance it looked rather like a Hurricane which misled the Germans on this first sortie. Not knowing about the rear turret, the German fighters attacked from astern and were blown out of the sky by the terrific fire power they met.

The Defiants shot down twice their own number on this occasion and all our aircraft returned safely. Unfortunately the press was informed of this victory and pictures of the Defiant were released and published in the national papers. This information obviously reached Germany very quickly, because when the operation was repeated three days later, the Germans attacked the Defiants head on and our casualties were very heavy and included Philip Hunter, the gallant Squadron Commander. Of course, the Germans would not have taken long to find the weak spots around the Defiant without the help of the press. By late July the losses were so great that the Defiant was withdrawn from daylight operations and re-painted as a nightfighter and in this role it proved a reasonably effective aircraft.

About this time one of our Spitfire squadrons was ordered to land at Manston and refuel before a patrol over Dunkirk. I flew down with them. When we arrived over Manston I was horrified to see about 50 or 60 aircraft all bunched together for refuelling in one corner of the aerodrome. One small bomb dropped in this bunch would have destroyed at least half a dozen aircraft. Over the RT I ordered our squadron to disperse at least 50 yards apart round the opposite side of the aerodrome after landing. When I climbed out of my Spitfire, I was greeted by an irate Group Captain who wanted to know why we had not taxied over to the already congested fuelling area. Equally crossly, I gave him the obvious answer, so the fuel tankers were driven to our dispersed aircraft.

While our squadron was patrolling (unfortunately LM had forbidden me to fly over France) to my amazement I saw my old Swordfish squadron (No 824 Fleet Air

Arm Squadron) come in to land. I went over and greeted them and found that my old friend Lieutenant Commander James Buckley was leading them. They had been sent down from Donnibristle in Scotland, with orders to load up with 250lb bombs, collect maps at Manston and dive bomb the advancing Germans behind Dunkirk. Out of nine aircraft only three returned from two sorties of this suicidal mission. James Buckley was shot down and made prisoner. Much later we heard that he had made a sensational escape, but was subsequently drowned in the Baltic. It was a sobering thought that if the war had come a little earlier, or if I had not had that minor carrier crash, "there but for the grace of God" was me.

From May to October 1940, we were all stretched to our limits of endurance, but we were not in the least downhearted or pessimistic. As Station Commander, I had to learn to snatch sleep in small doses. I had a camp bed in my office and one in a cubby hole in the Ops room when it was established at Sawston Hall owing to the bombing. At all times I had to be within reach of a telephone. Early in the piece we had a Tannoy broadcasting system on the aerodrome and this was in frequent use to call me to the nearest telephone. In that period I learnt to get the maximum benefit from even half an hours sleep in a chair.

We had no airborne radar in 1940 at Duxford and the searchlights depended on sound locators. When we sent up Spitfires or Hurricanes at night they had to depend on following the cone of searchlights to locate the enemy.

On one of the first occasions when the enemy sent aircraft over East Anglia at night, John Petrie, a flight commander in 19 Squadron was airborne and the searchlights held a Heinkel in their beams long enough for John to shoot it down. Unfortunately, just after John had hit the enemy, the searchlight cone switched on his Spitfire. John of course was blinded in the glare and the German rear gunner fired a last burst at our aircraft and then baled out. John's Spitfire burst into flames and he baled out. I was an eye witness to all this because it occurred right over the aerodrome.

My immediate concern was for John Petrie and after giving instructions for the civil police to be alerted to round up the enemy, I sent search parties out. I next learned that John Petrie had been picked up suffering from nasty burns and taken to the nearest hospital. After giving orders that the prisoners when captured were to be placed in the guardroom if unhurt, in the sick quarters under guard if injured, I set off in my car to see how John Petrie was faring in hospital. Poor John, his face was badly burnt, but his eyes had been saved by his goggles. I am glad to say that either Gillies or McIndoe (or both) made a magnificent plastic surgery job on his face. I next saw him as a highly decorated Squadron Leader in command of a Typhoon Squadron in 1943, as fit and as good looking as ever. Dawn was just breaking as I returned to Duxford and I was informed that the civil police had collected the prisoners and were bringing them into the guardroom. I left strict orders that there was to be no fraternising, when the prisoners arrived they were to be given a meal and cigarettes and left in cells until collected by the security people. As I had had no sleep for 24 hours, I then went to bed. At about 10.30am after a bath and a shave I asked about the prisoners. I was told that there were two German NCO's in the cells, but that the pilot, an officer, had been taken over to the Officers Mess.

I found the German pilot taking his ease in the guest room with a cocktail in his hand, chatting to Philip Hunter and several of our pilots. Our boys immediately stood up as I came into the room and said "Good morning, sir" but the Hun, an arrogant young Nazi of about 20, remained lounging in his armchair and insolently eyed me up and down but not for long, I got him to his feet smartly. Needless to say I had him quickly transferred to the guardroom cell. The boys thought me very hard-hearted and strict, but when the interrogation officers arrived to collect the prisoner they were very cross indeed, because, as they said "Chivalry is not understood by that type, they only regard it as weakness."

When I told the boys about how badly John Petrie was burnt, I think they understood my anger. Soon after the fall of France, Leigh Mallory rang me to say that No 242 Squadron (Canadian) were reporting to Coltishall and would be under the operational control of the Duxford sector. He told me that the Squadron had had a tough time in France and the ground crews had just been evacuated via Cherbourg, thanks to the resources of their adjutant, Peter MacDonald MP. Their own CO had left them to their own devices after the pilots had landed in England and the squadron, led by Flying Officer Stan Turner (as he was then) had landed at Coltishall, with nothing but the uniforms they were wearing. Tools, spares, kit, baggage the lot had had to be abandoned.

LM said "I've got to find them a new Squadron Commander and he's got to be good, because these chaps are Canadians and have had a rough time they are browned off with authority and need a good leader any suggestions?" At once I said "What about Douglas Bader?" LM replied "I thought you would say that. I think you are right."

So Douglas was promoted Squadron Leader and took command of 242 Squadron. The story of how, by sheer personal example, drive and leadership, he won the affection and loyalty of those tough Canadians and built up their morale and esprit de corps until they established themselves as one of the best fighter squadrons in the Battle of Britain has already been told in the book "Reach for the Sky" and shown in the film of the same name. I knew them all, Stan Turner, the chunky outspoken pipe-smoking Canadian, with whom I was to serve again at Tangmere and in Malta. Eric Ball, an Englishman from 19 Squadron, Powell Sheddon with an attractive stutter that almost disappeared when he spoke on the RT (we were also to meet again in Malta), Dennis Crowley Milling, another old friend, Willie McKnight (later killed after being awarded the DFC and bar), Ben Brown and Cryderman and the others who all became an enthusiastic team led by their single minded swashbuckling CO, Douglas Bader. Douglas, of course, was very apt to cut corners and ignore regulations or interpret them his own way in order to get on with the war. On one occasion when he had offended against some rule, I was given orders from higher authority to reprove him. He was ordered to report to my office and when he stumped in and saluted with his usual cheerful grin he noticed that I was wearing my cap and did not tell him to sit down which indicated an official interview. Douglas stood to attention and with an impish grin said "Woody, you're not going to be rotten to me are you?"

What could I do but laugh, then tell him to sit down? Needless to say, the reproof was more or less passed to him as a joke but the fact that it was passed on proved quite effective.

As all aircraft were housed in widely-dispersed shelter pens around the aerodrome, we had a larger hangar empty so we built a full-size stage and used the hangar for entertainment purposes. I discovered that Bill Whittle, a well known cinema organist was on the station as an aircraft hand so we bought a Hammond electric organ out of PSI funds and Bill Whittle and our amateur band played for regular dances. We bought roller skates, dozens of pairs and the concrete floor proved admirable as a roller skating rink.

Thanks to the adequate stage, we attracted some excellent ENSA parties with such famous artists as Beatrice Lilly, Noel Coward and many others, giving of their best. These ENSA concerts were usually held on Sunday nights when the artists had their only free night from London shows.

News was at times very depressing, particularly during June. We had been hearing of victories in Norway but on early in June, British forces withdrew from Narvik. Our initial jubilation on hearing that 43 Squadron and seven Hurricanes as well as 10 Gladiators from 263 Squadron had done the impossible and landed on HMS Glorious without arrester gear was soon dashed when we heard that Glorious was sunk by gunfire from the German battlecruisers Gneisenau and Scharnhorst with the loss of almost the entire squadron. Worse news (that was immediately suppressed from the country as a whole) was that the troopship Lancastria had been sunk by bombing off the mouth of the Loire River while evacuating troops and civilian refugees from France. We knew the death toll was bad and included personnel of several RAF squadrons but it was not until some time later that the grapevine informed us that more than 5000 lives had been lost. It was later confirmed that 98 Squadron had lost 75 confirmed and another 15 are still listed as missing to this day. There was a general feeling that Britain and its allies drawn from the former Empire were the final defenders of freedom against the Nazi onslaught, particularly after Italy had declared war on Britain and France on June 10 and France surrendered on June 14. Perhaps surprisingly, the more alone Britain became at that time, the more confident and determined the RAF seemed to become. It was as if our pilots relished the odds being against us and was a trait I was to witness several times during the war.

One Sunday, after an excellent entertainment we took the artists back to the Officers Mess for supper and refreshment and many of the officers were there with their girlfriends. Two Czech pilots were night flying locally, using a glim lamp flare path and a mobile Chance floodlight for landing.

Although I had telephoned the Ops room and been informed that there were no hostile plots on the board, we suddenly heard bomb explosions on the aerodrome. First telling the WAAF officer to get the guests down to the shelters, I dashed to my car and drove to the aerodrome, where I found that a stick of bombs had been dropped on the flare path. The airman operating the Chance light had been wounded by a bomb fragment just before he switched off the motor and four bomb craters were luckily on the centre line of the flare path T and two of the glim lamps had been extinguished.

In the meantime the two Czechs were still circling the aerodrome, with their navigation lights on, waiting to land, so having put the wounded man in the ambulance, I dashed to the watch office, rang the controller, told him to try to keep the Czechs in the air until we had fixed the flare path and the Chance light. I took one of the fire tender crew with me to the Chance and started the motor, but just then the intruder dropped another stick of bombs, the last of which was close enough to spatter the airman and me with earth. As we picked ourselves up, I said very feelingly "the bastard" the airman replied with equal feeling "You've said it, sir!"

Almost immediately the two Czechs landed without navigation lights, luckily one on each side of the flare path. It was miraculous that they did not collide.

Having sent the flying control van to lead the Hurricanes back to their shelter pens, we extinguished the flare path and I tried to assess the damage. We suffered several wounded, mostly Czechs at their dispersal, so when I had seen these casualties off to sick quarters, I made a tour of the camp before sounding the All Clear because I wanted to make sure that there were no further intruders about before allowing the off duty personnel out of the dug outs.

Luckily the living quarters had escaped damage and I found that Robbie, the senior WAAF officer, had shepherded all her flock and the guests down to the shelters and the WAAF's were brewing tea there but I couldn't find Robbie. At last I found her, sitting beside the bed of one of the girls. After rounding up her detachment to get them to safety, one was reported missing so Robbie searched the quarters and found the girl shivering with fright with her head under the bedclothes, so Robbie stayed with her as the girl was incapable of moving.

Everyone behaved extremely well on this occasion, particularly the women. The reason that the raider was not reported until he dropped his bombs was that he probably sneaked in low across the coast and so was not picked up by RDF. This attack by a single raider made us realise that wider dispersal was essential. The

Operations room as the vital control centre of the sector was too vulnerable, situated as it was on the perimeter of the aerodrome. Thanks to "Uncle Norman's" good offices, Sawston Hall was requisitioned and we went ahead with all speed to convert it to our requirements. The valuable ancient panelling was protected and preserved by means of temporary partitions and facings of hardboard. Our radio personnel and the post and telegraph department rapidly organised the communications side and we obtained three Aga cookers to install in the enormous old kitchen. The WAAF Ops crew had their sleeping quarters on the upper floors and when all was completed we had a more efficient operations room several miles from any obvious military target.

We fully expected an attempted invasion after the fall of France and the evacuation of our army from Dunkirk. We had no means of ground defence apart from about a dozen rifles and the revolvers which had been issued to most of the pilots, so our inventive engineer officer made pikes out of broom sticks with sharpened angle-iron wired on to the end. The transport officer somehow "won" an old heavy motor truck and with boiler plate, sandbags and a Lewis gun mounted on a Scarff ring, behind the cab, and made a primitive armoured car known as our "battle wagon."

After we had made these preparations, various army units were sent to take care of aerodrome defence, first a company of the London Scottish, relieved by a troop of the Queens Bays who had recently (to their annoyance) exchanged their horses for Whippet tanks and finally by a company of the Cameronians. The latter had been badly mauled in France and at Dunkirk and were almost praying that the Hun would invade so that they could have their revenge.

The administrative and operational tasks and problems increased daily and hampered as we were by a set of peacetime rules and regulations designed in the main to prevent petty pilfering, it is not surprising that everyone trying to do his job had to cut the "red tape" in order to get on with the war.

In this Douglas Bader and I saw eye to eye and we backed each other loyally in this matter of tape cutting. L-M as my AOC was always on my side too, which was very comforting.

In those harassing times it was good to have a man like Jimmy Copley as administration officer. Jimmy was an old RFC type who had been station adjutant at Duxford in peacetime and who was promoted to Squadron Leader (Admin) when I assumed command. As the Battle of Britain developed, my operational responsibilities were so heavy that we would have been in a sorry mess if I had not had such an excellent administrative team on whom I could rely implicitly. The Station strength had risen to 2500, including 450 WAAF ably commanded by little Flight Officer Margot Robinson (Robbie) who had already shown her qualities under the stress of bombing.

The operations team were grand too and with them I include the fighter controllers, Ops B officers, signals, cypher and teleprinter personnel of both sexes. All these had had to learn their job from a small nucleus of regular RAF personnel and they were good.

During that long summer of 1940 when even the weather seemed to favour the Germans, everyone on the Station was working hard and in spite of threats of invasion, bad news of sinkings by U boat and reverses in Greece and Crete, morale was high. Our casualties in the air were not light, but our victories outweighed them and we knew that man for man, we were superior to the enemy.

As we were fighting over our own country, we had a certain advantage in that the loss of an aircraft did not necessarily mean the loss of a pilot as well. On many occasions, hours and sometimes days after a pilot had failed to return with his squadron, he would walk into the Mess, or would be reported wounded and in hospital.

In the middle of the battle, No 19 Squadron was re-armed with new Spitfires with four 20mm cannon in place of the former eight machine guns. Whether it was because of faulty manufacture or not I cannot say, but those early cannon were not a success, they were unreliable. The cannon had stoppages after a few rounds almost every time they were used in action. On one occasion when the squadron intercepted an enemy raid over Debden in ideal conditions, every aircraft had stoppages before half their ammunition had been expended. We lost two aircraft and the enemy escaped with little damage.

This cannon failure was the culmination of a series of similar but not so serious problems, so I got on the telephone to LM and urgently requested that the squadron should have their eight-gun Spitfires back. The following afternoon the C-in-C, "Stuffy" Dowding himself, landed at Duxford without warning. I greeted him and he gruffly said "I want to talk to 19 Squadron" so I drove him over to Fowlmere, the satellite airfield where he met Sandy Lane, the Squadron Commander and his pilots. He listened to their complaints almost in silence, then I drove him back to his aircraft (he was piloting himself) and as he climbed into the aircraft he merely said "You'll get your 8-gun Spitfires back." "Stuffy" was a man of very few words, he listened to all of us, asked a few pertinent questions, then made his decision. It transpired that the mass-produced cannon merely needed the mechanism to be "run in," just as a mass-produced car engine requires to be run on a test bench before it is installed in the car. The cannon were fine after 400 rounds of practice ammunition had been pumped through them on the stop butts.

That same evening, as a result of Dowding's visit, the instructors from Hawarden OTU flew the eight gun Spitfires to Duxford and took back the cannon Spitfires. The battle went on, with a steadily mounting credit score on our side, until the peak day of September 15, 1940 when the total enemy destroyed for the day by Fighter Command amounted to 185. Out of this number, the Duxford Wing led by Douglas Bader, claimed 52 destroyed that day.

When our intelligence officers had sifted through the claims, the "confirmed" figures for the Duxford wing were 45 destroyed, 5 shared, 10 probables and one damaged. Two days later, the Times among other newspapers carried headlines showing 185 destroyed which included 7 by anti-aircraft fire.. Our losses were put at 29 aircraft and 12 pilots.

The figures were important as they were a great boost to our morale at a local level and also to the country as a whole. We all felt that we had reached a positive turning point in the conflict, that at last we were getting ahead in the battle.

After the war, the Germans produced so-called official records to show that the number we destroyed was only 79 and later the figure was amended down further.. I do not believe it. If their figure was correct, why did they stop? The fact remains that after September 15 they gave up large daylight raids and went over to night bombing. This gave us a lot of headaches, because airborne radar was only in the development stage and we had pitifully few night fighters. To combat this menace by night, we trained as many pilots in night flying as possible, but the Hurricane and Spitfires were of very little use except in conditions of bright moonlight. They could only circle the target being bombed in hopes of seeing an enemy against the glare from the fires on the ground and the risks of collision were high. An intensive gun barrage seemed to be best answer at that time, but there were insufficient guns to protect all our main cities.

On December 16, 1940, President Benes of Czechoslovakia, with his Foreign Secretary, Jan Masaryck, and the Chief of the Czech Air Force, Air Vice Marshal Janousek came to the Station to inspect No 310 Squadron. The President decorated a number of the Czech pilots, as well as Squadron Leader Douglas Blackwood and the two English Flight Commanders with the Czechoslovak War Cross (the equivalent to our DFC). To my astonishment President Benes then pinned one on my chest too. I was also presented with the Czechoslovak silver Flying Sword, which is worn on the right breast pocket to denote that I was a fully qualified pilot in the Czech Air Force and at the same time given written authority from the British Air Ministry for me to wear it.

I was touched, because although Sacha Hess and his Squadron had known of the award for some time, they left it to their President to announce to me as a surprise.

Towards the end of the year (December 18), Air Vice Marshal Leigh Mallory went to 11 Group and was relieved by Air Vice Marshal Saul from No 13 Group. Of course L-M was of such a stature that anyone would have found it difficult to step into his shoes. I will only say that where L-M led us, Saul thought it necessary to drive us. This did not make for happy relations between Group and Sector under the new regime.

I had grown more and more attached to our little WAAF officer, Margot Robinson and we decided to get married. I knew that if it was known that we were married or even engaged, Margot would be posted away so we married secretly in Cambridge on January 9, 1941 (which was my birthday) in Cambridge. The only people who knew were Air Vice Marshal Norman McEwen (who acted as best man), Marjorie Stiven our Cypher Officer (who was "best girl") and Corporal Barratt, my RAF driver. We only had 24 hours leave and were back on duty next day. The secret was well kept and we did not let anyone know until I was relieved in March.

(I never lived down my proposal to Margot. Shortly before Christmas 1940, I sent an airman to ask her to report to me in my office on some routine administrative matter. When she came in she stood to attention in front of my desk and it was only at that moment that I decided to pop the question which had been on my mind for some time. "I've got something to ask you. Will you marry me?"

"May I at least stand at ease before I answer that?" she replied. "And as we are both on duty here, will I be likely to face a court martial if I refuse?"

Of course, all I could do was apologise. (For the circumstance, not the question.)

As far as we were all concerned, another and much more notable event happened in January 1941. The King and Queen held an Investiture at Duxford. The King expressed the wish that it should be entirely a Station affair and that Group should not send any staff officers or inform the press. It had to be kept very secret because of the danger of a bombing raid if the news leaked to the Germans who, it was believed, had already deliberately bombed Buckingham Palace when their Majesties were in residence the previous month.

I was very nervous when the day arrived but was relieved that the whole of East Anglia was blanketed with low cloud with a base of about 300 feet, although of course, we kept a flight of Spitfires at instant readiness in case of emergency.

The King and Queen arrived by car, attended only by their Air Equerry, Wing Commander "Mouse" Fielden, who eased my mind by detailing the seating arrangements for lunch. In addition to those from our own Station, there were about 70 other offices to be decorated from neighbouring aerodromes. The dining room in the Officers Mess was not large enough to accommodate all these guests as well as our own officers so we had to arrange two sittings for lunch.

In spite of the King's wish, Air Vice Marshal Saul arrived to greet him and it was obvious that His Majesty was not pleased because after I introduced the AOC I do not think the King spoke to him again.

For the investiture we paraded all off-duty Station personnel in a large hangar. The airmen formed two sides of a hollow square, the WAAF detachment one side and the officers and men to be decorated lined up across the top of the square. Before the ceremony, the King briefly inspected the male contingent while the Queen inspected the WAAF.

The impression we were all left with was that they were not "inspecting" in a military sense they were presenting themselves for everyone (as Kipling says) "For to behold and for to see." Afterwards, Robbie told me that the Queen had a pleasant word to say to almost every one of her girls. She was so interested that the King had to send his Equerry to tell her he was waiting to start the investiture. After the ceremony, we went over to the mess for lunch. "Mouse" Fielden had arranged the top table, with the

King on my right and the Queen on my left, with a Group Captain who had received the CBE on her left. I forget exactly who was on the King's right, but I do remember that AVM Saul was relegated to the extreme end of the top table.

As the Queen was not attended by a Lady in Waiting, Robbie, as the senior WAAF officer was detailed for this most necessary responsibility. It was a most memorable occasion, our royal guests were quite charming to all of us they made us feel at home by making themselves at home. They were genuinely interested in everyone and everything they saw.

After lunch, when we were having coffee in the ante room, the Queen was taught the rudiments of "shove ha' penny" by our young doctor, Dr Apley. The King sat on the arm of a chair and watched. He idly picked up one of the "ha' pennies" (which were proper coins, smoothed off on one side) thank goodness, the "tail" sides were defaced and not the King's head side. He then said "You know, a lot of the best games come from pubs!"

After coffee, they had a friendly inspection of the station. We had some American lend lease Aircobra aircraft on the tarmac that the Air Fighter Development Unit (a lodger unit on the Station) were putting through acceptance tests. The Queen asked if we had any photographs of them. I replied "No, Ma am, but we'll soon have them photographed." She replied "That would be nice the children, would love to have copies." I then asked if I should send them to the Air Equerry, Wing Commander Fielden. She replied "No, address them to me, they'll get there quicker."

We then drove their Majesties to see our Operations Room at Sawston Hall. The King was of course very interested in the fighter control side, but the Queen went off under Robbie's guidance, thoroughly explored all the domestic arrangements and met a large number of the WAAF girls. While we were there a hostile plot crossed the coast. We "scrambled" two Spitfires immediately. Our fighters sighted the enemy over Norfolk, but he turned tail and escaped in cloud.

In March 1941 it was decided that all Sector Stations should be commanded by Group Captains. I was rather hurt to find that after commanding the Sector throughout the Battle of Britain, AVM Saul should decide to have me relieved by a Group Captain who commanded the Air Fighter Development Unit which had been at Duxford for some months as a lodger unit. Doctor Brown, our Station Medical Officer, who had been keeping his kindly professional eye on me, prescribed an immediate three weeks leave. I suppose I was rather tired.

Chapter 11

Tangmere Commander

On hearing that I was leaving Duxford, the "boys" hastily arranged a farewell party. When told about this, I asked if I could bring my wife too. They thought at first that I was pulling their legs when I told them that Robbie and I had been married for three months. However, when AVM MacEwen (who was of course invited to the party) told them that he had been at my wedding I was believed and the party became hilarious indeed. I felt more than a little sad, however, at leaving everyone after all we had been through together.

The next day, Margot and I set off on our deferred honeymoon which we proposed to spend in Somerset. Air Vice-Marshal Leigh Mallory, who of course had heard that I had been superseded and also been informed that I had a wife, telephoned and asked us to pause on our journey and have lunch with him at 11 Group Headquarters in Uxbridge. He was, as usual, extremely charming to both of us and wished us well. In parting he merely said "Don't worry, I'll be seeing more of you Woody."

We rusticated happily at a little farm near Waterrow in Somerset for a fortnight, when I was summoned to an investiture to receive the OBE at Buckingham Palace (April 8, 1941). Margot came with me of course and we met my sister Dorothy there. There were several of my Duxford friends there to collect "gongs" as well, so after the most-impressive ceremony, quite a gaggle of us with our wives, sisters and girlfriends, went across to celebrate in the ladies' dining room of the RAF Club. At the investiture, to my surprise and delight, I was told that I was posted to command Tangmere, with the rank of Group Captain. At the end of our leave, I took Margot back to Duxford where she resumed her duties as OC WAAF, then drove to Tangmere on April 22, pausing at 11 Group to thank L-M and receive his instructions.

At Tangmere I found that I was taking over command from my old friend Jack Boret, who had been promoted to Air Commodore and posted to Fighter Command. To my joy, I found Douglas Bader already there, now a Wing Commander and in the properly established role of Wing Leader. With him were a lot of old friends Stan Turner, promoted to Squadron Leader and commanding No 145 Squadron, Billy Burton, Ken Holden, "Cocky" Dundas and Denis Crowley Milling. When I met them again I thought "Wonderful, the AOC is keeping the old team together."

Douglas Bader, Chris Ulyatt (the RC Padre) and I shared one of the married quarters for sleeping. The Officers mess had been badly damaged by bombs just before my arrival and my most urgent task was to arrange dispersal so that all living quarters were away from the target that the aerodrome offered.

We were heavily bombed again only about a week after I arrived. The main runway was being extended and the new concrete work which was not camouflaged, was plainly visible even on a moonless night. On this occasion we had several Beaufighters in the air, but the enemy crossed the coast too low to be tracked by radar. The Huns first dropped incendiary bombs so I asked Douglas Bader to go to the Operations room to direct our night fighters and I dashed off in my car to direct the extinguishing of the incendiaries. Padre Ulyatt leapt into the car with me and gently chided me for not wearing a tin hat. Our drive was full of incident. Having smothered one incendiary with sandbags we were driving to the next blaze when I heard the scream of an aircraft, I braked hard and the Padre and I threw ourselves flat on the tarmac just as the bombs hit the runway. I thought for a moment I had been hit but it turned out the blow to my side was caused by the Padre spinning a tin hat to me from the other side of the car.

Chris Ulyatt was a grand chap, he had already distinguished himself when the mess was hit in the previous bombing and insisted on coming round with me in case there were any casualties needing assistance. Luckily, there were none on that occasion, but the runway was out of action and we had to order our Beaufighters to land at West Malling until the runway was repaired.

After this raid we completed our dispersal rapidly. We took over Goodwood racecourse and accommodated No 219 Beaufighter Squadron under the grandstands. The WAAF detachment were housed similarly at Fontwell racecourse. Hut accommodation was quickly constructed at Merstham and West Hampsted.

There were two grass airfields about three to four miles away. We requisitioned a country house near each of them as sleeping quarters for the pilots. Shopwyke House, a large country mansion situated almost in the centre of the triangle formed by the three aerodromes was already occupied by an Army Officer's school and they refused to move.

However, one night in April or May our Beaufighters shot down a Heinkel which dived into the grounds of Shopwyke House and exploded, leaving a large crater just outside the dining room windows and shattering most of the windows on that side of the house. The Army moved out at short notice and we moved in.

The Army unit left a perfect shambles inside but by using volunteer labour from our own personnel and supplying paint and materials out of mess funds, we quickly re decorated and repaired it and occupied it as a central officer's mess. We even dug out the crater made by the Heinkel, concreted it and turned it into a swimming pool. The owner, a Staff Colonel serving at the War Office, was so delighted when he saw what we'd done that he wanted to bring back all the family pictures which had been placed in safe storage. We did not accept this offer, but he insisted on bringing the expensive curtains out of storage and we were very grateful for these. With the furniture salved from the bomb-damaged mess and from the old officer's married quarters, we turned Shopwyke into a very comfortable mess.

Station Headquarters was moved to a smaller house close by, the Operations room was transferred to an adjacent school which had been closed down after the bombing and we established an emergency Operations room in the middle of Chichester. The Station Adjutant, Flight Lieutenant Freddie Ashton was a tower of strength and wisdom to me in my new command. A first war veteran, who had spent many years as an oil company executive in the Middle East, he had retired about 1938 and settled at Pagham. On the outbreak of war, he had offered his services to the RAF and had been Adjutant at Tangmere ever since. We owed much to his mature judgement and unfailing loyalty.

Another great character on headquarters staff was our Accountant Officer, Squadron Leader "Bill" Barrell, also a first war veteran who had come out of retirement to serve again. Another stalwart was Adrian Bell, our extremely efficient Squadron Leader (Administrative).

The untiring, unspectacular and in many cases unrewarded service given by officers, airmen and airwomen on station headquarters staffs during those years of war deserves special praise. Many of them elderly, like Freddie Ashton and Bill Barrell, they never spared themselves, were always on the job taking the administrative load, acting as buffers between the red-tape experts (with their quotations from King's Regulations and Air Council Instructions) and the people who were trying to get on with the war.

The extension of the main runway at Tangmere, made essential by the use of Beaufighters, was proceeding very slowly being a civilian-contract job. The aerodrome was visible and recognisable for miles, even on a moonless night, thanks to the scar made by the newly-laid concrete without camouflage paint. All our efforts to hurry the Ministry of Works and the contractors seemed unavailing.

Douglas Bader and I had fumed at the slackness displayed by the contractors' men, who came from somewhere near Brighton daily in several bus loads and then Douglas had an idea. He asked me if he could invite his golfing friend Henry Longhurst down to stay a day or two, casually saying "Of course he is a journalist, but he will be wearing his Home Guard uniform."

Henry Longhurst arrived and he and I stood for an hour watching the slow progress of the labourers. There were four or five boys who were employed solely in making tea and Longhurst asked one of these how much he was paid and the reply was 5 pounds a week. I was amazed and mentioned to Henry that the basic pay of a pilot officer in those days was only 4 pounds 17 shillings 6 pence a week, for which princely sum our junior aircrew were gaily risking their lives daily. The following weekend, a blistering article appeared in the Sunday Express about squadrons on a "certain RAF station" being endangered by the sloth of men extending and camouflaging the runway. In the same article a shrewd comparison was made between the rates of pay of a pilot officer RAF and a 15-year-old boy employed to brew up tea for the labourers. When Douglas and I read the article, we agreed that we'd probably started something and when I was told that Harold Balfour, the Under-Secretary of State for Air, was flying down to Tangmere I thought "here it comes." Douglas and I met the Under Secretary's aircraft and after greeting him, he politely said "May we go to your office?" On arrival there, he produced a copy of the Sunday Express from his briefcase, folded at the offending article and said "I think you are the Station Commander who is quoted here, Woodhall" and of course I had to admit it. He then went on to say very mildly and politely "you know this sort of article gives us a lot of trouble at the Air Ministry and I've been sent down to give you a rocket." At this Douglas could contain himself no longer and said "Well, sir, you can take the rocket right back to Air Ministry and tell them what to do with it. It was my idea to invite Henry Longhurst here to see what was going on. That runway has been like a beacon to the Hun bombers for weeks now and as we could not obtain any action by using the usual channels, something drastic was necessary."

Good old Douglas. Trust him to back me up loyally. I also said my say and it was a rather astonished Under-Secretary who meekly had lunch with us after delivering his rocket.

We had no complaints about idleness after this, the runway was completed within a week of Harold Balfour's visit, so our unorthodox action seemed justified.

In addition to three squadrons of Spitfires and a squadron of Beaufighters we had a flight of Lysanders based at Tangmere. These had a very special and hazardous role to perform and were based at Tangmere because we were such a short distance from the coast of France and because they needed the full benefit of all the meteorological and radio facilities we had.

Their role was to land British agents into enemy occupied territory and to bring them out again when necessary. This entailed very accurate night navigation to the dropping zone (DZ) or the landing ground concerned and careful identification by pre arranged signals on arrival.

The pilot used the Lysander's downward recognition lamp to flash his recognition letter, but the reception party's signal could only be flashed by a battery torch.

Only two or three days after I took over from Jack Boret, I was instructed to arrange a meal and accommodation for four agents who were to be brought down from London by an army conducting officer. The instructions stressed that the agents should not be seen or spoken to by anyone but me and the pilots of the two aircraft they were to fly with. This raised a security question because we had nowhere suitable to feed or accommodate them. We got over the difficulty the first time by using the former guest room in the bombed-out mess but I realised that something better must be arranged in future. Luckily there was a good-sized private house called Tangmere Cottage within the airfield boundary, close to the new perimeter track. We requisitioned this, turned part of the ground floor into the RC Chapel and made the first floor into a mess and sleeping quarters for our "Joes." ("Joe" was the generic term the RAF gave to the agents they infiltrated in and out of enemy territory).

I asked for special security guards and three RAF Service Police Sergeants were sent down to us. They turned out to be ex Scotland Yard and they took all security worries off our shoulders and in addition acted as cooks and batmen to the "Joes" when they arrived. Sometimes, the agents had to stay two or three nights in Tangmere Cottage awaiting suitable weather.

The Lysander pilots had to be very skilled navigators as well as pilots and the most outstanding of them was Flight Lieutenant Du Fort, the Flight Commander.

Du Fort and his select little band of pilots did a wonderful job. Thanks to their courage and skill, the French resistance was organised by the gallant French and British agents who they parachuted or landed into enemy territory. Among the agents passing through Tangmere were Odette, Peter Churchill, Nancy Wake and Violette Szabo.

A two-way traffic was maintained from 1940 until the Normandy landings, infiltrating agents and bringing them out again with their valuable information. This enabled us to make supply drops of arms and explosives to the resistance units who had been organised. Originally, Lysanders were used for the supply drops, but we eventually used heavy bombers.

With their short takeoff and landing ability, the Lysanders, were used for bringing out our agents right up to the end of hostilities and gave wonderful service in various theatres of war.

Some time in May 1941, another special squadron was based at Tangmere - a Turbinlight squadron. I do not know who invented the Turbinlight, but I know that Winston Churchill's imagination was caught by it and he gave orders that it should be thoroughly tried out.

The Turbinlight was a large searchlight which was installed in the nose of a twin engined Boston bomber. The searchlight required a lot of power to operate it so heavy storage batteries had to be carried in the aircraft. These batteries only supplied enough power to operate the searchlight for about four minutes.

The Bostons were also equipped with Aircraft Interception (AI) radar, but because of their heavy load of storage batteries they could not carry guns or ammunition so they operated with a pair of Hurricanes who flew in formation one each side of the Boston. The CGI (Ground Control Interception) which was a special form of radar designed to guide our night fighters on to enemy raiders would vector the

Boston into a position where the AI operator in the aircraft could pick up the enemy, then when close enough, the searchlight beam was switched on and the Hurricanes were supposed to shoot the enemy down. In fact, although the Turbinlight idea was very ingenious it was not successful enough to justify its continued use, although I believe 10 Turbinlight squadrons were formed. The Hurricane squadron that worked with our Turbinlight Bostons was the famous No 1 Squadron, which was allotted this role as a rest from day fighting. Some rest! There were two basic problems with the scheme. Firstly, the Hurricanes had to fly in very close formation with the Boston or they would lose it in the dark. (This also meant an extreme risk of the Hurricane colliding with the Boston.) Secondly, when the Boston turned its searchlight on, it not only blinded the Hurricane pilot, it also gave any German aircraft a beacon to shoot at.

No 1 Squadron was originally stationed at Tangmere before the war, went to France with the Advanced Air Striking Force in 1939 and did wonderful work in France and in the Battle of Britain.

Both flight commanders were New Zealanders, Colin Gray and Wally Raymond. Colin, who had earned a DFC in the Battle of Britain, was awarded a Bar to his DFC at Tangmere and shortly afterwards was promoted to Squadron Leader and took over command of the squadron. After commanding No 616 Squadron he 81 Squadron and was awarded a well-earned DSO. He commanded 322 Wing Fighter wing during the invasion of Sicily and eventually retired as a Group Captain in 1961 after a distinguished career in the RAF.

After I left Tangmere I did not meet Colin again until the 20th anniversary reunion of the Battle of Britain in 1960, when he joyfully reminded me of an incident that is worth recording here.

Colin Gray was flying his Hurricane as one of a pair in formation with a Turbinlight Boston one night and I was controlling in the Operations Room. They had been on patrol for an hour or so over the Isle of Wight, when a signal came through to me announcing the award of a Bar to Colin's DFC. There was no sign of enemy activity so I dispensed with the formality of using any call signs, picked up the microphone and said "Woody calling Colin, do you receive "a slight pause then Colin replied "Loud and clear er Sir" in a rather startled voice. I then said "Congratulations on being awarded a Bar to your DFC, Colin, the signal has just come through. There is no trade about so you had better pancake and we'll celebrate. Over . Woody." There was a considerable pause, then an even more startled Colin replied "Thank you Woody Roger out."

I think the "celebration" took the form of a bottle of beer and ham and eggs in No 1 Squadron's dispersal hut when they landed.

Another incident comes to mind which concerns Wally Raymond, the other New Zealander. Wally was the joint owner with two or three other pilots of an old car. With the stringent petrol rationing in force these boys found it difficult to run their car, which was their only means of getting off the station for recreational purposes in their free time. On the other hand, if there was a minor crash or an aircraft forced landed, the rules said that the aircraft tanks must be drained and the petrol could not even be used in service transport. I knew that those boys who were car owners frequently managed to salve a little of this crash petrol and I turned a blind eye to it. It must have been maddening to see so much petrol being drained on to the aerodrome and left to evaporate. Raymond and his pals had accumulated a small drum of this petrol (which of course was distinctively coloured to identify it as aircraft petrol) stored in a garage near Bognor. One night, this garage caught fire and one of the few things that did not go up in flames was the drum of petrol. The police identified it as aircraft petrol and then the trouble started. A Provost-Marshal Wing Commander was sent down from Air Ministry to investigate.

The Wing Commander was a hectoring unpleasant character who did not even have the manners to report his arrival on the station to me. He merely exhibited his Air Ministry pass to get past the sentries and after a day or two he barged into my office without saluting, slammed a paper on my desk and said "There is the charge, there are the names. You will take a summary of evidence on them immediately." This was too much for me. I said very quietly, "Get out and come in again properly." Rather shaken, he went out, then came in again, this time saluting. I then said "Show me your credentials." Having inspected his Air Ministry pass, I looked at the paper he had put on my desk. This was a report accusing Raymond and two or three other pilots of stealing government petrol. I then looked at the Provost Marshal and said "for a Provost Marshal you are amazingly ignorant of Kings Rules and Air Council Instructions. KR and ACI states that the Commanding Officer will first investigate the charges and should he consider them justified etc etc. In other words I threw the book at this character and then told him to take his unmannerly presence off the station.

I then sent for Wally Raymond and his friends, read the charges out to them and they all admitted that they had collected crash petrol to run their little car. I pointed out the seriousness of the charge and explained that, as they were officers, I could only punish them if they agreed to accept my punishment, otherwise it would mean a court martial. They unanimously accepted my punishment - I think I stopped their leave for a month and placed this punishment on record.

The reason for my action was that, apart from the fact that I had every sympathy with the boys making use of what was in effect waste petrol, I knew that a court martial could not fail to find them guilty of being in possession of coloured high-octane petrol. This would mean that pilots who had cost the country thousands of pounds to train and who were risking their lives by day and by night would probably be reduced to the ranks and have their wings removed.

Thank goodness in British law, you cannot be punished twice for the same crime, so, knowing this, my action was timely. I immediately telephoned the AOC, Air Vice Marshal Leigh Mallory and told him what I had done and why. L-M was silent for a moment or two then he said "You've been rather naughty, Woody, but I agree with you in principle. You'll be unpopular at Air Ministry you know, however I'm glad to have heard your version first. If there is any trouble I'll do what I can."

I forwarded a written report to L-M, giving full reasons for my action and I heard no more, though I suspect somewhere in the archives of the Air Ministry some pleasant little recording angel there added another black mark to the Woodhall dossier!

So far I have said little about Douglas Bader and the Tangmere Wing of Spitfires, chiefly because the exploits of the Wing that high summer have been so ably described in *"Reach for the Sky"* by Paul Brickhill and in *"Wing Leader"* by Johnnie Johnson.

Douglas was indefatigable and as at Duxford the year before, proved tireless in his efforts to defeat the Hun. The old team worked well together and by now our AOC had organised the 11 Group Wings into a formidable striking force.

In the group we had five Spitfire Wings, the Biggin Hill, Kenley, North Weald, Hornchurch and Tangmere wings, each led by a Wing Commander.

"Sailor" Malan who was then the top scoring fighter pilot, led the Biggin Hill wing. Douglas and "Sailor" were firm friends, but great rivals.

Douglas was a firm believer in the "finger four" battle formation which he brought to perfection and which I later used in Malta with great success when we were fighting against terrific odds over that beleaguered island.

Malan however preferred to stick to the line astern formation. The "finger four" formation was proved to be the best and was adopted almost universally throughout the RAF later on.

The advantages of the "finger four" formation were numerous. It was an easier formation to fly than the tight vic or line-astern and allowed each of two pairs of pilots to see the sky around each others tail and therefore provide protection. In the line-astern formation it had been quite common for the "tail-end Charlie" to be shot down without his loss even being noted until a flight landed and found the trailing aircraft had simply disappeared.

After the first fighter sweeps over France, it was found that the Hun failed to react to fighters alone and as our object was to bring him to battle and shoot him down, L-M persuaded Bomber Command to co operate, first with a force of Blenheims, then with Stirlings with their much heavier bomb load. This entailed very careful planning and timing.

First the bomber force had to rendezvous with their close escort fighter wing over a pre-arranged easily identified landmark, at the same time the top cover wing or wings had to position themselves above and up-sun of the main force to deal with the high flying 109's. In addition there were the escort cover wing, the high cover wing and the withdrawal support wing. The last named was timed to meet the bombers as they crossed the enemy coast and assist any damaged aircraft that were straggling. It was a formidable force, which Douglas Bader christened the "Beehive" because the sedate bomber formation flying in perfect formation, surrounded by a weaving mass of faster Spitfires, looked just like a swarm of bees circling their parent hive and so Beehive became its code name.

In April 1941 I heard that my old friend Alan Grace was in the Midhurst Sanatorium, recovering from TB. As soon as possible I visited him there and found him very cheerful, but champing at the bit to get into the war.

I had a yarn with the surgeon in charge, Paul Wood, who was a very clever Australian (he was from Tasmania although he was actually born in India) who had specialised in lung disease. He told me that Alan had been partially cured and returned to ground duties some months previously, but unfortunately the posting authorities had sent him to a bomber operations room job. As a result of being confined for long hours in an operations room with little or no fresh air, he had suffered a relapse and been returned to the sanatorium. There his lung was collapsed again and he was almost recovered for the second time, but the surgeon told me that he would only allow Alan to return to duty if he could be sure he would be employed in an open air job. As it happened, I had already applied for a relief for the satellite aerodrome commander at Westhampnett.. I telephoned Leigh Mallory who immediately arranged for Alan Grace to be posted as administrative CO of the airfield.

Alan more than justified our choice. He proved an able administrator and although he was not allowed to fly at altitudes above 2000 feet at first, he was passed fit enough to command an Air Sea Rescue flight by the end of the year. He achieved some remarkable rescues thereafter and on several occasions after picking aircrew in the Channel, he taxied his amphibian Walrus many miles across to the English coast because the aircraft was too overloaded to take off. He did much to improve the efficiency of the Air Sea rescue service and was awarded a well-deserved DFC for his efforts.

Eventually his Air Sea rescue unit was enlarged to include some Mark II Spitfires for escort duties with the Walrus amphibians. By that time, Alan was nearly fit again and frequently flew a Spitfire himself although he was still restricted to flying below 5000ft.

When the V1 flying bombs opened their attacks on London, Southampton and Portsmouth, Alan further distinguished himself by shooting one down. This was no mean feat in a Mark II Spitfire as the flying bomb was much faster than the Spitfire II once it had reached its full velocity.

This was what Alan did. He had spotted a VI launching site in the Pas de Calais, so making use of low cloud cover, he kept it in view until a bomb was launched. He then dived through the intense flak that the Germans had established round their launching sites, caught up the flying bomb just after it left its launching pad and before it had reached its full speed, shot it down. When it is considered that Alan Grace was invalided out of the RAF before the war as unfit for further duties because of a TB infection which developed as a direct result of his crash at Penang in 1938 his subsequent achievements deserve the highest praise. Of course, Paul Wood, the surgeon responsible for Alan's recovery and whose skill resulted in the cure of so many sufferers from the same disease, both service and civilian, deserves no small place in history. When I met him he impressed me as such a kind, humane and efficient man.

From June 1941 onwards, the Tangmere Wing was carrying out two or three sweeps a day over enemy-occupied territory. Douglas Bader always led the Wing himself. He never spared himself and by this time he was a legendary figure. These sweeps required such accurate briefing, involving as they did such large numbers of Spitfires in addition to the bombers they were escorting, that it became necessary for Leigh Mallory to hold a conference of Sector Commanders, Wing Leaders and Squadron Commanders at Group Headquarters two or three times a week.

On these occasions, after the last mission of the day, Douglas and I and either Ken Holden (CO of 610 Squadron), Stan Turner (CO of 145 Squadron) or Billy Burton (CO of 616 Squadron) would climb into our Spitfires and fly to Northbolt where we were met by car to take us to Uxbridge. These briefing conferences were most rewarding. Leigh Mallory with his usual courtesy, encouraged everyone to express opinions, listened to arguments and then laid down his plan of further action. After the conference, we visitors would have a quick cup of tea in the Mess and then fly back to our sectors.

Shortly after we landed back at our own aerodromes, complete and detailed instructions implementing the decisions made for the next operations would arrive by teleprinter, headed "Operation orders for Circus Number".

These "Circus" operations made the enemy react quite seriously and although we had some losses, the balance was considerably in our favour (or so it appeared at the time). They were also intended to pin down a German fighter force on the Western front which would otherwise have been sent to the Russian front when Hitler launched his attack to the East in June.

On the odd occasions when evening weather conditions were such that in Air Force parlance "the birds were walking" that is, low cloud or fog made enemy night bombing impossible or extremely improbable, we would declare a "thrash" in the mess. We had an excellent amateur dance band and when required they were delighted to demonstrate their talents for our benefit. On one of these "thrashes" (and an occasion there were no women present), after a few beers I was persuaded to produce my piano accordion and a sing song was started. Douglas loved a sing-song and made a very able chorus master, beating the time with one hand and resting the other hand on my shoulder he roared out the old flying songs and songs like Rolling Round the Mountain, Little Angeline and My Brother Sylvest, that he had learned from his Canadians in 242 Squadron. Then the inevitable high-spirited games started. I unwisely got mixed up in a "scrum down" that developed and of course Douglas enthusiastically joined in. I was somewhere at the bottom of a laughing, struggling heap of pilots when something very hard and painful hit my right elbow. It was one of Douglas's tin legs! My arm was less painful after another drink or two but next morning it was very stiff and sore and our MO Squadron Leader Simpson diagnosed it as an impacted fracture and put it in a sling.

That day Leigh-Mallory came to visit us so I hurriedly discarded the sling and hoped the AOC would not comment if I saluted left handed. But when Douglas and I met the AOC, I forgot my injured arm and instinctively tried to salute, with miserable and painful results. Douglas, with what I thought was an unneccesary chuckle explained that it was entirely his fault for falling on me and of course L-M thought it was equally funny but told me to put the arm back in a sling. With a twinkle in his eye he said "you mustn't be rough with your Station Commander, Douglas, he's older than you are!"

All through the summer, the Wing carried out two and frequently three sweeps a day over enemy territory and Douglas led every one himself. Although he insisted that all his pilots stand down from operations and be given leave at suitable intervals to prevent them getting stale, he never stood down himself.

We had ample reserves of pilots because each squadron had at least 18 pilots available to fly 12 aircraft, so the rotation of the pilots was easy. But we only had one Douglas Bader and my only criticism of him is that he drove himself too hard. Towards the end of July it was obvious to me that he needed a rest and I told him he must take at least 14 days leave and suggested that he should go right away to somewhere like St Andrews and play golf. His old friend and Adjutant in 242 Squadron, Peter MacDonald (later Sir Peter MacDonald MP) backed me up and promised to arrange accommodation for Thelma and Douglas at St Andrews. Douglas was stubborn so I telephoned the AOC who agreed with me and came down to Tangmere the next day with the intention of ordering Douglas to take leave.

Over lunch, Bader used all his charm on L-M sand said "the shooting season" will only last until the end of August, sir, I would like to go until then, please." The AOC allowed himself to be persuaded, but told Douglas that he would definitely be sent on leave on September 1 and after leave would be taken off operations for a time. As L-M said so reasonably, all the other Wing Leaders had been taken off operations for a rest and Douglas had carried out more sweeps than anyone else in the Command. By this time the Wing regarded Douglas as invulnerable, their confidence in his leadership was unbounded and all ranks looked up to him with a sort of wondering affection. Thelma, who of course knew him better than anyone, was also deeply concerned that he should have a rest. Peter MacDonald, in an endeavour to clinch matters, booked accommodation at St Andrews for Douglas, Thelma and himself for August 11.

On August 8 another "Circus" operation was laid on and as usual Douglas led the Wing. The German reaction to this sweep was immediate and heavier than usual. I kept "Dogsbody" informed of everything that the radar plots indicated and very soon it was obvious from the RT that the Wing was heavily engaged The last I heard from "Dogsbody" was to the effect that he was diving on some 109's.

I listened hard for Douglas' well-known voice in order to get a radio "fix" on his position and then after a few minutes called him on the RT without result. After a pause Johnnie Johnson replied "We have been heavily engaged I last saw Dogsbody diving on a 109 but haven't seen him since."

Full of foreboding, I drove out to Westhampnett to meet 616 and 610 Squadrons as they landed. I knew that "Cocky" Dundas, Johnnie Johnson and Jeff West had been flying in the "Dogsbody" finger four.

Jeff West, a stocky New Zealander had been flying as No 2 to Douglas and he told me that when Douglas dived on the 109's, he said to the rest of the Squadron "Follow me down Ken, (Ken Holden of 610 Squadron) you stay up top and cover us." With that, Douglas went into a screaming dive leaving his No 2 and the other pair well behind. There was quite a dog fight and after the first attack when the 109's appeared to be caught napping, Douglas had not been seen or heard from.

Some enemy aircraft had been shot down and several parachutes had been seen, but no one could give definite news of Douglas. Jeff blamed himself bitterly for not being able to stay with his leader, but I realised only too well how impossible it could be to keep sight of one particular aircraft in a dog fight.

Buck Casson had also failed to return. After quick refuelling and arming, Cocky Dundas took off with "Nip" Hepple, Johnnie Johnson and Jeff West and flying low over the sea, searched along the coast of the Pas de Calais in case Douglas was down in the sea. All they saw was an aircraft dinghy, but it was empty.

The Air Sea Rescue was of course alerted and were also carrying out a search while Group enquired at all possible aerodromes where Douglas could have landed.

I then drove out to Bay House and broke the news to Thelma. The search continued until last light, but with no result.

Two days later I received a call from someone at Air Ministry to the effect that our monitoring service had intercepted a message from the Germans in plain language to the effect that Wing Commander Bader was in St Omer hospital, unhurt, but that his right artificial leg was damaged. The message went on to say that when we had a spare leg ready, the Germans would give a safe conduct for an unarmed aircraft and would tell us where to land the leg. I telephoned the good news to Thelma immediately and then made arrangements for Douglas's spare leg to be sent to Tangmere at once. I also told the Station the good news over the Tannoy loud speakers. I telephoned the AOC personally and told him that I was making arrangements to fly the leg across in a Lysander (I did not mention that I proposed to pilot the aircraft myself) but he told me to await further orders. However, just to be prepared I carried out a few "Circuits and bumps" in one of our Lysanders as I had not flown one since I tested the prototype in 1934. The leg duly arrived and we found that it would not go into the standard cylindrical parachute supply container, so we had to make a special box for it. With Thelma's aid, the hollow leg was filled with a variety of comforts, stump socks, talcum powder, toothpaste, soap, chocolate, a supply of Douglas' favourite tobacco and so on.

In the meantime the AOC had decided (quite rightly) that the offer of a safe conduct was a subtle propaganda move and that the leg would be dropped on a normal bombing raid. Accordingly, on the next Circus operation, the leg was delivered by one of the Blenheims. The Tangmere Wing, led by "Paddy" Woodhouse, acted as close escort to the bombers.

The orders for the bombers were that they were to fly over St Omer, drop the leg on its parachute and then proceed to their target which was some 20 miles or so further inland.

The Blenheims arrived over St Omer in perfect formation and then it was found that the case containing the leg, being very little smaller than the escape hatch, was jammed there by the slipstream, half in and half out of the hatch. So the Blenheims did three circuits of St Omer accompanied by the escorting Spitfires, while the perspiring rear gunner struggled to force the container out and away. In the meantime, although the sky was full of flak bursts, there was no German fighter reaction at this stage. Eventually in the Tangmere operations room we heard Paddy Woodhouse report "leg gone" then speaking very slowly in English he broadcast "Wing Commander Bader's spare leg has been dropped over St Omer. I repeat, Wing Commander Bader's spare leg has been dropped over St Omer."

I understand that this message was duly received by the Germans, in any case the leg reached Bader safely. We later heard that the Germans repaired the damaged leg and that Douglas escaped before we dropped his spare leg.

The escape organisation to bring him out by Lysander was all ready to go as soon as we knew he would be mobile, but unfortunately he was recaptured and shipped off to prison camp by then, although his spare leg went with him on the train.

So ended my two years of close association with Douglas Bader in war I treasure the memories of those days and of a man whose example, leadership and courage in the face of almost impossible odds have placed him in a niche of his own. I unreservedly agree with Johnnie Johnson who described Douglas as "the greatest tactician of them all."

A few days before Douglas was reported missing Stan Turner and his squadron (145) had been withdrawn for a rest and replaced by No 41 Squadron, commanded by Piet Hugo, a South African who subsequently became highly decorated. No 616 Squadron were also to be replaced within the month by No 65 Squadron, so the old team was being split up. Billy Burton and Cocky Dundas, who had been in the "team" from the Duxford days were sent for a rest in spite of their protests. Burton was promoted to Wing Commander and 616 Squadron was taken over by Colin Gray, the New Zealander. Cocky, after what must have been the shortest "rest" ever, forced his way back to operational flying in command of a Typhoon Squadron and subsequently became the youngest Group Captain in the RAF with the DSO and DFC. I was very pleased that Cocky achieved so much – only a few months before this, I spoke to him very severely about his drinking when he and Johnnie Johnston had been hitting the bottle in an attempt to alleviate the stress of battle and the grief at losing friends. I am pleased to say they both took me seriously and not only survived but went on to long and successful lives.

The very day that Bader was missing I had recommended him for a bar to his DFC (he already had a bar to his DSO) so as soon as we knew he was alive this recommendation went forward and the award came through.

Jeff West was awarded the DFM and recommended for a commission, Johnnie Johnson was awarded the DFC and promoted to Flight Lieutenant. I forget the number of decorations earned by the Tangmere Wing under Douglas Bader's leadership, but it was large enough to make all ranks proud to be associated with the Station, the Wing and the Squadrons.

So far I have barely mentioned our night fighter Squadron. This was No 219 Squadron equipped with Beaufighters and commanded by Wing Commander Tom Pike (later Air Chief Marshal Sir Thomas Pike, KCB, CBE, DFC, Chief of the Air Staff from 1 January 1960 to 31 August 1963 and then Deputy Supreme Commander Allied Powers Europe until his retirement in 1967 as Chief of the Air Staff).

Tom Pike was a softly spoken, quietly-impressive man who had that combination of courage, ability and efficiency which deservedly brought him to the peak of his profession. As a night fighter pilot he was outstanding and he did much to develop and improve our techniques in dealing with enemy night bombing raids. I think he was the second ex-Cranwell cadet to become Chief of the Air Staff, his predecessor, Sir Dermot Boyle, having been the first to achieve that distinction. Tom Pike was a firm believer in the principle that the first duty of an operational squadron commander was to fly and to fight. This belief he shared with Douglas Bader and the two were firm friends although of completely different character. No 219 Squadron under Tom Pike's command was a unit that any Station Commander would be proud to have on his station. With the end of the summer, the weather deteriorated and our day operations decreased, but No 219 Squadron's efforts increased with the longer nights.

As the weather made Circus operations impossible on most days, the day fighters carried out more and more "rhubarbs." This was the code name for low-flying sorties into enemy territory carried out by not more than four aircraft making use of cloud cover and seeking what targets they could find. The ideal target was of course an enemy airfield with aircraft on the ground and just taking off or landing. These airfields were heavily defended by anti aircraft guns, so such targets were reserved for days when a cloud base of about 300ft made complete surprise possible. Troop trains, goods trains, motor vehicle convoys, bridges all were given appropriate attention.

These "rhubarb" operations required careful planning at Group level. To ensure reasonable success they needed the most up to date information about gun defences, aircraft disposition, troop movements and of course, the most accurate weather forecast possible. Our planners at Group served us well in these respects and kept the Sector constantly posted with the latest intelligence, weather and photographic reconnaissance reports.

At the beginning of the New Year (1942) the AOC told me that I was due for a rest. I asked him what this meant and he said it would probably mean a posting to a staff job. I protested, but he pointed out that I had been commanding Fighter sectors longer than any other Station Commander in the Command and he thought I needed a rest. Three or four days later, the C-in-C Fighter Command, Sholto Douglas (later Marshal of the Royal Air Force, Lord Douglas), telephoned me and asked me if I was prepared to go to Malta at short notice. (I thought to myself, this sounds like some rest!) I accepted the posting of course and the C-in-C told me to report as soon as possible to the Director of Overseas Operations in London for briefing. The following day I found the DOO was established in deep bomb-proof offices, well below ground in a building somewhere near Waterloo Station. I remember being conducted (after passing security checks) into a lift which delivered me into a series of underground offices with neon lighting and air conditioning. I was taken to the Director, Air Commander Alec Coryton (later Air Chief Marshal Sir Alec Coryton) who told me that I was posted to a newly created appointment to be known as Group Captain, Malta Fighters. He explained that the fighter defences were quite well organised but they needed someone with up to date experience in Fighter control and organisation to take charge and improve them. My first question was "What fighters have we in Malta," the answer I was given was "Five squadrons of Hurricanes." My next question was "What about aircraft serviceability, replacements and spares?" To this Coryton rather vaguely replied that he thought the serviceability was very high because the main workshops at Kalafrana had been augmented by various garages and workshops in other parts of the island. He was doing his best to send spares out by air and submarine and he hinted that a convoy could be expected in the near future.

He also said that Spitfires would be flown out from an aircraft carrier very shortly. I was then given orders where and when to report for passage to Malta. My service tunic was removed and my photograph taken wearing a woollen pullover. Before I left to return to Tangmere that evening I was handed a civilian passport which described me as a "Government servant." It was explained that as we would be landing in Ireland

and Portugal, I was to wear civilian clothes until we arrived at Gibraltar. I had an uneasy feeling at my briefing about conditions in Malta and that Alec Coryton was being deliberately optimistic and vague, or that he just didn't know. On looking back I can only think that he did not want to depress me and that he was under strict orders from the security people to hide the true facts at the time.

It was not until many years later when I read Sir Basil Embry's book Mission Completed that I knew it was on his advice that the appointment of Group Captain Malta Fighters was established.

Basil Embry had spent several days in Malta in December 1941 when on his way back from an advisory mission in the desert and he knew the facts. On his return to England he advised Air Ministry accordingly. Considering the importance of the job, it seems a pity that I was not sent to him for briefing.

Chapter 12

Taking Control at Malta

On my return from London, I told my wife about my posting, handed over the command of Tangmere to Charles Appleton and found the boys had arranged a farewell party for us. My wife was living in Bognor in a cottage called Rookery Nook, where my elder son had been born on November 27, 1941. Although Margot had been there since June, my duties had been such that I had only been able to see her on very rare occasions for a hurried meal together and on perhaps three or four occasions when the "birds were walking" and no flying was possible. I had no time to make any other arrangements for her, so I could only leave her in the cottage and trust that she could make a further agreement when the lease was up.

My first impression after the painful business of saying goodbye to my wife and two-month old son, was how impersonal the whole organisation was. At a Bournemouth hotel I was checked in as a civilian and all articles identifying me with the Service were taken forcibly away from me. I embarked at Poole with several other senior officers of the other Services, plus four enthusiastic young Fleet Air Arm pilots, in a Sunderland Flying boat. Incidentally, this was the first time in 14 years I had ever been flown. I had always flown myself before so I felt quite unhappy about it! We took off and arrived at Foynes in Eire. Arriving there we were greeted by the usual customs authorities plus an Army officer who was apparently in charge of security.

The Eire subaltern scrutinised my passport which stated that I was a Government official. He asked me what kind of official I was. I glibly stated "Air Ministry clerk." His reply was "thank you very much, Group Captain." I discovered that the next in turn, a Major General, was also detailed as a Government official. His replay was "War Office clerk" the security officer answered, "Thank you, General."

Over a glass of Guinness later it transpired that the Subaltern had a brother who had been awarded the DFC in the Battle of Britain and he also had an up to date list of the Navy, Army and Air Force, so I presume that his deductions were easy.

That evening I was talking to a Subaltern in the Irish Army of about my own age, (we had to stay the night in a very hospitable hotel in Limerick). I noticed that he was wearing the Great War and Victory medals. When we knew each other well enough, I tactfully asked about these. His reply was "I fought wid ye, an' aginst ye in the last war and now the bastards won't let me fight at all!" The following morning we took off and flew blind for some three hours in dense cloud until we saw sunlight and the north coast of Portugal and in a surprisingly short time landed at Lisbon. We spent the night in Lisbon at a very comfortable hotel where we had excellent food and service. The next day we landed at Gibraltar after a very short flight. We took off in the dark for Malta after two nights at Gibraltar where I found everything amazingly cheap and plentiful, (there was practically no rationing and apparently no profiteering). We arrived at Malta about half an hour before first light. By this time I had persuaded the pilot to allow me to take over the controls. I had no sooner taken over when I saw a lot of flak coming up to port and although it was dark on the ground, light was just breaking at the height we were flying. At this moment an aircraft cut across our bows and shook me considerably. I looked around for the pilot to make sure that he agreed that it was not an enemy aircraft, but he was busy at the chart table. I then decided that it was a Wellington, whose pilot must have been as frightened as me. We remained south of the island until the flak died down and then as day was breaking, landed at the seaplane station of Kalafrana.

I was greeted by the Station Commander, Group Captain Cahill, who immediately provided me with a much-needed bath. We then proceeded to a breakfast of fried eggs which struck me as being marvellous for besieged Malta. He assured me, however, that the hens were never fed, but were so used to laying that they did not know how to stop!

During breakfast there was a lot of banging and it all sounded very frightening to me. I asked Cahill if he thought we were all right and he replied "don't worry, there is a chap on the roof who will tell us when to duck."

This was typical of the spirit of the Services throughout Malta in the bad times.

I then went and reported to my AOC, Air Vice Marshal Hugh P Lloyd (later Sir Hugh) and he rather shook me at first, although he said he was glad to see me. He asked what I knew about fighters. I told him and his reply was "they're all yours and God help you if you fail." That frightened me still more, but I saw at once what a man he was.

I went out to the fighter aerodrome at Takali expecting to find five squadrons of Hurricanes, as I had been told that was the fighter force available when I left England. On arrival at Takali, I found seven Hurricanes with the pilots waiting at readiness at their dispersals. This I found was the total serviceable fighter force in the island. I then returned to the Operations Room and took stock there. I found that the plotters were civilians, wives and daughters of service personnel who had not been able to get away from the island and members of an ENSA troop who had been marooned. These were extremely good. We had no disciplines, except the discipline produced by goodwill and the desire to win the war. In 99 per cent of the cases it worked. There was a sprinkling of airmen who produced the necessary stiffening when times were really tough. I had no sooner arrived in the Operations Room than a hostile plot of 3 plus came on the board over Comiso, 65 miles away, at 12,000ft. I sat back to see what would happen. The Controller ordered "stand-by" to the pilots, which meant that they were in their cockpits and capable of taking off within 60 seconds. The next plot showed the enemy at 9 plus. The controller, in a rather panic-stricken voice over the RT ordered the pilots to disperse. I asked what this meant and found that they taxied down into the fields, stopped their engines and waited and "took" the attack because they were not considered sufficiently numerically strong to fight. This I thought was extremely bad for morale.

That night I called all the fighter pilots together, deliberately "raised their back hair" and we had a most informative discussion as a result. They told me all their moans about the Operations side and we swapped ideas generally. We finished up by drinking the last of the beer in the Mess and the AOC and the GOC who were present at the discussion agreed that we were "getting places."

The scheme we formulated was this. As long as we had four aircraft to fight we would always fight, because four made a team; less than four left at least one of the team unprotected. Another maxim which we laid down was the sun can be the greatest friend or the greatest enemy of the fighter pilot therefore we adopted it as our friend.

The following day the usual Hun activity boiled up and eight Hurricanes were scrambled. They climbed into the sun with no orders whatever from me until I knew from the time factor, that they were, at least as high as the Hun. I then produced a running commentary over the RT, telling the boys exactly where the enemy was, where he appeared to be going, his numbers and so on. The result of this was that for the first time for some months the fighter boys, although inferior in numbers, found themselves in a position to choose the time, the place and the height of their attack. These tactics proved worthwhile. This was broadly speaking, the principle which governed the whole of our defence of Malta during the bad times.

When Italy came into the war, after the fall of France, the defences of Malta were by no means complete and as all material, guns, ammunition, petrol and spare parts had to be imported, together with the bulk of the food of the island, poor Malta was in a perilous state by the beginning of 1942.

We had a fair supply of aircraft petrol, but other fuel , aircraft spares, AA ammunition, flour and milk for babies were becoming very short.

Certain supplies were brought in by air and by submarine, but these were very limited, consisting as they did, mostly of vital technical stores for guns, aircraft and ships.

The first question I was invariably asked on arrival was "when are we getting a convoy?" The first question my fighter boys asked was "when are they sending us Spitfires?" I could only answer "soon I hope!"

The majority of the fighter pilots in Malta in February 1942 had been there for nine months at least and some for 18 months or more. With virtually no relaxation for them and nowhere to go that was free from bombing, it was obvious that they needed a change. The only female society in the island was Maltese (apart from a few Service wives who had been unable to leave the island, or had chosen to take a chance and stay with their husbands). The beer ration was one bottle, locally brewed, per head, per week. Perhaps. A certain quantity of spirits, good and bad, was available, but I discouraged pilots from using hard liquor (not that they need discouragement, they were too sensible), because the mixture of hard liquor and flying is the surest way to sudden death that I know.

The picture theatres kept going as long as possible, but the films were old and worn and had been seen by most people before leaving England. The only real relaxation the boys could get was at the rest camp which was established at St Paul's Bay. This was a most delightful spot run most efficiently by the kindly and cheerful Flight Lieutenant Bosworth, formerly of the Air Sea Rescue Service, who was affectionately known as "Uncle" by us all. At Uncle's establishment one could bathe and laze to one's hearts content.

The only drawback to St Paul's Bay was that it was just as much in sight and sound of the daily battles going on overhead as any other part of the island. At night, one's rest was as disturbed there, as anywhere else.

Another distressing feature of our life was the growing shortage of food. At the beginning of February 1942 Malta only had a partial rationing scheme; eggs were obtainable and in certain little cafes one could get pork and chicken, although the service ration consisted solely of bully beef and "Maconochie"ham.

By April, we were down to half ration of everything, including bread which was the staple article of food for the Maltese.

Added to this was the prevalence of "Malta Dog" (a most weakening form of dysentry) and sandfly fever.

It was obvious, under these conditions, that a pilot could not give his best for very long and the AOC agreed that replacements be arranged after three months in strenuous times and six months in less strenuous ones.

Those "old" Malta fighter boys were a grand crowd, keen as they are made and only anxious to meet the Hun on something approaching even terms. They only had Hurricane II's against the Hun with his Me 109's. The old Hurricane could not catch a Ju 88 full out in level flight, the 109's could out climb them and walk away from them in level flight. Our pilots used to pray for the Hun to send over some Ju 87 dive bombers. They said these were a "piece of cake."

"Rags" (Wing Commander Rabagliati, DFC) was the Wing Commander Flying in those days. He was a slightly-built young South African who had all the boys right behind him. He was a very gallant leader and a most tenacious fighter. Jack Satchell, the Wing Commander commanding Takali, was another notable character. Almost my first day in the island I found him at "readiness" with the boys and that morning he destroyed one Me 109 and damaged another. He said he wanted to demonstrate that a Hurricane could shoot down a 109. Jack never stopped, he was always on the job. When his office was blown down for the third or fourth time he established his headquarters in a tent on a bluff overlooking the aerodrome and about 150 yards from the perimeter. His clerks, stores, etc, were in a cave just underneath. Above, at the top of the bluff was a Bofors gun position.

He had a small gun pit made just outside his tent and erected twin machine guns on a home made mounting made from bicycle parts. When there was a raid on, the Bofors gunners would shout the "gen" to him in his gun pit and from that position he was credited with one enemy aircraft destroyed and 12 damaged. He never put in a claim for himself, other eye witnesses made his claims for him.

He issued as many rifles as he could obtain to the ground crews, together with condemned aircraft ammunition and gave them orders to shoot at any low-flying Hun. The airmen forgot about shelters if they had a rifle in their hands. The results possibly deterred the Huns - they certainly frightened us! Jack Satchell was later awarded a well-deserved DSO.

Then there was George Powell Sheddon, DFC, who after having earned his DFC in the Battle of Britain, went to Malta and developed the Night-Fighter Defence of the island with Hurricanes. He was then given the job of Wing Commander "Bomb 'oles" at Luqa as a rest!

Wing Commander "Bomb 'oles" was officially second-in-command of the Station, but his main job was to see that the aerodrome remained serviceable. This meant marking unexploded bombs, organising their removal or explosion and filling in all bomb holes on the aerodrome as quickly as possible after each raid. Hardly a rest cure!

George had achieved a certain amount of fame in the Battle of Britain from an occasion when he called for help while under attack from four or five 109's. A pilot coming to his relief could see Powell-Sheddon being pursued by several aircraft while turning in a tight circle and radioed "I'm nearly with you, hang on and I'll get some off your tail." Powell-Sheddon with his slight stutter replied "N-n-no rush, I s-seem to have the bastards s-surrounded."

Squadron Leader Dennis Westmacott, DFC, took over the Night-Fighter Unit from George Powell Sheddon, still equipped with Hurricanes.

Dennis had been badly burned about the face, but had been patched up marvellously.

His pet form of amusement was to go over to Sicily at night and bomb trains and German staff cars. Another famous Hurricane pilot was Flight Lieutenant "Don" Stone DFC, a most courageous fighter and leader. When off duty he was always getting into trouble with the authorities through his high spirits and love of practical joking. A most lovable character, in spite of (or because of) his mischievous habits.

There were many others, all gallant chaps whose names I have not mentioned. They all did a first class job under nasty conditions, with aircraft that were patched up and slow, against odds that were almost impossible, but in spite of everything proved that they were better than the Hun.

Great and almost insurmountable difficulties had to be overcome to service the fighter and most aircraft in Malta during that year.

It must be realised that the total area of the island is approximately one-sixth that of Greater London and it was impossible to camouflage or hide the aerodromes.

In addition, the Italians helped to build the Civil Aerodrome at Takali in peacetime and used it jointly with Imperial Airways so that they had complete and accurate maps and photographs of the island and its defence.

When war broke out there were well-equipped and up-to-date aircraft and engine repair shops at the seaplane base at Kalafrana, but these were almost destroyed soon after the Germans came to Sicily in 1941. Luckily there were several well equipped motor workshops and garages on the island. These were taken over by the RAF and produced most efficient service.

Wing Commander Wooberry, OBE, the Command Engineer Officer, organised this dispersed repair service. He even repaired airscrews, a job which in England was only done by the manufacturers.

When an aircraft was damaged beyond repair by the normal Station Headquarters facilities, the wings were whipped off and it was towed on its own wheels (in the case of the Hurricane) to whichever workshop it was detailed. This meant a slow journey along the narrow winding Maltese roads for several miles.

When Spitfires arrived however, matters were complicated because the under carriage of the Spitfire comes off with the wings. As we had only one "Queen Mary" this is the name given to the long salvage trailer so often seen carrying aircraft in England) this was worked overtime and Wooberry improvised several trollies to carry the aircraft and augment the "Queen Mary" service.

Most of the damage was done to aircraft on the ground and early in 1942 we had very few aircraft shelter pens. The need for these was so great that all hands were set to build them, using empty petrol tins filled with earth. The Malta police did first-class work in this respect. They worked right up to the last possible moment in a raid and were back on the job again before the dust from the bombs had settled. The fighter pilots constructed some of the more efficient pens too. They appreciated only too well the value and necessity of these pens. All resources were pooled on each aerodrome. We organised what we called runway crews, whose job was the rapid refuelling and re-arming of aircraft; and also maintenance crews, whose job was routine inspections and small repairs within their scope. By this means, we increased the serviceability from seven to 27 Hurricanes within a week of the scheme being started. Alas, this serviceability did not last very long, because very soon the increased scale of attack and the lack of spares nearly got us down. For nearly a fortnight in April we had to sit and "take it" and leave the island's defence entirely to the guns, while we worked night and day to make aircraft fit to fly. By the law of cussedness it was always the aircraft that was nearly serviceable that was hit. It was heart- breaking because we all knew that, given the aircraft, we could beat the Hun every time.

In those black days the Hun kept a standing patrol of from two to four Me 109's flying low just out of AA range round the island.

At this time we had to keep our few precious Hurricanes to deal with big raids and we could not afford to weaken our defending forces by even one pair of Hurricanes. The result of this was that the Huns became quite saucy and used to give acrobatic displays within sight (but out of range) of the island. My boys were hopping mad at this naturally and often asked me to let them go and chase the 109's.

Unfortunately I always had to refuse in those days because we had to save our pilots for bigger game, namely the bombers. These came over regularly at least three times a day, about 12 to 18 strong with an escort of up to 50 fighters. Following each raid the Hun then sent a further force of fighters to try to catch our fighters when they were landing short of ammunition and fuel. To deal with this we organised our fighters (when we had enough!) into a main attacking force (four aircraft!) and an aerodrome defence section (two aircraft).

The main force would be "scrambled" as soon as bomber activity was seen over Sicily and they climbed rapidly into sun. At the last possible moment before the Huns reached the island the aerodrome defence section were "scrambled" and climbed to a position about 10 miles south of Malta where they awaited instructions from me.

I kept RT silence until 15 minutes had elapsed. By this time I knew the main force would have reached 25,000 feet, then started a running commentary on the RT giving my boys all I knew about the Hun, his strength, composition, course and position.

It would go something like this: "Hello Johnnie, Woody calling. There are 18 to 20 Big Jobs 20 miles north east St Paul's Bay, course south west, angels 18. About 50 Little Jobs at angels 21, two miles behind them. Ten Little Jobs patrolling Zonkar Point, angels two five. Over."

Back would come the laconic reply: "OK Woody, Johnnie, over." Then would come Johnnie's orders to his fellow pilots: "Fingers out, chaps, there they are. I'm going straight for the Big Jobs."

They would try to attack the bombers head-on and after the first attacks they were invariably mixed up with the escorting fighters. When their ammunition was finished they would dive down to sea level in pairs so as to watch each other's tail and make for Takali. At this time, owing to shortage of ammunition, the Bofors guns at Takali were the only ones to be allowed unrestricted fire. I therefore made Takali the "sanctuary" where our fighters with no ammunition could circle low and obtain some protection from our guns. When I knew our main force was trying to land I would call the leader of the Aerodrome Defence Section something like this: "Hello Buck, Woody here. Come in now, come in fast. Little Jobs over St Pauls Bay making for Takali, angels 10." This pair of fighters would come rocketing in and chase off the 109's and enable our ammunition-less fighters to land. As can be imagined, there was never a dull moment either on the ground or in the air.

Pilots on the ground who were having a stand off would shout excitedly (and uselessly!): "Turn Hurricane, turn, there's a 109 on your tail!" then the Hurricane pilot would see the Hun, turn into him and the Hun would sheer off because luckily he wasn't sure that our pilot had no ammunition left and he was unwilling to risk getting in his sights.

There was one fearless pilot who was caught alone and set on by four 109's when he was at about 300 feet. He could not reach Takali because he had to turn into each attack. This he did and suddenly he called out on his radio: "Oh boy! Just watch how these Hurricanes can turn!"

He actually managed to gain height until the Huns attacked from two directions at once and they got him at last. Luckily he baled out and escaped with a few bruises and abrasions.

The RT control of these fighter boys was a very personal affair. They all knew my voice and I knew theirs. I flatter myself that I knew most of them by their nicknames or Christian names and I could recognise their voices over the RT. I knew from my own experience what a difference it makes when the controller calls one by name. I certainly found and I think any of my Malta boys who read this will agree, that the friendly personal relations between us did a lot to build up the confidence and trust we always had in each other. It made an otherwise almost unbearable job very worthwhile to me.

The outstanding personality of the defence of Malta in 1941/42 was Air Vice Marshal Sir Hugh Pughe Lloyd, KBE, CB, MC, DFC. A comparatively young man, he was a born leader and more than any other man, I consider that he saved Malta in her darkest days. He worked all his subordinates hard, very hard, but he worked himself harder still. Wherever trouble was worst, there he would be found encouraging, helping and directing. When he put his hand on your shoulder and said "well done, well done," you felt that you were really doing a worthwhile job.

He had piercing eyes that seem to see through everything and yet there was always a twinkle lurking somewhere at the back of them. He always backed his subordinates to the hilt if they did their job, but, he was ruthless with shirkers and incompetents. He was so quickly on the spot when an aerodrome was being bombed that his presence on an aerodrome made the chaps expect a raid any moment after his arrival. His example and personal influence were such that his subordinates would willingly and daily attempt the nearly impossible and achieve it. Soon after I arrived, the AOC was distressed at the readiness of some of the ground-crew to take cover in shelters and the resultant loss of man hours put in on our precious aircraft.

As it happened a little WAAF officer, Section Officer Aileen Morris, MBE, visited the island on special technical duty about this time. The AOC asked her if she was afraid of bombing and her reply was, naturally "Yes." His reply was, "So am I, but if you are willing, we'll go out to Luqa and try something out."

They went out to the aerodrome and, sure enough, the sirens went and it became obvious that the target was Luqa. Throughout this raid those two, AOC and Section Officer, walked calmly up and down the tarmac, smoking cigarettes. Stout-hearted little Aileen told me afterwards that she had never been so frightened in her life! Foolhardy? Perhaps, but it worked!

Aileen Morris organised our Y Service (as our radio interception was called). She was an accomplished linguist as well as a radio technician. Thanks to her efforts we were able to listen in to the German controllers in Sicily and to their aircraft transmissions. This proved of inestimable value to us as it gave us information of raids building up before they were shown on the radar screen.

It was about this time, early in February, that the AOC established a system of flag warnings on each aerodrome, similar to a system already in force in the Dockyard. This was simple, a red flag which was hoisted in a prominent place when the Huns were obviously making for that particular target. A siren had to be sounded for civilian purposes when the Huns were 35 miles from the island.

Until the flag scheme was introduced this meant that all work stopped, both on the aerodrome and in the dockyard, until the "all clear" went and as warnings were frequently on all day, the amount of work lost can be imagined. The flag system worked very well and was controlled by the Operations Room. The result of this was that personnel would remain at work until within five minutes of the bombs dropping and would be back at work five minutes after that raid was over.

Also at the beginning of 1942, a visual reporting system was established to augment the control system. For this, we posted an officer at the Signal Tower on top of the Governor's Palace in Valetta. This covered a view of practically the whole of the island and when the Huns were over the island, this controller would chip in with warning to our fighters and indications of where the enemy were. Flight Lieutenant Birtwhistle rendered magnificent service from the roof of the Governor's Palace. With a tin hat and a portable RT set, he persistently stuck to his post until he actually saw the bombs leaving the aircraft, apparently coming straight for him. He would then say hurriedly over the telephone to me "well, goodbye for now, I'm getting down quickly" and would tumble down about two flights of stairs until the explosions took place. He would then run back and breathlessly say "OK now, but they're rotten shots!" and would get on with the job again.

This was our only visual reporting post to begin with. Later I established five posts on the Observer Corps system, which fed the information into the Operations Room. To man these posts we had to train Maltese, chiefly university students who were locally enlisted in the RAF and gave very valuable service.

At this period we had heard rumours of the long hoped-for convoy. As the life of the island depended on the safe arrival of this convoy, we made every preparation possible to help it in safely. With our small force of Hurricanes things looked pretty black. Then came the news that Spitfires would shortly arrive. Everybody's tail went sky high at the mere prospect.

When the day of the Spitfires arrival dawned we had every possible Hurricane standing by as a reception committee, because we knew these Spitfires would be very short of petrol after having flown 550 miles from the carrier which launched them. Just before their arrival I was extremely glad to greet my old friend from Duxford and Tangmere days, Wing Commander "Stan" Turner, DFC, who came by flying boat with other reinforcement pilots. "Rags" had been posted away, so I promptly appointed Stan as the Wing Commander Flying. He had at that time flown some hundreds of operational hours and was by far the most experienced pilot I had. He was also Bader-trained and was an enthusiast for the "Finger four" formation, which I considered so essential for the fighting over Malta.

In his first flight in Hurricanes over the island he and the three other pilots of his section, shot down their own weight in Huns without loss. Unfortunately, two or three days afterwards his aircraft was badly damaged and he was unable to bale out because his hood was jammed, but he managed to crash land with only minor injuries near the aerodrome at Luqa.

With the arrival of the Spitfires I realised that our forces would have to be dispersed. The Hurricanes were accordingly moved to Halfar, as this was a smaller aerodrome and not so suitable for Spitfires. We decided the Spitfires should be split between Luqa (the bomber aerodrome) and Takali.

Fourteen Spitfires arrived and although the Maltese had never seen one in their lives before, in no time the whole island was cheering and shouting "Spitfires." Unfortunately, those aircraft required about 48 hours work before they were fit to fight, as the cannons had not been harmonised and in many cases, the wireless required complete checking. Before these Spitfires were ready to fight the Hun managed to damage and destroy several on the ground, so that our total fighter force to assist the convoy was soon down to eight Spitfires and 14 Hurricanes.

The morning of March 23, 1942 when the convoy arrived, it appeared the Lord was on our side. For the first time for weeks, the sky was overcast and the cloud base was 1500 feet. This meant that to attack the convoy the Hun would have to break cloud. It also meant that we could patrol and defend the convoy with the minimum of fighters.

The poor convoy and its Naval escort had a rough time the day before it was within range of our fighters and it was timed to be within 40 miles of the island at first light. Our fighter patrol picked up three merchant ships about 12 miles away at dawn, but a fourth, the Clan Campbell, was partly disabled and lagging about 30 miles behind. This was unfortunately sunk early in the day. The other three came steadily on and then the Huns started. Owing to the cloud cover they came singly or in pairs which just suited us. Our radar picked them up long before they got anywhere near and we could thus position our fighter patrol to intercept them as they broke cloud. Our boys had a grand day and during the afternoon we intercepted a message from one of the German bombers that said, "Cannot reach convoy because of intense fighter barrage."

The Grand Harbour guns, the Royal Navy ships and the merchant ships themselves, of course, put up a terrific barrage around which our fighters patrolled and through which they frequently flew when chasing the Hun.

Two ships, Talabot and Pampas, came into the Grand Harbour with the bastions around lined with cheering Maltese. The poor old Breconshire, an old friend which had run the gauntlet to Malta several times before, was disabled by a lucky bomb which went down her funnel and wrecked her engine room, so she had to anchor just outside awaiting a tow.

By nightfall, the weather had become worse and with the cross sea running it was hopeless to attempt to tow Breconshire into Grand Harbour, particularly as there was only one ancient paddle tug available.

That grand cruiser, HMS Penelope, affectionately known from this time on as HMS Pepperpot (because of all the gunshot and bomb-splinter holes in the hull) had come in with the convoy with all her ammunition expended and her decks littered with empty cartridge cases. In spite of the fact that none in the convoy had had any sleep for days, Captain Nichol, DSO, the Captain of the Penelope, undertook to take charge of the towing of Breconshire round to Kalafrana Bay.

The civilian crew of the one dockyard tug refused to undertake the job, so Captain Nichol manned the tug with a volunteer crew from his own ship. Our meteorological forecast promised thick low cloud and conditions generally unfavourable for a night attack. In spite of this the civilian stevedores refused to unload the ships that night. Volunteers from the Navy, Army and Air Force had already come forward for the job, but were rejected by the "powers that were," we were told. Not a hatch cover was removed from the two ships that night.

The Pampas and the Talabot escaped any serious damage for two days in which vital cargoes should have been unloaded and then the next day were both sunk in harbour when the German bombers and fighters swamped our fighter defences in clear weather. The same day, Captain Nichol and his stout volunteer crew towed Breconshire round to Kalafrana Bay, a magnificent piece of seamanship, because she could not be steered. Later that day (March 26) poor old Breconshire was also sunk in shallow water in Kalafrana Bay.

A considerable amount of cargo was eventually salved from all these ships, in fact, when I left Malta at the end of July, oil fuel and stores were still being taken off the Breconshire.

The loss of this convoy in harbour, after all the blood and sweat it had taken to get it in made us realise that we really had to tighten our belts. All our stores of food, ammunition and petrol were becoming dangerously low. All Military Transport had to be withdrawn from the services, except for transporting essential stores, rations and petrol.

The pilots had no transport whatever and had to toil up a long hill to their billets carrying their parachutes after a strenuous day's fighting. It made us all rather sick, however to see that the civilian labourers, who were being paid danger money to fill in bomb holes, always arrived in motor buses and refused to come to the aerodromes at all unless these buses stood by to drive them away as soon as the siren sounded. The work they put in was negligible, so much so that the AOC asked the GOC, Major General Beake, VC, for help. The GOC promptly allotted an infantry brigade, one battalion per aerodrome. These soldiers were magnificent. They took on the job of arming, refuelling, filling bomb holes, constructing pens and generally were indispensable. In fact we could not have flown without their help. The co-operation the whole time between the Navy, Army and Air Force was first class.

The Malta Police, the Malta Artillery and the King's Own Malta Rifles were also beyond praise and I quite believe that the civilian labourers would have shown up better if a firmer hand had been taken with them.

Not long after this our serviceability got so low again, that we had to stop flying and "take" the attacks for days, in order to make our aircraft serviceable. We, literally, could not put four Spitfires or Hurricanes into the air.

Just about this time, through not having been out of my clothes for over a fortnight, I collected some strange bug which developed into blood poisoning. However, the Takali doctor, Squadron Leader Squires, dosed me with large quantities of M and B and, apart from being delirous one night and apparently controlling thousands of fighters from the ramparts of Rabat, outside my billet, I recovered slowly. I was sent to St Paul's Bay as soon as I was fit to move and thereafter every 48 hours for a fortnight I worried the doctor to let me get back. Doctor Squires was an interesting character. He was decorated by the Serbians in the last war. Between wars, he ran a very lucrative general practice in the south of England. Then he went to Greece as Squadron Medical Officer and brought back the ground crews of his Squadron from there, then took them to Crete and was lucky enough to escape from there. Not satisfied with this he came by submarine from Alexandria to Malta to carry on the job. About this time we managed to fox the Hun in no mean fashion. We had a radio listening service and so we knew, had the Hun. This meant that any orders or messages given on the RT in plain language could be translated by either side as soon as they were given.

On one of the days when we had no fighters to send off, three or four of my fighter boys had come in the Operations Room to see me, when our radar gave us warning of considerable enemy activity over Sicily. I suddenly decided to try a little "Humgufery," ie try to make use of the Hun's listening service, so I told one of the fighter pilots ("Buck" MacNair, a Canadian who had an unmistakeable voice, with a typical Canadian accent) to go to the "stand by" RT cabin and answer all my instructions on the RT exactly as if he were leading a squadron in the air.

The "stand by" RT channel was an ordinary battery-operated aircraft transmitter and receiver which we kept available in case the main transmitter was knocked out.

The Hun raid developed into a force of about 12 bombers, escorted by roughly 30 ME 109's. I transmitted orders just as though we had a squadron of fighters in the air and "Buck" played up magnificently from the "stand by" cabin, answering me exactly as he had done so many times when actually fighting the Hun.

Very shortly, our listening service reported that the German control in Sicily was reacting and warning the ME 109's of British Spitfires. With calls of "Achtung Schpitfeuer" over the radio, the Hun fighters themselves got the "twitch" to such an extent that two of them enthusiastically shot each other down about 10 miles out to sea. They were seen to hit the sea by our AA gunners, so on this evidence I put in a claim for "Pilot Officer Humgufery - two ME 109's destroyed."

Early in February, two old friends of mine, Teddy Daniel and Peter Oakes who had served with me at Tangmere in No 219 Squadron, landed in two Beaufighters on their way to the Middle East. They were delayed in Malta for 48 hours and after seeing the night raids on the island, they decided that it was the Night Fighter Pilot's Paradise. They promptly rang me on the telephone and asked to stay. As it happened, the squadron they were joining in the Middle East had already been asked to supply four Beaufighters for the defence of Malta. I told them to deliver their aircraft to their Squadron, get them properly equipped for night fighting, (they were stripped of a lot of essential equipment for the ferry trip) and apply to come back. Sure enough they were back with two more crews within four days.

Malta was now the proud owner of four Beaufighters, which very quickly began to take toll of the night raiders to such an extent that a larger and larger percentage of bombs was dropped in the sea as time went on.

At this time the only way of getting aircraft to the Middle East meant ferrying them from England, with Gibraltar and Malta as refuelling bases. The reinforcement aircraft, largely Wellingtons, would pass the Narrows, between Tunis and Sicily after dark, then land at Luqa, refuel and take off again before first light for Egypt.

As they usually had very little reserve petrol left by the time they reached Malta, they had to be brought in to land at once and frequently this meant landing in the middle of a raid. The scheme we devised was as follows. The ferry pilots were briefed at Gibraltar to cross the coast of Malta below 3000 feet, between certain limits which avoided the Grand Harbour barrage. The guns around Luqa aerodrome were given freedom of fire between 3000 feet and 12,000 feet. The searchlights put up a cone over Luqa so that the enemy's aim was completely dazzled; the barrage made him unwilling to come below about 13,000 feet and the Beaufighters had freedom of action above the top limit of the barrage. In the meantime, if an aircraft wanted to land, all landing lights and runway lights were put on, including the Flood Light and the delivery pilot came in below the barrage.

It is amazing that I never heard of a single aircraft being hit by our barrage, in spite of the fact that many must have flown through a stream of shells, although they were below the bursts.

This was rather a hectic time for the delivery pilots and crews, who were, in the main "sprogs," ie newly-trained crews who had not had any operational experience.

It was found necessary to arrange for relief crews to take the aircraft on from Malta, so that the crew who arrived one night would turn the aircraft over to another who took it to Egypt. The first crew then rested for 24 hours and took another aircraft the next night. We did not dare to keep an unnecessary aeroplane on the ground during the day. We had lost too many that way from day bombing. The German day fighters were too numerous for us to risk flying unescorted bombers in or out of the island by day.

The Beaufighters started to pay a dividend almost immediately, although we were handicapped from the start by the lack of spares and trained ground crews. To begin with, we had no one on the ground staff side who had ever maintained a Beaufighter before; we also lacked the proper toolkits. In spite of this, thanks to the initiative of the pilots and observers, plus that of the Command Engineer and Armament Officers, we maintained a surprisingly high state of serviceability.

On Safi Strip (a taxi track connecting Luqa and Hal Far aerodromes), there was what was commonly known as the "Boneyard." This contained the burnt-out and badly damaged heavy aircraft that had been hit on the ground by day. This produced many spares for our Beaufighters, because there were several coastal Beaufighter wrecks in it, that had been hit on the ground when they were refuelling after a successful dawn attack on Sicilian aerodromes in 1941. I am afraid, however, that the Maintenance Schedules governing the inspection of aircraft were not adhered to. We hadn't a copy of one on the island anyway. The precious Beaufighters were dispersed by day, usually at Takali as that aerodrome had more room for them and they were operated at night from Luqa as they had better night landing facilities and concrete runways there.

Before this first Beaufighter team left the island for a rest about June, Teddy Daniel distinguished himself by shooting down three Italian bombers in one sortie and the four crews between them destroyed, at least 12 night raiders and had many more "probables" and "damaged" to their credit. At the end of May or the beginning of June they were relieved by six more crews from 89 Squadron in the Middle East. These did equally well, notably, Flight Lieutenant "Moose" Fumerton DFC, who destroyed four night bombers in his first two nights in the island.

"Moose" was a big, loose-boned Canadian who never used an unnecessary word. (He finished the war as the leading RCAF night-fighter pilot with 14 confirmed kills.) The total bag of this squadron over Malta from mid February to mid July was something like 37 destroyed at night, including two that were "frightened" down! These fell to "Moose" later on and they were both JU87 dive bombers, which the Hun was then using at night. They both did the same thing. The enemy rear gunners saw our fighter before the latter opened fire and the Hun took avoiding action by diving. This they both did with such enthusiasm that one went into the sea and the other into the island, near St Paul's Bay. "Moose" never fired a shot.

The whole night defence of Malta was an outstanding example of team work, between guns, searchlights and aircraft. The searchlight and RA personnel were very largely Maltese and they were beyond praise. These chaps had been "taking it" and "giving it back" the whole time and they stood up to the job magnificently.

Another very fine body of men were the Malta Police, who were 100 per cent Maltese. The discipline and courage of these men was marvellous and no job was beyond them. They cleared the debris from the streets, rescued the buried and injured, built aircraft shelter pens, filled in bomb holes in our aerodromes all in addition to their police duties. They were the absolute backbone of all the Malta ARP and NFS services.

We had two Matilda tanks from the Royal Tank Regiment working with the Luqa RAF Crash Party and these were used principally to tow wrecked aircraft and clear the runways after a raid. In charge of one of the tanks was Bob McManus, a tenacious little Corporal from Dundee, Scotland. On one particular occasion, a Beaufort crash-landed with a live torpedo still aboard and McManus shooed everyone away and then went out with his tank and towed the Beaufort and torpedo onto the grass so that incoming aircraft could again use the runway. He should really have waited until the torpedo was disarmed but simply said "I couldna leave it out there but I'm glad it didna go bang on me." Some while later, one of the Matilda tanks was seen driving a little erratically around the perimeter of Luqa for no apparent reason. Jumbo Gracie investigated and found one of our Australian pilots at the controls with Bob McManus coaching him. "He's an Aussie," McManus explained. "He couldna go back home without having a drive of a Matilda could he?" Jumbo was intending to hand out a reprimand but could only laugh.

While I was convalescing early in April, the C in C Middle East, Air Chief Marshal Sir Arthur Tedder, GCB, visited the island. The only Officers Mess that was fit to entertain guests at that time was the Fighter Mess at Takali. This was in a lovely old

Baron's Palace that overlooked almost the whole of the island from the Battlements of Rabat (or Citta Vechia, as the old capital used to be called).

Air Vice Marshal Lloyd asked the C in C to lunch there to meet as many of the pilots as possible. Sir Arthur Tedder was delightful and charming as always, but at the same time one realised that in his quiet way he did not miss a thing.

We were all chatting on the balcony which overlooked Takali aerodrome, but also commanded a view from St Paul's Bay, past Sliema to Valetta and round to Luqa aerodrome. Hal Far aerodrome was hidden by a slight hill, but aircraft taking off from there were visible from the balcony almost as soon as they were airborne. We had not been on the balcony very long when the sirens went and shortly afterwards AA bursts appeared south of the island. Eventually we spotted the Huns, 18 to 20 JU88's with a fighter escort and the target was Luqa aerodrome. While the attack was developing, Sir Arthur Tedder produced a small sketch book and rapidly sketched an impression of the whole scene.

Incidentally this was one of the days when we had no fighters to put into the air and we just had to sit and "take it" leaving everything to the stout-hearted gunners.

Before the smoke from the bombers had subsided over Luqa some low- flying ME109's started beating up Takali. One saucy blighter first fired a burst into a damaged Spitfire in a shelter pen about 400 yards away and then flew along the valley below us, firing an occasional burst.

He was actually below us and we were looking down into his cockpit as he went past not more than 20 yards away.

Sir Arthur asked if we had wired Kesselring to lay on a show especially for his benefit.

As our next reinforcement of Spitfires was dependent on aircraft carrier transport to within flying distance of the island, the C in C promised us an additional squadron of his precious Hurricanes. These were flown over from Egypt a few days after he returned to the Middle East and they did first-class work against the enemy.

Just about this time, the Hun delivered a mass attack on Takali at dusk. I had released the day fighters a little before dusk and had just arrived at the mess at Rabat when the first wave of bombers came in. This wave was about 12 strong and laid a pattern of incendiary bombs right on the domestic and administration site of the aerodrome.

The succeeding waves, about 150 aircraft in all, dropped their high explosives on these incendiaries. The incendiaries were obviously dropped as an aiming mark, because there was very little to burn in the island and I think the Hun sent his "first team" to drop these, while the less experienced ones used them as target markers. The bombing was certainly good and it took nearly an hour for the smoke and dust to die down. We thought that there must be frightful casualties because a lot of ground crews had been working late and more were in their barrack huts. Jack Satchell organised all the pilots into search parties and stretcher parties and these toured the whole area with the result that they found one killed and four wounded. Ever since, I have been a firm believer in slit trenches.

The poor chaps on the aerodrome had lost most of their kit and needless to say were very badly shaken. We collected them all as soon as possible and put them in tents about two miles away. In the meantime, the aerodrome was a mass of bomb holes and there were unexploded bombs to be dealt with all over the place.

The few serviceable aircraft were flown off to the other two aerodromes next day and in 48 hours the aerodrome was in full use again, but we decided not to repair the damaged buildings.

One building we were delighted to see could not be repaired and we had great joy in blowing it up ourselves. This was a quaint and rather opulent looking house on the edge of Takali that we called the "Mad House." It was reputed to have been built by an eccentric who was afraid of having his horse stolen. He accordingly had a stable built in a turret on the roof approached only by a winding stair that not even a goat could have climbed. I cannot vouch for this, but the story caused us to christen it the "Mad House." We were glad to see it go though, because not only was it a "flying obstruction" but we always felt that it was such a prominent landmark that it neutralised all our miserable attempts to camouflage the rest of Takali.

This heavy raid taxed our signals staff very heavily because afterwards there was not a single land line serviceable. There was no spare telephone cable in the island, so they had to "mend and make do."

The Takali Station Signals Officer set a marvellous example at all times, but he excelled himself on this occasion. He was a little chap who looked (and I believe was) terribly ill, but he never let up and was never discouraged. His standard reply was "We'll fix it, sir!" and he did.

I remember one night, about 3am, a dirty dishevelled figure appearing at the window of my bedroom which overlooked the battlements at Rabat. Apparently my telephone had been out of order and he had traced the wire himself by climbing in the dark around the battlements. I asked why he did not give the job to a linesman and he said "Oh, the boys are very tired, sir, so I thought I'd let them rest. They'll have a hard day tomorrow." Just another example of the enthusiam that kept Malta going. Also he knew that unless my telephone was in order I should have to sleep in the Operations Room, because I had to be on call at all times.

After the arrival of our first 14 Spitfires in a non-operational condition, ie with the cannons unharmonised and with many of the wireless sets unserviceable, we decided that something drastic must be done to ensure that the next consignment arrived fit to fight as soon as they were refuelled.

I suppose it was hard to people at home to visualise the conditions in Malta. When a new Spitfire (or any other type of aircraft for that matter) is delivered to a squadron in

England, the Squadron fitters, riggers, armourers, electricians and wireless mechanics fall on it and check all their own items thoroughly.

This means that the guns have to be lined up with the sight, then fired on the butts which meant in the case of the cannons that at least 200 rounds were necessary to "run them in".

The wireless connections have to be checked, correct crystals fitted and so on, so there is a good 48-hours work to be done on each aircraft before it is ready for operations.

This is easy in England, but in Malta the delay proved fatal. No adequate air tests could be made because every flight in those days was in the face of the enemy.

Added to this we were becoming short of petrol and ammunition and we had to conserve both for use against the enemy.

The AOC therefore sent Squadron Leader "Jumbo" Gracie home by air to make certain that the next consignment of reinforcements were completely operational before they were embarked in the aircraft carriers. Unfortunately there was too little time between his arrival in England and the embarkation date, although everyone worked night and day in their efforts to help. The result was that many of the next batch arrived in the same non-operational state as before, as for many reasons the sailing date of the carriers could not be put back.

However, the great day arrived, April 20, 1942, when our new Spitfires were expected.

Naturally, we had every available Hurricane and Spitfire ready to cover their landing. This they did so effectively that none of the new aircraft were lost from enemy action when within range of our fighter cover.

Each flight was briefed to call me on a certain wireless channel when within range and I then detailed them to land at the appropriate aerodrome. We split these Spitfires between Luqa and Takali, in order to facilitate their refuelling and rearming.

An experienced Malta pilot was waiting to take over each Spitfire, because the pilots who had flown them in would be tired and they did not know the "form."

Long after the others had landed and we were trying to "count noses" I suddenly heard a rather panicky voice call: "Gondar, Gondar, give me homing," repeated several times. We got a quick bearing and found that the man in trouble was north of the island. I told him to steer 180 degrees and then a lone Spitfire was sighted low coming in from the north.

He flew straight across the island and disappeared to the south. I kept calling him with no result until I suddenly heard again: "Gondar, Gondar, give me homing." This time I told him to steer 360 degrees and he eventually arrived almost out of petrol and crash landed.

Apparently he was very inexperienced and having lagged behind his leader did not dare to open his throttle to catch up because he was afraid of wasting petrol.

He first sighted Sicily and thought it was Italy, steered south and then when I gave him 180 degrees to steer he thought Malta was Sicily and also thought that my voice was a Hun controller trying to spoof him. I'm afraid I sent that boy back as being too inexperienced and too expensive! Incidentally he turned up again with the next batch in May and I had to send him back again. He was certainly keen!

One pilot who was supposed to arrive with 603 Squadron did not turn up on Malta. This was an American, Sergeant WB Walcott who was later listed as "defecting." He had decided the Malta was no place for him and flown to Algeria after leaving USS Wasp . As he was not a British subject he could not be called a deserter.

The new Spitfires were two complete Squadrons. 601 was commanded by Squadron Leader Bisdee DFC and Squadron Leader Lord David Douglas Hamilton lead 603 Squadron. I naturally had to share the aircraft out amongst the other Squadrons. My Squadron Commanders were now (249) Stanley Grant, DFC; (126) "Admiral" Barton, DFC; (603) David Douglas Hamilton; (601) John Bisdee, DFC; (185) "Laurie" Lawrence and Squadron Leader Dafforn (229).

The latter two squadrons still had Hurricanes and they used to call the Spitfire pilots the "Glamour Boys!" The new pilots were in the main quite experienced and were a first-class keen bunch of fellows, which made it all the harder for me to send those of them back who had had no operational experience before they left England.

It was the only thing to do though, because we knew only too well that an inexperienced pilot is not only a danger to himself but a liability to his leader. In Malta if they did not learn quickly they were dead. It was very seldom that the Hun allowed one of our pilots to make more than one mistake.

That evening the AOC met all the new arrivals and had a yarn with them in the mess at Rabat. It was just dark I remember and as he wound up by saying "You have come to a great little island and one of these days people will talk about Malta and you will be proud to say, I was there," when the Hun dropped a stick of bombs unpleasantly close. We could hear the whistle of the bombs and then the explosions as each of the "stick" approached until finally the last of the stick whistled over the roof and exploded at the bottom of the battlements. The AOC didn't bat an eyelid but I don't mind admitting that most of us wanted to get under something. I looked round the startled faces and they were all looking at the AOC who just repeated softly "You will say, I was there." They realised what a man they had to lead them. After the AOC had left we sat around on the balcony and I got to know them all and I don't think I have ever been bombarded so with questions. I loved those evenings with the boys, no one who has not met them on their own ground, so to speak, can realise what a splendid mixture they are, of youth and commonsense, of naivete and guts, of humour and gaiety and (sometimes) sadness, of sentiment (well hidden) and hard boiledness (usually assumed), of thoughtfulness and irresponsibility. In fact, they are the cream of the earth.

One of the most important jobs in Malta, particularly during the "lean" times when we were so short of aircraft, was Photo Reconnaissance. On the information we had about strength and disposition of the enemy's ships and aircraft depended the use to which we put our miserably small force of bombers and torpedo bombers. Early in 1942 we only had one Beaufighter fitted for this work. The aircraft was stripped of practically everything, guns, ammunition etc, in fact, she carried nothing but a pilot, an observer and a camera.

The pilot was Squadron Leader (later Wing Commander) Adrian Warburton, DSO, DFC, a most tenacious and gallant officer. He had the reputation of always "delivering the goods." He would fly off low in a southerly direction to fox the enemy radar, make a wide sweep round and eventually appear over Naples or Taranto and take his photographs and then come haring back, usually at sea level, because low down, his stripped Beaufighter was as fast, if not faster than the ME 109's. If low cloud prevented him from taking photographs he would come below cloud for a few seconds over his objective and bring back an accurate sketch of the disposition and numbers of the shipping or aircraft we wanted to know about. He was, of course, chased back many times by enemy fighters and we frequently had to send out Hurricanes or Spitfires to chase off his pursuers and enable him to land.

Warburton's ability to "deliver the goods" was legendary, the ground crews adored him and the Maltese almost made him a saint.

Thanks to the information he brought back we knew when the Hun was assembling a convoy, moving the Italian Fleet to Taranto, reinforcing his Sicilian airfields or building new airfields. Later Warburton was reinforced by two very stout reconnaissance pilots with their photo reco Spitfires. They also did invaluable work and were both decorated.

Whenever our photo reconnaisance showed us suitable targets we would try to "prang" them at night with Swordfish and Albacores of the Fleet Air Arm based on Hal Far and with Wellingtons from Luqa.

The "Stringbags" as we affectionately called the Swordfish and Albacores did a wonderful job from Malta. They were old and slow but very manoeuvrable, their top speed was about 100 knots, but their pilots loved them. One day, I hope that someone with all the facts at his disposal, will write the "Saga of the Stringbag." They have operated from every theatre of war, from the decks of aircraft carriers, from landing strips in the desert; they have dive bombed tanks and bridges at Dunkirk, torpedoed the Bismark, attacked U boats with depth charges and shadowed enemy shipping.

In the early days in 1942, there was, we found, no future in keeping night bombers in Malta because they were invariably damaged on the ground in the day raids.

When worthwhile targets were available therefore, Wellingtons were sent over from Middle East, refuelled, bombed up and briefed in Malta and they returned to Middle East as soon as possible after completing their mission. Even so, many Wellington "bones" were left behind in our "graveyard" on Safi Strip. The Swordfish and Albacore Squadron were out searching for enemy shipping along Rommel's supply lanes to Africa almost every night and although I never remember them having more than four serviceable, they put up a marvellous show.

Some incredibly gallant flights were put up by the Stringbag pilots and crews and we, in the RAF felt it very deeply when we learnt that an "immediate award" of a decoration was very seldom given in the Fleet Air Arm. I certainly never knew of one. This meant that after one of the chaps had put up a good show, he would be recommended by the AOC for a decoration but the actual award never came through in less than six months because it had to go through normal Naval channels before being approved.

The value of the decoration was therefore reduced considerably, because when it did arrive, either the recipient had left the island or all his friends had and no one knew what it was all about. It means a lot when a pilot gets a "gong" if the others who were with him when he earned it can help him to celebrate the occasion.

Halfar aerodrome where the Stringbags and Hurricanes operated from, had very pleasant memories for me. I had of course flown from it in 1927 when the hangars were canvas and our offices, flight stores and workshops were improvised from aircraft packing cases.

Then in 1928 and 29 very fine barrack block hangars and messes were built, in fact, I think the Halfar Officers' Mess was one of the most comfortable I have ever been in. It made me sad, therefore, to see how the place was knocked about, not a barrack block or building was habitable and we had our meals in the only room left standing in the officers' mess the kitchen.

Halfar was the nearest aerodrome to the coast, the south west boundary was only about 200 yards from the edge of the cliffs. This made it the easiest and least expensive aerodrome to attack from the enemy's point of view they could nip in from the sea, drop their bombs and break out to sea again without having to fly over the island for more than a minute or so.

I have seen JU88's and JU87's release their bombs before crossing the coast and the bombs with their forward speed at the time of release have reached Halfar. With the arrival of our reinforcement Spitfires on May 9 the Hun became very wary, sending over only a small number of bombers with 50 or more fighter escort. The latter flew very high and began to show a marked reluctance to "mix it"; most of the fighting took place at 20,000 feet and for several days the island was free from raids.

On May 12, Pilot Officer Bert Mitchell, from Marlborough, N.Z., flying with 603 Squadron became detached from his fellow pilots but took on a formation of more than a dozen 109's. He was witnessed shooting at one aircraft but then turned away with a German firing on his tail. He was seen to go into a long dive and just before he hit the water he called me on the RT. "So long Woody, I've had it." There were several others who heard those final words and they all quote him as saying "Goodbye Woody". I prefer my memory.

Two convoys were expected about June 14 and every conceivable preparation was made to receive them; dispersed dumps were prepared all over the island for petrol, food, ammunition stores etc and all available transport was mobilised. In the meantime, our stocks of petrol were so low that no training flying could be allowed and the only transport allowed was that required for moving essential food stores and equipment and the buses that stood by to take the civilian labourers to safety when the siren went.

On June 13 we were all "tee'd" up and prepared to receive the convoys at first light the following day, when we heard that the one coming from the East (and the larger one) had been attacked so heavily that the Naval escort and most of the convoy had run out of ammunition and so they had to turn back. However, the convoy from the West was on its way, so we were keeping it covered by a continuous escort of coastal command Beaufighters from the time it was off Tunis.

The Beaufighters were sent to the island especially for this job from the Middle East and they covered the convoy from the time it was within 400 miles of Malta. We only had 12 Beaufighters to carry out this job, so we sent them off in pairs. Each pair did 60 minutes over the convoy when it was at extreme range and was relieved after 45 minutes by the next pair. This meant that for 15 minutes in every hour there were four Beaufighters patrolling. This was a small enough fighter cover in all conscience, but it paid handsomely.

We mustered all the long-range Spitfire tanks that we could and arranged to cover the convoy with four Spitfires continuously from the time it was within 120 miles of the island. At this extreme range our Spitfires only had enough petrol to allow for 30 minutes fighting and the return to base. We could only raise 48 long-range Spitfire tanks so "Brookie" (Wing Commander Brooks, who had become Command Engineer Officer) provided a tank which we called a "Brookie special." This was a 45 gallon Hurricane tank which he modified to fit a Spitfire. It was very bulky and took off a lot of speed but the "Brookie specials" filled the gap admirably.

At about 11am on June 14, although the convoy was still 160 miles away we had run out of serviceable Beaufighters so I had to send off four Spitfires and arrange to relieve them every 20 minutes. These Spitfire boys were grand, they shot down a claimed 60 Huns that day and from the time they established their "umbrella" over the convoy the Huns never got in close enough to get even a "near miss."

During the afternoon, one of our aircraft reported that two heavy Italian cruisers, two light cruisers and several destroyers were closing the convoy from the north west. The gallant Cairo (she was only armed with 4.7 guns and her primary role was that of an AA cruiser) and four destroyers went to intercept. The only striking force we had in Malta consisted of three "Stringbags" and these three were ordered off to torpedo the enemy ships who were approximately 160 miles away. We could only give them Spitfire escort for 100 miles because our long range tanks and even our "Brookie specials" were all used up.

It must be understood that this 100 miles escort meant one hours flying in a Stringbag, therefore to escort them, the Spitfires had to fly in figures of eight because of their superior speed. This only left the Spitfires half an hour's petrol to return to the island.

The first four Spitfires escorted the Stringbags to a point just north west of Pantellaria and then had to come back, so thereafter I sent further relays of four every 15 minutes to try to pick up their charges on the way back.

The story of these Stringbags is an epic. After they left their escort, they were attacked several times by ME109's and two of the Stringbags shot down a Hun each.

Their methods of bagging Huns were identical. When the observer saw the 109 coming in to attack he would tell his pilot something like this "109 coming in starboard quarter from above" the pilot would then throttle back, pull up the nose of his aircraft until it was practically stalled. This unexpected reduction of speed of an already slow aircraft caused the Hun to overshoot and present a belly shot to the pilots, who in each case shot down their Hun as he overshot the Swordfish, using the single front Vickers gun.

On reaching the enemy ships the Swordfish dropped their torpedoes and scored hits on two cruisers.

One Swordfish was never seen again, but the remaining two decided that they would fox the Hun by flying almost to Sicily at sea level and then south to Malta.

Our relays of Spitfire escorts, of course, saw nothing of them. The next thing I knew was that an unidentified plot appeared about six miles north of Malta, moving very slowly. I sent four Spitfires to investigate and on sighting the Swordfish, the leader came through to me on the RT "It's all right Woody, they are Elephants we'll bring them in." (Elephant was one of our pet names for Swordfish).

The Hun in Sicily who, we knew could listen in to our RT, heard this and our listening service heard the Hun controller pass to his fighters "Achtung! Achtung! There are Halifax's about!" These gallant Swordfish did their job well. The result of this forlorn hope (I felt that I was ordering them to certain death when I passed the instructions to the Squadron over the telephone), was that the Italian ships once again turned tail and never delivered an attack on the convoy.

About an hour before dark the convoy and our fighter cover were near enough to be plotted on our operations table, so I automatically took over control of the Spitfires. The controller in the Fighter Directing Ship, one "Peto" Bennett, told me afterwards that this happened just in time, because thanks to heavy gunfire and "near misses," the radio telephone and radar of the ship was almost out of action and he was finding controlling impossible.

Just before sunset two large plots appeared "on the board" over Sicily flying in a westerly direction. I judged that they would circle round and try to attack the convoy by keeping as they thought out of range of our fighters. I "scrambled" 249 Squadron led by Laddie Lucas and gave him a course to intercept the Huns about 30 miles north of the convoy. When they were converging on the Huns about 10 miles away I told Laddie "You should see them now, ahead of you and to starboard and a little below all Big Jobs." There was a pause then a whoop of "Tally Ho! There they are, in we go" and in the boys went. They went into these JU88's head on and the Huns all scattered and ran for home. The boys only claimed two destroyed and five or six damaged as far as I can remember, but I should be very surprised if more than half of the 18 JU88's escaped without damage.

Laddie and his boys had to land in the dark, but they brought it off safely.

This was the end of a glorious day the boys had destroyed or damaged at least 60 Germans and although only two merchant ships reached Malta, what they brought was vital and being unloaded that night. The safe arrival of even that small part of the convoy from the West eased matters considerably, but we were by no means out of the wood.

Lord Gort, the new Governor, exhorted us all to tighten our belts because rationing was still necessary, in fact, so short were we of paraffin for instance, that communal cooking had to be organised. At the end of June no meals could be obtained in restaurants or clubs, people had to bring sandwiches (if they could get them) to their work, communal kitchens were set up where housewives could take their rations to cook; thin people became thinner and fat people were reduced to normal.

Poor Malta was looking very much worn by this time, although she was still extremely serviceable. The Hun, true to form, had been very systematic in his attacks and his plan was obvious, but in every stage he did not quite achieve his object. He started by bombing aerodromes but we always got them serviceable again. He destroyed and damaged a lot of aircraft on the ground, but we always managed to repair enough to continue the fight.

He attacked AA gun sites and inflicted many casualties, but never enough to affect our gun defences. He then attacked the dockyard and the submarine base and caused a lot of damage, but he never laid out the power station which was in the dockyard. The submarines had to submerge in the base by day for a while, but they still operated from Malta.

Next the Hun attacked communications, which, of course only consisted of roads. The two roads leading out of Valetta were each hit, but only half destroyed, so they were never entirely unusable. The water, gas and electric mains which were cut, were very soon repaired. Finally he went for our stores of wheat and any other stores that he thought he knew about. The ancient granaries in Floriana were plastered with bombs, but, as far as I know, not a bushel of wheat was destroyed. One or two flour mills were badly damaged, but there were always enough mills working to just feed the population.

The granaries were hewn out of the solid rock during the Turks siege of the island. They were bottle shaped inside and were sealed at the top with a sort of stone stopper. I believe one or two of these stone stoppers were cracked but that was all. Of course, during all this bombing, much irreparable damage was done, chiefly to ancient buildings such as churches and Knights' palaces. I do not believe a single church in the island escaped damage.

Luckily, practically no wood is used in the construction of Maltese buildings, so there was hardly any fire risk.

The Opera House which was comparatively modern, was completely destroyed and more than half the buildings in Valetta, Sliema and most of those in the Three Cities around the Dockyard were damaged or destroyed. But life went on and we managed to keep cheerful in spite of everything.

After the arrival of our new Spitfires in May, the enemy raids diminished and for some days ceased altogether, then Kesselring started sending over his second team, the Italians. The first time we saw them we could hardly believe our eyes, five three engined bombers flying in a perfect Vic formation at about 25,000 feet. Unfortunately, on this occasion, they were sent over just after a Hun raid and all our fighters were either re fuelling or just coming in to land short of fuel or ammunition. However, the bombing was so poor as to be almost funny.

The Italians sent over from three to five bombers escorted by Macchi's and sometimes ME109's at odd intervals during May and June and we usually shot down at least one and damaged others until early in July, we shot down all three bombers in one raid. After that the Italians never came alone or in force again.

From April onwards the enemy employed mixed forces of Italian and German fighters, the Italians used at first Macchi 202's and later we encountered some Regiani 200's. The latter were small and beautifully streamlined and finished (we got one almost intact after the pilot had made a very clever wheels up landing on the island). They appeared to be very manoeuvrable but our Spitfires could "see them off."

One amazing thing we discovered was that the Regiani had no armoured windscreen and only a small piece of armour at the pilot's back, so it was very vulnerable.

One of the outstanding Spitfire pilots of the island, Flight Lieutenant "Johnnie" Plagis DFC, a Rhodesian by birth, Greek by parentage and endowed by nature with a most aggressive spirit, had, as it turned out afterwards, a most amusing battle with six Italian fighters.

He had chased a JU88 almost to Sicily before he shot it down and was returning to Malta without ammunition when he ran into six Italian fighters. He could do nothing, but continue to turn into the Italians attack until in despair he prepared to ram one. The Italian was so frightened that he dived his aircraft into the sea in his anxiety to escape. The other five decided there was no future in that kind of fighting and beetled off home.

The next thing I heard was Johnnie calling me up saying "Give me a homing, Woody, I'm nearly out of gravy." I gave him his course with great relief and sent a pair of Spitfires out to meet him in case his petrol ran out before he reached Malta, so that we would at least know where to send the rescue boat if he had to bale out. For a few dreadful minutes I feared we had lost Johnnie, but he made his base safely.

Johnnie was one of our top scorers in the island; very shortly after he arrived he shot down four Huns in one sortie. He, with Laddie Lucas, Stanley Grant, Raol Daddo Langlois, "Buck" McNair, "Buck" Buchanan, Geoff West and Ronnie West, Paul Brennan and Ray Hesselyn, came out with Stan Turner and they were the backbone of our team of Spitfire pilots.

With the May contingent of Spitfires we had some American pilots; all the Americans were keen to be in the same squadron so "Admiral" Barton, the CO of 126 Squadron, put them all into B Flight of his squadron. These Americans were most capable fighters and delightful and amusing messmates. The Flight Commander, Bob Tilley, came from the "Deep South" and it took me some days to understand his southern drawl as it came over the RT.

There were two inseparable Americans, little Jimmy Peck and big "Mac" McLeod, who had been trained together in America and had stuck together ever since. Jimmy was small and wiry and quick as a terrier and aged 19; Mac was big and hefty, rather slow, always good humoured and aged about 26. Apparently when they were learning to fly in America, Mac was senior pupil and he put all pubs and saloons out of bounds to Jimmy because of his extreme youth.

In Malta, the youthful Jimmy was promoted Flight Lieutenant and awarded a DFC (Mac had had to bale out and was put off flying for about a month). So Jimmy proceeded to get his own back on Mac for his out of bounds orders at training school. Their crosstalk was a joy to listen to and, of course they were really the firmest friends.

In their first fight together over Malta I vectored them on to two ME109 fighters carrying bombs approaching the island and they intercepted them just off the island and "bounced" the Huns beautifully. They were very excited, Mac said "You take the left, I'll take the right, Jimmy oh boy, ain't this grand!" and Mac shot down his. Jimmy's was a bit more difficult to finish off so Mac shouted "I got mine, Jimmy, have you shot yours down yet or do you want me to come and show you how?" Jimmy replied "You big . . . !" followed by a lot of unprintable things and shot down his Hun.

From then until they landed this irrepressible pair were back chatting to each other to such an extent that I felt bound to ring them up and read them a lecture about unnecessary chatter over the RT. However, Mac rang me first and said "Say, I want to speak to that guy Woody." I quickly said "Speaking." Mac said "Say, Woody, I want to stand you a drink, what's your real name and rank? That was a peach of an interception," and more enthusiastic stuff on the same lines. When I could get a word in edgeways I told him my name and rank and he dropped the telephone like a hot coal and said to Jimmy "Gees, why didn't you tell me, why didn't ya stop me?" and so on. That evening a very sheepish Mac came up and tried to apologise. I was so amused that I nearly forgot to read them the intended lecture. Needless to say we were great friends from then on.

By May 9, 1942, we had seven squadrons of fighters in the island, five of them being equipped with Spitfires and two with Hurricanes.

Although we were numerically not half as strong in fighters as the Hun, morally we had achieved air superiority. As I said before, the enemy bomber effort decreased considerably and the fighter escort increased while this escort flew very high and was very shy.

We had not been raided for several days so I decided that the time had come to start a little "Hun baiting" as we wanted to keep the enemy "on the hop," instead of allowing him to lick his wounds and repair his damaged aircraft.

I arranged that "Admiral" Barton should take four Spitfires and do a sweep at 25,000 feet over the German fighter airfield at Comiso to entice Hun fighters into the air. As soon as the "Admiral" reported that the Germans was reacting, I was to "scramble" two or more squadrons to deal with whatever was put up. When the "Admiral" was about half way to Sicily I had indications that a huge bomber force was assembling and their fighters were joining up over Comiso.

Over the RT, I told the "Admiral" "stick around where you are, there is some trade on it's way." Back came the "Admiral's" husky reply "OK." He never wasted words! He was beautifully placed to bounce the Hun because his section was 25,000 feet up sun and on the flank of the enemy's line of approach.

In the meantime, I scrambled two Squadrons of Spitfires who climbed straight up and intercepted the enemy about 25 miles north of the island. Our boys went right in and attacked, one squadron going for the bombers and one for the fighter escort.

Once the fight developed into a "mix up" there was a certain amount of excited chatter, dominated by Canadian and American voices.

The "Admiral" who was by now at 30,000 feet "up sun" of the fight chose a lull in the chatter to say huskily over the RT "Take it easy, boys, take it easy, there's one each apiece all round!" then led his section in and they shot down four Germans.

The effect of Admiral's transmission was immediate there was almost complete RT silence from then on! As far as I remember only two enemy bombers out of that raid of about 20 reached the island and they were so shaken that they hit nothing.

The battle and tactics that day were in fact a turning point as far as Stan, Laddie and most of our pilots were concerned. We were at last in a position to take the fight to the Germans on our own terms and attack the bombers before they arrived over their target. It was also a vindication of the offensive policy put forward by Douglas Bader back in the Battle of Britain days at Duxford. He had always wanted to be scrambled in time to intercept the German bombers as they left France. Of course, AVM Keith Park, within the month was refining the techniques and putting forward his own "Forward Interception Policy". But I feel quite strongly that it was back during the hard-pressed days of April and May (1942) that the Malta team under Hugh Lloyd had turned the tide and despite the convoy and supply difficulties had effectively won the battle for Malta. When they were so few in number as in the early months of the year, the tactic of taking the time to get our fighters at good height and up-sun was a very necessary one to give our out-numbered pilots a chance of a decent attack and more importantly, survival. To send a few aircraft to attack a superior formation from a position of disadvantage was to me similar to the Great War when infantry were made to advance across open land into the mouths of machine-guns. In Malta we were not likely to win a battle based on attrition and constant reinforcement. We had neither the men nor the equipment. And I hope we had more sense by now.

The Admiral was a great character and a magnificent leader albeit he was thought unorthodox. He was an old friend of mine I had taught him to "deck land" in aircraft carriers in 1936 when he was a Lieutenant R.N. He left the Navy because he found in the early days of the war he was doing more watch-keeping than flying. He then joined the RAF as a Flying Officer, was awarded the DFC in the Battle of Britain and got a "bar" to his DFC in Malta.

I sent him back to Gibraltar at the beginning of May with some other experienced Malta pilots to help lead in the reinforcements who were being flown to us from the aircraft carriers. These chaps had to wait a few days and stayed at the Rack Hotel in Gibraltar. They naturally and excusably arrived in a rather untidy condition because they had only been allowed to bring 45lb of kit from England in the first place. Thanks to losses from bombing and pilfering, my pilots had not even one decent suit of uniform and uniform was almost impossible to replace in the island. Until these fellows could buy more in Gibraltar their dress was "fancy" to say the least of it.

During their first dinner (which incidentally was the first decent meal they had eaten for weeks) an officious Wing Commander who had been living in fat ease and comfort in Gibraltar under almost peacetime conditions, sent a waiter to ask "Admiral" to report to him at his table and then, in public, handed him a "raspberry" for being improperly dressed.

As the "Admiral" humourously put it when he told me about the incident on his return "I was only wearing one khaki sock and one blue, khaki slacks, a blue tunic and scarf. It was all I had to wear and the blighter hadn't even got wings on his chest! It makes you think you know, sir!" I was furious, of course and I tried to locate the Wing Commander concerned when I passed through Gibraltar on my way home at the end of July, so that I could invite his criticism to my dress. It is perhaps as well that I did not meet him. I wonder why it is that people who have soft, comfortable, safe and (usually unimportant) jobs, become self complacent, critical, intolerant and full of their own importance.

"Admiral" Barton was one of my finest Squadron Commanders who was loved and respected by us all. His subsequent death in a flying accident in England was an irreparable loss to the Service.

Another fine officer and leader was Squadron Leader "Stan" Grant DFC. An ex Cranwell cadet who had a lot of experience of fighting over England and the Continent, he was given command of 249 Squadron almost as soon as he reached Malta. His fine leadership, his calm voice over the RT and his unfailing sense of humour, together with his sound commonsense contributed to his Squadron being the highest scorers in the island.

They celebrated their 100th victory over Malta before I left. Then there were two grand youngsters, Sergeants Paul Brennan and "Ray Hesselyn," an Australian and a New Zealander respectively, who wrote "Spitfires over Malta." I am glad to say that I recommended both for the commissions they obtained later they were grand fighters and most likeable characters.

Brennan and Hesselyn were "cobbers" and they were always fighting and in trouble generally together. They made a perfect team of two and developed into very fine leaders.

Brennan won the DFC and DFM. Both were Sergeant Pilots at this time and in the confines of Malta particularly, the distinction (and pay difference) between NCO and officer pilots was often a cause of uneccessary friction. I always felt that all pilots especially on a battlefield such as this, were more or less equal. We were fighting the same enemy in the same aircraft so it was ridiculous to have the old-fashioned British segregation of officers and men within Squadrons. Obviously, we needed flight and squadron commanders but each pilot was in fact in command of his ship and therefore should have been an officer. During the Battle of Britain, two of the highest-scoring allied pilots were Ginger Lacey and Joseph Franticek, both Sergeants.

One evening I walked into an "Officers Only" bar in Valetta to find Paul and Ray already in there drinking – they had been unable to find a decent place to relax and had put up fake officers tabs on their shoulders to gain admittance. They were horrified to see me of course, they were committing a Court Martial Offence in impersonating an officer. "Hello boys, good to see you," I said. "Let me buy you a drink." I bought them a whiskey apiece and gave it to them and said "Now you'd better drink up and scarper before anyone else recognises you!"

(I didn't tell them then, but I had already been party to recommending them both for commissions so it was only a matter of weeks before they could invite me back into the same bar for a drink.)

Paul was unfortunately killed in a landing collision with another Spitfire in Townsville, Australia on June 13, 1943. Ray was shot down over Beauvias on October 3, 1943 while flying with 222 squadron. He was shot down by a Fw190 and barely escaped his burning Spitfire. He was immediately taken prisoner and remained in Germany for the rest of the war although he escaped briefly on one occasion. He already had a DFM and Bar (from Malta) and was awarded the DFC 20 days after being shot down. He was liberated by the Russians in May 1945 and for his work in prison camps he was awarded the MBE in December 1945.

One promotion from Flight Sergeant to Pilot Officer was set up beautifully by Laddie Lucas. Jack Rae's promotion came through while he was in hospital recuperating from a leg wound and Laddie organised for an Army sergeant to go into the ward and order Jack to hand over all his clothes. Poor Jack was wondering what was going on and why he was being treated in such a fashion when fellow pilots arrived and wheeled his bed into the "officers" ward where a Pilot Officer's uniform was hanging up waiting for him.

What constantly impressed me was how young all these boys were (the "Admiral" was about the oldest at 26) the others were all in their early twenties and some were only in their teens. It made me feel dreadfully old sometimes and yet at others, absurdly young, just to be with them.

When these fighter boys first arrived in Malta, they looked on fighting as a game. A grim game where the loser lost his life, but still, a game where one's opponent played according to the rules.

Our chaps unconsciously placed the Luftwaffe on the same level and credited them with the same sporting instincts as they had themselves. They were soon disillusioned. When they had been in the island a short time they had to believe the evidence of their eyes.

The Hun not only shot up our pilots in their parachutes after they had baled out, but also shot them when in their dinghies in the sea.

There were three rescue launches in the island and all these were badly shot up at various times, even on occasions when going to pick up a German pilot.

Another pleasant trick of the Hun's was to fly so close over the top of the parachute canopy that the parachute collapsed and our wretched pilot dropped like a stone, I can vouch for this, I saw it happen to Douggie Leggo, one of our Rhodesians in 249 Squadron (March 20, 1942)

Laddie Lucas also witnessed this incident and there were a number of pilots who believed a similar fate had befallen Ken Murray some two weeks earlier.

I can also vouch for the fact that one pilot was picked up dead in his partly deflated dinghy with such wounds on him that he could not possibly have baled out, much less have climbed into a dinghy so the wounds must have been inflicted while in the dinghy.

On another occasion there were three pilots shot down and in their dinghies, two being Germans and one British. As luck would have it, the first one to be picked up was the German. After the rescue launch had pulled him on board, the skipper set course for the other two pilots and the German cried "No, no! back to harbour, 109's will shoot" then he realised what he had given away and merely quaked with fright until the boat had picked up our boy, the other German and returned to harbour.

Our rescue launch crews were extremely brave and rescourceful. Their casualties were very high at this time, but they were always on the job and were prepared to put to sea in any weather, day or night.

It was not until we had shot down two German Air Sea Rescue flying boats and one Italian seaplane, all heavily armed and in each case heavily escorted by fighters, that the Germans stopped their vile habits. There was a lot of invective on the Rome radio about the brutal English, but no-one shot our pilots in their "brollies" or in their dinghies again.

I suppose in total war, it is logical to try to complete the destruction already wrought by making sure the pilot does not fight again after shooting down his aeroplane, but to my mind it is no more justifiable than shooting a prisoner of war.

One of the best friends of the RAF in Malta was Godfrey Caruana, the jovial proprietor of "Captain Caruana's Bar." This was a pleasant little tobacconists shop cum bar in Strada Reale or "Kingsway" as it is was later called. Godfrey, plump and always smiling, welcomed one as no one else can and when he sang his "Raspberry Song" for you, you knew that he had really taken you to his heart.

In times when liquor was very scarce and profiteering was often met, Godfrey always sold the real stuff at something under the controlled price. When any of his RAF friends left the island he would open a bottle of his precious champagne and this would be "on the house."

Godfrey was also a cinema proprietor and he kept his cinema and his bar open as long as possible in spite of the bombing. A brave, generous and resourceful friend.

Another remarkable man was the "Chocolate King" (I cannot remember his name, can only quote what was written over his shop). His bar was in Sliema and we used to call in for a "sundowner" after a strenuous day on our way back to supper. He too was the personification of "business as usual" and straight dealing.

Again there was Squadron Leader "Pop" Mallia, the Camp Commandant of the RAF Headquarters Unit in Malta. Pop had many years service in the Navy. I first knew him as a Chief Petty Officer when he was our Messman in the Wardroom of HMS Eagle in 1927 and afterwards in HMS Courageous from 1928 to 1930. He was awarded a well-earned MBE for his services during the bad times in Malta. He ran the Headquarters Unit efficiently and well and could always find that little item one was short of and nothing was too much trouble. His men, English and Maltese, all loved and respected him.

Another outstanding personality was Miss Mabel Strickland. She was the proprietor and editor of the Malta Times and although I only met her once she was one of the most striking personalities I met on the island. If anyone kept the flag flying, Mabel Strickland did. The Malta Times was published every day without fail, blitz or no blitz. Her offices were blitzed, her printing press was blitzed, but she carried on and courage was the keynote of the paper she directed and edited. A great woman who deserved well of Malta and of the Empire she so staunchly upheld.

All these were typical of the real spirit of Malta they were frightened, yes who was not, but they carried on.

The latter part of June and most of July 1942 were comparatively quiet. The Hun treated the island with respect and what fighting there was had to be looked for by our fighters mostly at about 25,000 feet. It was obvious, however, that another convoy was needed badly, Malta could not live without fighters, but she needed food as well as fighters.

Everyone had lost weight and we all realised that without more food, petrol, ammunition and spares in the very near future, Malta would have "had it," but we knew that supreme efforts to get another convoy through would be made and everyone was amazingly cheerful, largely, I think, because we knew that now we had our Spitfires. We had made the Hun wary, if not actually "windy."

Three freighters and most importantly the tanker Ohio (although severly damaged and without power or steering) eventually got through in August 12-15 in the Operation Pedestal convoy and everyone knows what an epic fight this convoy and the island put up to bring it to Malta.

Among the pilots sent back to Gibraltar early in July to lead a new batch of Spitfires to Malta was Flight Lieutenant "Buzz" (Noel) Ogilvie, one of the Canadians from 185 Squadron. With poor visibility on the last leg to Malta, he called for a homing vector and almost immediately a fake Oxford accent came on the air and a German controller replied "Hello Bullet One. Steer 040." I immediately cut in with "No No No. Bullet One, Steer 105." Buzz told me later that he had no doubts which was my voice and that I nearly blew the earphones off his head.

"You've got a voice like a Russian who has been drinking vodka all day and singing The Volga Boatman from the bottom of a well. There's no mistaking you."

The German controller was trying to home the Spitfires on Pachino in Sicily. Almost two years earlier they had successfully managed to so confuse the pilot of a Wellington that he was forced to land in Sicily. Unfortunately, among the passengers was Air Vice Marshal Owen Boyd who was on his way to Egypt to take up his posting as Deputy AOC Middle East.

Poor Owen did not have much luck, nor the career he deserved. He escaped from an Italian prison camp, was recaptured and subsequently released when Italy surrendered but he died only six months later of a heart attack.

In the middle of July, Marshal (later Air Chief Marshal) Sir Keith Park came to take over command from Sir Hugh Lloyd. By this time I was rather worn I had lost over two stone in weight and as I had completed my job, namely, organised the fighter defence of the island and done my best to make it a "going concern" Sir Hugh Lloyd told me he would send me home for a rest.

While the two AOC's were together, Sir Keith Park sent for me and after commenting very kindly on what he had heard of my work, said he would like me to stay on a bit longer. Sir Hugh Lloyd, growled from his armchair "You keep Woody in Malta over my dead body I have nearly killed him already." I was ordered to hand over to "Dusty" Miller forthwith and be prepared to leave by Hudson the same night after having kept a date with Sir Hugh Lloyd at Captain Caruana's at 6.30pm. (I have often wondered if this was one of the wrong turns in my RAF life. Park was known to be unforgiving of those he saw as coming from the Leigh-Mallory camp and wasted no time in getting known Bader-supporters, such as Stan Turner, off the island. But he did listen to my tactical viewpoint and took on many of the ideas as his own and I suspect if I had been able to stay with him, we may have worked well together.

When the boys heard I was going, "BB" (Air Commodore Bowen Buscarlet, our SASO), Stan Turner, Jack Satchell and a lot of others came to Caruana's "to see me off."

It was also Sir Hugh's farewell party, as he was leaving for the Middle East the next day. Godfrey Caruana of course, brought out some of his precious champagne and sang his "Raspberry Song" and after a rather rapid "session" we went to the Mess at Luqa to wait for my aeroplane to arrive from Gibraltar. There "BB" gave us his famous description (with sketches), of his epoch-making aeroplane, the "cat o scratch o plane" the chief motive power of which is a cat that is dosed with an emetic but I must not infringe patent rights! While we were waiting in the Mess, the Hun (I felt it was an unfriendly desire to have one last crack at me!) staged a raid on Luqa, but we carried on with the party, until the Hudson was due to leave.

I awoke at first light, lying on my Mae West, to find that we were at 15,000 feet with nothing but sea and sky in sight. We landed at Gibraltar at 9.30am and after an enormous breakfast I slept again until about 5pm. I began to feel the result then of not having had more than two to three hours consecutive sleep for some months. I looked at myself in the mirror and found that in my blue uniform I looked as though I was wearing borrowed clothes belonging to someone twice my size.

Next day we left Gibraltar at 9.30am only to be ordered back by signal when halfway to England. Apparently, all aerodromes in the south of England were fogbound. However, the day after that we left again at 9.30am and landed at Hendon at 6.30pm.

We had one bit of excitement on the way. When we were about 40 miles west of Brest, flying at 15,000 feet, I spotted another aircraft approaching us from the east. It was about 5000 feet below us and crossed our track about a mile astern, flying on a westerly course. Flight Lieutenant Potter, our command navigator, from Malta, who was also on board, agreed that it was an ME110. I naturally informed the pilot who merely fired a few rounds through his two forward guns to test them, (the rear turret had been taken out to make room for freight and passengers) and continued on his course. Either the Hun did not see us, or he had much too important an engagement to worry about us.

Over a very welcome pint of English beer in the Mess at Hendon, I telephoned my wife at Arundel. In the train from Victoria there was an RAF Officer who offered me the Evening Standard. In it I saw an article headed "Bader's Old Chief is now in charge of Malta's fighters" I thought that's me that was!

One very sad story I heard on my return to England was about two friends and colleagues, Squadron Leader Humphrey Gilbert DFC, the CO of 65 Squadron and Flight Lieutenant Gordon Ross (a controller) who had died in a very silly flying accident on May 2, 1942. They had been drinking at a local pub and then decided to borrow a Miles Magister and attend a party. In view of their condition, a flight sergeant wisely declared the Magister unserviceable so the clots decided to squeeze into a Spitfire instead. Ross was a big man and inevitably the Spitfire, after taking off from Great Sampford, Debden, crashed at Cutlers Green. There had already been a number of reported incidents where amorous puilots had taken their girlfreinds (usually WAAFs) up in single-seat fighters and got away with it, but the Gilbert-Ross crash brought home the idiocy of such antics. Humphrey Gilbert had just become engaged to Diana Barnato, the daughter of Joel Woolf Barnato who was one of the "Bentley Boys" with Glen Kidston in the early 1930's.

Chapter 13

Towards D-Day

The day after my return to England I reported to Air Vice Marshal Bottomley at Air Ministry and after making a brief verbal report to him I was given the services of a stenographer and dictated my official report. It took 48 hours to complete this and then I took a copy with me to hand to the C-in-C Fighter Command, Air Chief Marshal Sir Sholto Douglas.

After a long interview with the C-in-C in which he questioned me shrewdly about our fighter tactics in Malta, he expressed concern at my obvious loss of weight and sent me on a month's leave, with the assurance that I would be given command of a fighter station at the end of it.

So I returned to the bungalow at Walberton, near Arundel, where my wife had established herself with our eight-months old son and it was the most enjoyable leave I ever remember.

At the end of my leave I was posted to No 57 Operational Training Unit at Hawarden in Cheshire, where I took over from my old friend, Basil Spackman. Here, Headquarters staff and the instructors were accommodated in Hawarden Castle which had been Lord Gladstone's residence and was a most comfortable officer's mess.

Soon after my arrival I was delighted to greet two of the Malta fighters who had left Malta shortly after me. They were Flight Lieutenant Denis Barnham from 601 Squadron and Flying Officer Jack Rae and I was very glad to have two such able instructors to pass on what they had learnt in the hard fighting we had just left.

Denis Barnham has since written an excellent book called "One Man's Window" which vividly describes what the fighter boys went through in those hectic times. Jack Rae, who is another New Zealander, was subsequently shot down the following year after his return to operations and was a prisoner of war with Bader and like Bader, made several attempts to escape. (Jack Rae has subsequently written "Kiwi Spitfire Ace" about his time as a fighter pilot and prisoner of war.)

When Douglas Bader visited New Zealand in 1956, he arranged a most memorable reunion with Jack Rae, Jeff West (who had been in the Tangmere Wing as well as in Malta) and me, but that is another story. At Hawarden I found that the serviceability of our Spitfires was distressingly poor. This was chiefly the result of an acute shortage of tyre replacements. At this time, owing to the blockade and the fall of Singapore, synthetic rubber was being used for aircraft tyres. These synthetic tyres had a very short life and very soon more than half our aircraft were grounded because we could get no new tyres. I found a large dump of damaged tyres in stores which I was told could not be repaired.

As luck would have it, I discovered a middle-aged airman employed as an instrument repairer, who in civil life had been the maintenance specialist for one of the large tyre companies. I took him to the dump of damaged tyres and asked him if they were repairable. He replied "Of course, given the proper materials and equipment." Thanks to his influence with his old employees and by cutting a little red tape, we obtained the necessary vulcanising equipment and helped by two unskilled assistants he soon repaired sufficient tyres to enable all our aircraft to fly. We promoted him to Corporal and thereafter he and his little team had a full-time job and he was subsequently commissioned as an Equipment Officer.

After about three months at Hawarden, I was posted to Fairwood Common, a recently-constructed fighter station near Swansea. My old friend, Rupert Leigh came to relieve me at Hawarden and I remember we had a most hilarious dinner party with our wives to celebrate. his promotion and first command of a station and my return to an operational command.

At Fairwood Common. I found that my predecessor was David Atcherley who had succeeded his twin brother Dick some six months before. The aerodrome was composed of three concrete runways and a perimeter track laid out on heath land where wild Welsh ponies used to roam. All the domestic buildings were widely dispersed Nissen huts connected by fairly narrow tar-sealed roads

To my delight I found that my old Malta friend, "Rags" (Wing Commander Rabagliati) was Wing Leader at my new command. David Atcherley had already gone to his new posting but he and his brother had left an efficient station although there were some remarkable legacies.

Amongst these was a battery of old 18-pounder guns which the RAF Regiment could man for defence purposes. Unfortunately there was only salt-filled practice ammunition for these. The Station Commander's car was a large American vehicle that had been requisitioned and it still had a radio installed (this was quite illegal in war time).

Almost every airman and airwoman had been issued with a bicycle because of the distances they had to travel between their sleeping quarters, their eating quarters and their work. All the roads within the station boundaries had reflecting "Catseyes" in the middle. Every Mess, airmen's, airwomen's, NCO's and Officer's had a piano, "on loan."

I have never known a station so recently completed to be equipped with so many unofficial refinements.

The Atcherley twins bequeathed a very happy station even if some of the equipment was unorthodox. Their refreshing individuality and drive were well-known throughout the RAF and they both rose to high rank by the end of the war.

In early July 1943, we were very grieved when "Rags" was killed. I felt his loss particularly because we had shared the worst period in Malta only a year before and we had become firm friends. He was flying a Typhoon with 195 Squadron from the satellite airfield at Matlaske on a Roadstead (anti-shipping) operation when he was hit by flak off the Dutch coast near Den Helder. He baled out and his parachute opened but like so many others on that type of operation was not rescued nor seen again.

His successor was Wing Commander Peter Townsend, DSO, DFC, who had achieved a great reputation as a gallant fighter pilot and leader. Peter impressed everyone with whom he came in contact. His unfailing courtesy, quiet efficiency and modest bearing, combined with his outstanding courage and ability as a fighter and leader established him firmly in the affections of all with whom he served. Those of us who knew him could well understand and sympathise with the love affair between him and Princess Margaret that surfaced in the 1950's. It is sad that an unbridled and unprincipled press should been able to misuse it's much vaunted "freedom" in vicious and unrelenting pursuit of so called "news" and thus cut short a promising career and make it impossible for a very gallant gentleman to live in his own country.

Early in 1943, we were given orders to keep a standing patrol in daylight hours over the Bristol Channel in order to make sure that no German reconnaissance aircraft could approach the area while a very hush-hush operation was being tried out. This was the full-scale trial of PLUTO (Pipe Line Under The Ocean) which was later used so effectively to supply fuel for our aircraft, tanks and motor transport in France after the invasion.

The pipe line was laid from a point on the Gower Peninsula in South Wales across to the north Devon coast. To do this an enormous floating drum was constructed, large enough to wind on some 40 or 50 miles of armoured flexible pipe.

In the centre of the drum there was a revolving axle to each end of which a tow line could be attached. With the end of the pipeline attached to the shore in south Wales powerful tugs towed the drum which revolved as the pipe line unwound itself on the sea bed.

PLUTO was successfully laid and tested across the Bristol Channel and as is well-known now, it was laid across the English Channel to France the following year and played an invaluable part in supplying our invasion forces with fuel and oil for the remainder of the campaign.

In April 1943 the AOC No 10 Group, Air Vice Marshal "Dicky" Dickson (who later became Marshal of the Royal Air Force, Sir Richard Dickson and was Chief of the Air Staff in the 50's) sent for me from his headquarters near Bath. He told me to take command of the Exeter Sector as soon as possible and warned me that I would find a certain amount of chaos partly due to the station being knocked about in one of the so called "Baedeker" raids some months before.

(On March 28, 1942 the RAF had attacked and destroyed the German port city of Lubeck with incendiary bombs in a raid that really had no purpose except to test the new "fire-storm" bombing technique. Lubeck had no military and little strategic importance but was a city of great antiquity with beautiful buildings. In revenge, Hitler ordered that five English cities of similar nature should be targeted and selected Exeter, Norwich, York, Bath and Canterbury. The air raids were nicknamed "Baedecker Raids" after the well-known travellers' guide book. There were four raids on Exeter, on the nights of April 23, 24 and 25 and the final and most devastating on the night of May 4, 1942. German aircraft attacked for about an hour and a half from 1a.m. and dropped over 10,000 oil and incendiary bombs as well as a large quantity of high explosive. The bombers came down to 500 ft to improve accuracy and their gunners relentlessly shot at rescue workers and any persons caught in the open. Unaccountably, Exeter Cathedral was left practically unscathed and there was much debate as to whether this was on purpose, or by design. In other words, did the aircrew disobey orders or were they simply inaccurate. Or was it one of those "miracles" of the Church?)

Air Vice Marshal Dickson was chiefly dissatisfied with the administrative side of the station and gave me a free hand to deal with matters as I found them. When I arrived at Exeter I found that my predecessor had already gone overseas and when I looked into details I realised that the AOC was indeed justified. In carrying out his orders to "clean up" the problems at Exeter I made some difficult decisions and at least one enemy.

The aerodrome at Exeter was originally a civil airfield which had been hurriedly enlarged. Concrete runways and a perimeter track had been constructed and a Beaufighter Squadron manned by Poles and a Rhodesian Typhoon Squadron were accommodated there. In addition, satellite airfields at Hope Cove and Harrowbeer (near Plymouth) were included in the Exeter sector.

Hope Cove was commanded by my old friend Squadron Leader K K Horn and another old friend from Duxford days, Squadron Leader John Petrie DFC was commanding the Typhoon Squadron at Harrowbeer.

The operational responsibilities were extremely heavy as we also had the Czechoslovak Spitfire Wing, which included No 310 Squadron as well as the Spitfire Wing from Ibsley led by the New Zealander, Wing Commander "Cam" Malfroy DFC..

The Typhoon Squadron's chief role at this time was to defeat the low-flying Focke Wolf 190 sneak raiders that the Germans were employing to bomb our south coast towns. Exeter was also used frequently for the refuelling of the Thunderbolt escort fighters used by the American Air Force in stepping up the daylight raids into enemy territory. Basil Embry, then an Air Commodore, was SASO (Senior Air Staff Officer) at No 10 Group and for four months he was acting AOC. He was an inspiring man to serve under and we all missed him when he left to command his Group in the second TAF (Tactical Air Force).

In September 1943, Air Vice Marshal Dickson took command of No 83 Group, which was a newly formed mobile fighter Group designed specially for the coming invasion. I was posted shortly after to command No 483 Group Control Centre.

This was a sort of mobile sector headquarters, complete with Operations Room with VHF transmitting and receiving sets with their own generators, the whole unit with field cookers, tents, caravans and vehicles could pack up and move forward at short notice. The fighter aircraft in the Group were established on quickly-constructed airfields along the south coast, from (and including) the Romney Marshes to Chichester.

The airfields were made quickly by laying runways of Summerfield track across the grassland. This was a coarse wire netting with rod and flat steel bracing laid and pegged down on to the grass which was used extensively for the quick construction of temporary runways from that time onwards.

The Group Control Centre was set up on Lympne racecourse when I joined it. The fighter squadrons were organised in Wings of three Squadrons, each with its own Wing Leader. The already famous Johnny Johnson led the Canadian Wing, from their airfield at Wittering near Chichester.

A large mobile offensive fighter force was formed into two Groups, No 83 and 84 Groups that winter of 1943-4. They trained "on the job" so to speak, by carrying out Fighter Sweeps, disrupting road and rail communications, escorting bombers and generally softening up the enemy forces in France.

Fighter Command became Air Defence of Great Britain, with Air Marshal Sir Roderick Hill as C-in-C.

Air Chief Marshal Sir Trafford Leigh Mallory was the Air Commander at Supreme Headquarters Allied Expeditionary Force (SHAEF) of which Eisenhower was Supreme Commander and Montgomery was in command of the British Army.

The South of England was stiff with troops for months before D-Day, which made it all the more surprising that the initial landings in Normandy achieved the success and surprise that they did.

In 1944 we carried out a dress rehearsal called Exercise Spartan by embarking our vehicles and personnel in landing craft with the object of carrying out practice landings on the Dorset Coast.

It was good practice for an embarking rehearsal, but the weather deteriorated so badly that everyone was very seasick and there were some near disasters owing to the high seas.

An even larger rehearsal involving principally American personnel called Operation Tiger followed "Spartan". Some 3000 local residents in the area of Slapton in Lyme Bay,

Devon, were evacuated in order to provide a secure area for practice beach landings as a prelude to the Normandy invasion. Slapton Sands was selected because of its similar features to what would be known as Utah Beach (an area between Pouppeville and La Madeleine) on the French coast). Although some valuable military lessons were learnt, the final day of this operation turned into a nightmare for practically all concerned. The Royal Navy was providing seaward protection for the assault troops with two destroyers and several motor torpedo boats and gunboats against the threat of German E-boat flotilla based at Cherbourg. Due to a series of unhappy "breakdowns in communication" eight LST's (Tank Landing Ships) were attacked by nine E-boats early in the morning of April 28, 1944. Two LST's were sunk and a third severely damaged with the loss of at least 600 men and the E-boats, although fired upon, withdrew without loss.

At the time of the attack, only the corvette, HMS Azalea, was escorting the nine LSTs and was leading them in a line, a formation which later drew criticism since it presented an easy target. HMS Scimitar, a World War I destroyer and the second ship supposed to be present, had gone into Plymouth for minor repairs. The American forces had not been told this. When other British ships sighted the E-boats earlier in the night and told the corvette, its commander failed to tell the LST convoy, assuming incorrectly that they had already been told, but the American forces and British naval headquarters were operating on different frequencies. The shore batteries defending Salcombe Harbour had seen silhouettes of the E-boats but had been instructed to hold fire so the Germans would not realise that the area was defended. Earlier still, a Blenheim on night patrol had seen and fired upon the E-boats as they left Cherbourg and this information had not reached either the Royal Navy nor the Americans.

The debacle continued when the remaining LSTs landed troops on Slapton Beach. My old ship from 1921, HMS Hawkins, had been brought out of retirement and following an order from General Eisenhower, the Supreme Allied Commander, who felt that the men must be hardened by exposure to real battle conditions, HMS Hawkins shelled the beach with live ammunition. (I think this is the only time a Royal Navy ship has deliberately fired upon England.) A Royal Marine observer on Hawkins recorded that many American troops were being killed by the barrage. On the beaches they had a series of white tape lines beyond which the Americans should not cross until the live firing had finished but the assault troops were going straight through the white tape line and getting blown up. At the end of the operation, total casualties reached over 900 and were not divulged to the general public or even victims' families until well after D-Day.

Shortly after "Tiger", I was posted to ADGB to relieve my old friend Jack Boret as Air Commodore (Operations) at Bentley Priory. After I had been there a few days (luckily I had waited to put up the broad stripe until official orders were published) the practical-joke department at Air Ministry decided that the appointment should be reduced to Group Captain. This was quite a shock to both Air Vice Marshal Dickson and Air Chief Marshal Leigh Mallory, who had each told me that the posting was a promotion one.

Sir Roderick Hill instructed me to take a survey of ADGB Operations and make any organisational recommendations I thought fit. The first thing I discovered was that a very large percentage of the operations personnel of all ranks and both sexes had been "sitting pretty" at Stanmore for four years! Most of them had never seen a Sector Station and until then, they had a very comfortable war.

I recommended posting everyone who had been more than two years at Command HQ to Sector Stations. Those who had spent so long in tough isolated places like the Orkneys and other outlying bleak spots should relieve them at Stanmore. These suggestions were not popular but I believe they were eventually implemented.

It was while I was at ADGB that I heard the story of a loyalty and bravery of a young Australian pilot, Flying Officer Bob Tuff, and his devotion to his squadron commander. I never met the Australian but I knew Geoff Warnes, the squadron commander very well. As a youth, Geoff Warnes was mad on flying and learned to fly with the Yorkshire Aeroplane Club, taught by none other than "Ginger" Lacey. Before the war he tried to join the RAF as a pilot but failed the entry requirements with his eyesight. He joined the Equipment branch and in 1939 he was a Flight Lieutenant in a non-flying role. After many interviews with the medical authorities, he managed to enlist the sympathies of no less a person than Group Captain Livingston who was then the eye specialist for the RAF. Livingston was a most gifted occulist who later became medical director general of the RAF. He was a very charming personality and his one object was not to turn people down but enable them to overcome any defects. Eventually, Livingston fitted Geoff with contact lenses and he was passed fit to fly. I believe he was the first person to fly with contact lenses which were a very new thing in those days. Geoff resigned from the Equipment branch and dropped three ranks to Pilot Officer. He soon passed his RAF flying instruction and was posted to 263 Squadron. Within a year he was commanding that squadron and had been awarded the DSO and the DFC. A Yorkshireman, Geoff was an athletic, broad-shouldered man of more than medium height, he was always cheerful and with a dry sense of humour that was invariably in use. He was a fearless pilot and leader and by his personal example and tireless energy, set a very high standard for his squadron. Pilots and groundcrew alike appreciated his even-tempered efficiency and all ranks held him in such respect that a quietly-spoken request became an order to be obeyed without question. He made it his business to look after the comfort and well-being of his men and everyone from the C-in-C downwards held him in high esteem. He was quite a character who often drank a pint of stout after his early-morning bath and smoked a cigar immediately afterwards. ("Might not get another chance of such a luxury all day," he told us.) When drinking n the local hostelry with the boys he sometimes had the disconcerting habit of tapping one of his contact lenses with a pencil, or loosening the lenses and washing them in his glass of beer, usually to the astonishment of any strangers in the bar.

When I knew Geoff, his squadron was equipped with Westland Whirlwinds, a twin-engined fighter with very high performance at low levels. They were used chiefly as fighter bombers and a great deal of their job was to attack the flak ships which the Germans used to protect their coast-wise convoys. They were also used of course in attacks on the convoys themselves using cannons and bombs. This was one of the most hazardous jobs I know. Frequently, they would take off before dawn and Geoff would lead the squadron in the dark at no more than 10 feet above the wave-tops to escape radar. The attacks were made in the dim light before sunrise at mast height in the face of very heavy anti-aircraft fire. Geoff and his squadron did magnificent work with their Whirlwinds operating from Angle when they were under my operational control from Exeter and I can vouch for the havoc they wrought.

There was one occasion when Geoff came back after dark after attacking a convoy at dusk and his Whirlwind was badly damaged by flak so I advised him to land at Exeter where we had a longer runway and full night-landing equipment. His hydraulic system was damaged, the flaps and brakes were out of action, so we gave him all the lights we had although we knew enemy bombers were in the vicinity. (In fact, one of our Beaufighters was chasing a German bomber overhead when the lights went on.) Geoff made a perfect landing in spite of his necessary high approach speed and when I greeted him his first question was "Are all my boys down safely? We got split up after the attack and I told them to find their own way home."

I was able to assure him they were safe but he wasn't satisfied until he got on the telephone and heard their stories himself. His only remark about his own performance was to say "Gosh. That gave me a thirst," when we had a beer in the mess.

After a rest posting to 10 Group HQ, Geoff resumed command of 263 Squadron, by this time equipped with Hawker Typhoons. The new aircraft were faster, heavier and could hit harder and the role of the squadron was now trainbusting, bridge destruction and disruption of general enemy communications but I suspect Geoff still hankered for the anti-shipping attacks.

On February 22, 1944, Geoff took off from Harrowbeer with nine Typhoons from 263 Squadron. Their mission was a sweep over France but the weather report was not very accurate, their target area was blanked out by low cloud and they were recalled. On the way back, Geoff decided to make a low-level search between the Channel Islands and France in the hope perhaps of catching a coastal convoy as in the Whirlwind days.

Geoff may have caught a wave because right down near sea level, his engine suddenly cut. He only had time to radio "Engine's packed up. I'm ditching." He was seen to climb out of the cockpit before the Typhoon sank. The rest of the squadron immediately climbed until they were picked up by the home station and could transmit a Mayday and position for the Air Sea Rescue service. Geoff's number two, Flying Officer Tuff, circled and saw that Geoff's dinghy, which should have been attached to him, was now detached and blowing downwind much faster than the pilot could swim. Tuff realised that unless Geoff could get into his dinghy he had no chance of surviving until rescue arrived. If a pilot baled out over the English Channel in winter there was little chance of survival for more than half an hour unless he was in his dinghy. In this instance, it was a bleak February day, with low cloud and strong whipping up white horses on the very cold waters.

"He can't make his dinghy, I'm baling out to help him," Tuff called out over the RT. He inverted his Typhoon and parachuted down. He obviously thought that as a strong swimmer and a younger and fitter man than the 29-year-old Warnes, he would be able to get the apparently injured squadron leader into his dinghy. The remaining seven Typhoons circled for half an hour and the weather became worse, the wind rose and the rain came in tearing, freezing blasts with visibility practically nil. Although an Air Sea Rescue boat arrived and searched, neither pilot was ever seen again.

In my opinion, Bob Tuff's very gallant attempt to save Geoff Warnes life was the finest example of devoted and calculated, cold-blooded bravery I have ever known.

As I was at ADGB, I was witness to the flurry of debate that followed a recommendation that Tuff should receive the George Cross for his sacrifice. Astonishingly, the award was reduced to a Mention in Despatches because it was concluded that Tuff did not knowingly sacrifice his life, in other words, he thought he could succeed in the rescue. There was talk of either an Albert Medal or another Royal Humane Society award but this avenue was discouraged in wartime as it was felt such awards could sway personnel from their military objectives.

The Chief of the Air Staff wrote on the file that while he had every admiration for the gallantry displayed, he was bound to comment that Tuff's action was not justifiable on military grounds since he threw away an aircraft for an extremely improbable chance of saving his Squadron Leader's life.

I should mention here that Group Captain Livingston had also made it possible for me to continue flying at the outbreak of war when I was diagnosed as having one short-sighted eye. Under the rules, any pilot who required eyeglasses was grounded because it was forbidden to wear glasses under flying goggles. Livingstone pointed out that if I could master the wearing of a monocle, there was nothing in the regulations to keep me from continuing as a pilot. And that, in case anyone was wondering, was why I had that trade-mark monocle during the battle of Britain and beyond. (Incidentally, the word was that the same Ishihara colour-blindness test that grounded me on HMS Eagle was defeated by Geoff Warnes because he borrowed the book of charts and memorised the correct answers – but I was never able to verify this tale.)

The development of Hitler's much vaunted "secret weapon" the V1 Flying bomb had been known for some time and our constant bombing attacks on V1 launching sites as they were discovered undoubtedly delayed their use. However, on June 13, 1944 the V1 attacks commenced and ADGB was kept busy in trying to combat this menace.

The V1 attacks were a rude shock for England. The D-Day landings had begun on June 6 and all was apparently going in our favour when the "doodle-bugs" suddenly started falling on London. On the first Sunday of the V1 attacks there were nearly 300 casualties from one bomb which hit the Horse Guards' Chapel in St James Square in the middle of morning church service. I believe there were a further 200 or so deaths from a bomb which landed in the street outside the Air Ministry's Ad Astral House.

The Hawker Tempest which had just entered service was the best aircraft with the low-altitude speed necessary to catch the V1 so 150 Tempest Wing was brought back from its ground-attack role in France. The wing leader, Wing Commander "Bee" Beamont, , had been a test pilot with Hawkers in developing the Tempest and he had immediate success against the V1 after he harmonised his cannon at 300 yards. All other aircraft in the Wing soon followed this example and the unit destroyed over 630 of the flying bombs. Roland destroyed 31 himself, a feat only exceeded by Squadron Leader Berry from 501 Squadron with 59 kills. Shooting them down at such close range was very dangerous as with an 1800lb Amatol payload, the V1 could easily destroy the destroyer. Some of the really skilled and brave pilots found they could tip the V1 over by flying so close that they disrupted the airflow over one wing. The ubiquitous Mosquito was second only to the Tempest in bringing down the V1 and accounted for over 400. The Griffon-engined Spitfire XIV when tuned and polished also had some success (300 plus destroyed) and the P51 Mustang dealt with another 232. The twin-jet powered Gloster Meteor was rushed into service in a further attempt to combat the menace but although it had ample speed it suffered badly from cannon jams and only accounted for 13.

AA Command and Balloon Command were also called upon to assist in bringing the V1 down before they reached any densely-populated area. Hundreds of AA guns were moved to the coast and the real break-through came when radar-guided guns and proximity fuses were deployed. The threat was virtually over by the end of August 1944, when the coastal guns were shooting down 80 per cent of the missiles.

Quite a number were brought down to explode harmlessly in open country, but a lot of indiscriminate damage and casualties were caused in greater London and the coastal towns like Southampton and Portsmouth.

Most of the V1 launching sites were sited in the Pas de Calais in order to place them within range of London, their primary target. As soon as the invasion was well under way, these sites were eventually overrun and destroyed.

My official posting to ADGB was for six months Sir Roderick Hill was adamant about this he said I needed a "rest" from operations. It was very trying however to know that the invasion was launched and after June 1944, most of my friends were in France, so I applied for a posting overseas.

Eventually, just before my six months had expired, I was posted to Italy to command a newly- formed mobile Spitfire Wing to operate from the South of France.

The Wing Headquartes personnel, vehicles and equipment were due to leave by sea in 48 hours. As I had to be inoculated and vaccinated against cholera, typhoid, smallpox, yellow fever, plague the lot I left by air a week later, still feeling ill from the various injections that had been pumped into me.

We left Lyneham by Lancaster, landed in North Africa, transferred to a DC3 and then landed at Caserta near Naples.

The Headquarters of Mediterranean Allied Air Force was in the former Italian Royal Palace at Caserta. My orders were to report there but after nearly six hours of being passed from one office to another, I discovered that the South African Air Force had arranged to man the new Spitfire Wing and I was told to take local leave until a command could be found for me. As I stood on the steps of the palace feeling a little disheartened at my treatment, I met an old friend from the Duxford, my former Ops B Controller, Teddy Morton. Obviously my feelings were showing for he commented "You're not looking so good. Have you had some bad news?"

"It seems the RAF doesn't have a place for me any more," was all I could reply. Bless him, he took me to task for that. "What a load of nonsense, there wouldn't be an RAF without you."

Morton told me that my old AOC from Malta days, Hugh Pughe Lloyd, was now commanding the Mediterranean Coastal Air Force so I sought him out. He was delighted to see me and immediately suggested that I should spend a few days in Malta. He put a little Fairchild Argus monoplane at my disposal and I flew to Malta, refuelling at Catania on the way. It seemed unreal to fly over Italy, Sicily and finally Malta in a little unarmed aircraft after the battles that had raged over the island only two years before.

I flew over much of the route that I had driven in that Austin 7 only seventeen years earlier. It seemed more than a lifetime ago, which was hardly surprising.

Malta I found to be on the crest of a wave of prosperity, with no shortages of food and all sorts of luxuries in the shops. I spent a very pleasant week there meeting old friends and visiting old haunts, then flew back to Naples to find there was still no job for me. I then flew to Rome and after about four days I was recalled to Naples for orders. I was instructed to report to Balkan Air Force Headquarters at Bari. Here I met my new AOC, Air Vice Marshal "Bill" Elliot (now Air Chief Marshal Sir William Elliot, KCB, DFC) who told me I was to take command of No 334 (Special Duties) Wing at Brindisi. After briefing by the AOC and his staff on my new command, I was driven down to Brindisi the following day.

(Bari was the scene of one of the most devastating Luftwaffe raids of the war some nine months earlier when on December 2, 1943, 105 Ju 88's attacked the port which was the main support and supply base for the British 8th Army and the 15th United States Air Force in occupied Italy. Seventeen Allied ships were sunk and another eight damaged in under 30 minutes and Bari became known, at least locally, as Britain's "Pearl Harbour". The defences were caught totally unprepared when the first wave of bombers found their main targets, the ships being unloaded at the docks, floodlit. Embarrassingly, Air Vice Marshal Sir Arthur Coningham told a press conference the afternoon before the raid that the Luftwaffe was defeated in Italy. "I would regard it as a personal affront and insult if the Luftwaffe attempted any significant action in this area." The day after the bombing many of the personnel who had received minor injuries started dying and doctors at the three local hospitals suspected the Germans had used chemical weaponry. The Americans quickly brought Lieutenant Colonel Stewart Alexander, a chemical warfare expert, in to investigate and he very soon suspected some form of mustard gas was causing the casualties. Alexander, a thorough and methodical investigator, refused to believe the authorities, both British and American, who denied that any of the sunken ships had been carrying gas bombs or canisters. He carefully studied the distribution of casualties and came to the conclusion that an American freighter, John Harvey, was the focal point of the poisonings. At that stage he had no evidence, as the ship had been completely obliterated, no trace of crew or ship remained. His suspicions were confirmed when a naval diver found fragments of a bombshell with clear markings identifying it as an American 100lb mustard-gas bomb. Confronted with this evidence, the port commander admitted that he had been informed after the raid that the John Harvey was carrying 100 tons of mustard gas bombs as well as many thousands of tons of high explosive bombs. A detachment the US 701st Chemical Maintenance Company was on board the ship but as no-one survived, no gas alarm was given. Alexander was understandably angry that authorities had tried to blame the Germans for the gas casualties as he realised the awful consequences that could have arisen if a retaliatory gas attack had resulted from such subterfuge. He also pointed out that many deaths could have been avoided if doctors had known from the outset that they were dealing with mustard gas. Following Alexander's report, there was a complete cover-up. Churchill decreed that all references to mustard gas, or even to Lt Col Alexander and his position as consultant in chemical warfare medicine, should be removed from medical and military records. Casualties were to be diagnosed as burns due to enemy action or listed as "not yet diagnosed." I believe they remain so to this day in British records although the Americans recorded 617 cases of chemical poisoning and 83 directly-attributed mustard gas deaths. Surprisingly, this disastrous raid did have one positive result as Alexander's meticulous compilation of data and collection of pathology specimens confirmed an earlier study on the effects of nitrogen mustard on white blood cells, lymph nodes and bone marrow and lead to the foundation of chemotherapy as a means of fighting cancer. Although all the data and tissue samples he sent to the British (Porton Downs) Chemical Warfare Centre were never acknowledged, a duplicate set safely reached the United States' Edgewood Arsenal. This may seem like a long digression, but it was a story I heard initially when I was in Bari. It was later brought up by some of the American pilots with me at Brindisi because the raid had a serious effect on supplies for the 15th Air Force. The medical side of it was told to me by a USAF doctor and later, when I was living in Canada after the war, the chemotherapy aspects were in an article forwarded by an old USAF colleague, then back in civilian medical practice.)

Chapter 14

Special Duties Wing

Brindisi aerodrome had been a civil airport in peacetime with an adjoining military seaplane station. An RAF maintenance unit now used the formerly Italian seaplane workshops and living quarters and No 334 Wing and its squadrons occupied the aerodrome and adapted the former civil airport buildings for use as Headquarters Officers, Operations room, living quarters and so on.

On the operational side we were equipped with a diversity of aircraft. No 148 Squadron was armed with Halifaxes with an attached flight of Lysanders, No 1586 (Polish Flight, later to become No 301 Polish Squadron) had Halifaxes and Liberators, at Bari there was a British Squadron of Dakotas (DC3's). In addition the Wing had a Russian manned Dakota Squadron at Bari, two US Air Force Groups of Dakotas at Brindisi which were soon joined by another USAF Group of Fortresses and Liberators and at Lecce, two squadrons of Italian Savoia Machetti bombers, under its operational control.

The Americans, the Russians and the Italians were administratively self-contained. 334 Wing had Intelligence, Meteorological and Operations sections and each of these sections had a most capable and experienced officer in charge of it.

I was amazed when I first surveyed all the complex demands that were made on the Wing and the diversity of tasks that were given to aircraft and crews to perform.

The "Agencies" who made the demands were, amongst others, ISLD (Inter Service Liason Department), LRDG (Long Range Desert Group), SOE (Special Operations Executive) (M), OSS (Office of Strategic Services) (USA), No 1 Special Force, SAS (Special Air Service) and PWB (Political Warfare Bureau).

Each of these agencies had headquarters in Southern Italy and missions in the various enemy occupied countries in which they were interested.

Every "agency" had its own school where the agents were trained and briefed for missions assigned to them.

There was also a heavily-guarded secret packing depot not far from the aerodrome. Here, complete stores of clothing, boots, rations, medical supplies, explosives, sabotage materials, and weapons including everything from field guns to revolvers plus ammunition for every type of weapon were stored. When I visited this packing depot, I was allowed into the strong room and under close surveillance of an armed guard, I was shown golden sovereigns and five dollar gold pieces, all ready to be sent in to the Partisans.

The reason for this gold currency was that the Germans had flooded the occupied countries with quantities of counterfeit British, American and Italian paper money which could only be distinguished from the genuine article by experts.

Gold, therefore, became the only currency which was readily acceptable anywhere. The missions that the aircrew of 334 Wing were briefed to carry out under the omnibus description of "Special Duties" called for special skills and a very high standard of courage and determination. Of course, the very nature of the operations demanded secrecy and absolute security.

At 9am each morning a briefing conference was held in the Operations Room. These conferences were attended by Squadron Commanders or their representatives, in addition to the Wing Intelligence and Meteorological officers and me, as well as representatives from each "agency."

The first essential was to study the weather forecast for each country concerned. Our Met. forecasters faced some difficulties as our theatres of operations included Poland, Czechoslovakia, Northern Italy, Yugoslavia, Romania, Bulgaria, Hungary, Albania and Greece.

The terrain within the triangle bounded by the Western Alps, Poland and Greece is well known for its topographical diversity and it as it was mostly enemy-occupied it was the part of Europe which had least meteorological information available, either from past study or from current reports.

After deciding on the countries where the weather probabilities made operations reasonably possible, each agency would ask for specific loads (and often personnel) to be dropped or landed at each target. The priorities for each night's operations were sent down each day by Balkan Air Force Headquarters. All passengers, whether military or civilian agents were given the generic name "Joes" by the RAF and as a matter of security, the real names and purpose of the agents were not known to the aircraft crew. This secrecy meant that nobody could divulge information if captured but also made it very hard to keep track of which agent had gone where, especially when enemy action or bad weather resulted in missed or mistaken drop zones.

When loads and missions had been allotted to the Squadrons, the crew of each aircraft was then specially briefed for their particular operation, by Met, Intelligence and Signals.

The aircraft were loaded up during the day and an armed guard posted on each aircraft because the local population were so desperate after the Italian collapse and the years of German domination that they would steal anything.

The guards were drawn from Yugoslavia partisans who were so trigger-happy that they soon discouraged the thieves. Just before the aircraft took off, the "Joes" would embark. These "Joes" were often British officers in uniform, amongst whom I remember Brigadier Fitzroy MacLean, Major Randolf Churchill and the New Zealander, Doctor Lindsay Rogers who has described his experiences in "Guerrila Surgeon."

The intensive operations the Wing carried out into and out of Yugoslavia were only made possible by an unusual organisation known as Balkan Air Terminal Services or BATS parties, who in my opinion deserve very special mention.

In the Balkans, the partisans were having a bitter fight, their only advantage was that they were fighting on their own ground. The Germans had the troops, the armour and the supplies; all the partisans had were the knowledge of their own country, the help of their countrymen and countrywomen and the ability to "live off the country."

Their country was rugged, with high mountains There was a coastal belt of cultivated land, extensively cultivated patches in the valleys between the mountains and there was a heavy rainfall. From September or October onwards, there was snow and ice and throughout the year, winds would whistle up the valleys so that flying was not particularly pleasant, especially when flying below the mountain tops.

The Partisans in the Balkans were in a bad way, they were short of medical supplies and had a considerable number of wounded on their hands. They were poorly armed, short of food and clothing and the Germans with their tanks, guns and aircraft, had the odds heavily in their favour.

Early in 1944, the Balkan Air Terminal Services or BATS parties were formed to meet the most pressing need to establish landing grounds and reliable communications with the allied missions so that wounded could be evacuated and supplies flown in to the Partisans.

In all, nine of these BATS parties were formed and although only five of them became operational before the end of the war, those five parties did wonderful work. It was part of our job in the Special Duties Wing to parachute them in.

Each party consisted of an officer and two sergeants the officer was the airfield controller and the sergeants were radio operator and technician respectively.

Their duties were to locate and construct landing strips with the aid of the Partisans and establish radio communications with Balkan Air Force and 334 Wing Headquarters. They could then pass on details from the allied missions and the partisans of the supplies required, numbers of wounded to be evacuated and finally to direct aircraft in to the landing strips at night.

In the early stages the supplies had to be dropped by parachute, in fact this method had to be resorted to many times when the parties had been forced by enemy attack to abandon a strip.

The first BATS party, led by Squadron Leader Bell, was dropped in to Yugoslavia on May 14, 1944 and after many difficulties prepared a strip and several aircraft were landed. On May 25, however, the Germans located the strip and attacked it with dive bombers and fighters wounding and half-blinding Squadron Leader Bell. In spite of his injuries, Bell led his party, together with members of a Russian mission, about a hundred miles across almost impossible country, to a place called Ticevo. On this trek they suffered incredible hardships, because they had practically no food and were moving so fast that they had very little time for sleep. However, at Ticevo another landing strip was constructed and on June 9, about three weeks later, Bell and his party and the Russian mission were flown out by four Dakotas to Italy.

The General in charge of the Russian mission reported "The reputation of the British has gone up many hundred per cent when non-infantry personnel led by a half-blind, wounded officer, find their way without guides across this country at such speed and show such endurance and cheerfulness."

After a brief rest and before his wound was properly healed, Bell again took his party in to Yugoslavia and they were landed on a strip at a place called Kavoskopolje, on June 26.

They operated this strip for two weeks when they were driven out by a German tank attack. They then constructed a new strip at Ubdina which was ready a fortnight later. While there, the party directed the fire of British Spitfires onto German tanks and troops attacking partisans and broke up the enemy forces so seriously that the attack failed.

They continued the good work, fighting, retiring to the hills, constructing new strips and bringing in aircraft and evacuating wounded until August 21, when they were themselves evacuated to Italy.

In May 1944, Squadron Leader McGrath and No 2 BATS Party went in and after several adventures joined up with Marshal Tito's 3rd Division, who were retreating and were in dire straits owing to lack of food and ammunition. McGrath and his party joined in the fighting and eventually gave a position to our Wing where parachute supplies could be dropped. The same night 10 Dakotas dropped much-needed supplies and ammunition and thus enabled the fight to go on.

On June 4, after heavy fighting between the partisans and German paratroops, Marshal Tito and his staff, together with the British and Russian missions were evacuated and Squadron Leader McGrath and McGregor were on the run again. They continued in hiding in the hills until June 30 when they were flown out from Megabudja in Montenegro together with a number of British and American air crew and over 200 wounded Partisans. McGrath and McGregor were extremely tough and valiant and they, as well as Squadron Leader Bell, Squadron Leader Wells, Sergeant Jopson and the other NCO's deserved much higher decorations, in my opinion, than they received.

The job which the five small BATS parties did in the Balkans in the period of their operations was very impressive. As a result of their efforts, No 334 Wing carried out 11,500 successful sorties, took in 7800 personnel and evacuated over 20,600 wounded partisans, British and American aircrew, British and

American and Russian Mission personnel and many important political personages. Amongst others we took in or brought out Fitzroy Maclean, Randolph Churchill, Marshal Tito and the New Zealander Lindsay Rogers. (Maclean's "Eastern Approaches" and Rogers' Guerilla Surgeon" are both excellent accounts of the operations involved and the intricacies of dealing with the various ethnic and political groups.)

Tito was a most interesting character to meet, he showed much more independence and confidence than most of the Communists I met. His name, incidentally, was a nickname coined from the way he allotted tasks and responsibilities. In Serbo-Croat "Do this, do that" comes out as "Ti, to!" (His real name, largely forgotten, was Josip Broz.)

I made several trips over Yugoslavia as "spare"pilot and in order to see for myself what the missions entailed. We would take off from Brindisi just before dusk with parachute containers on the bomb racks, parachute bundles inside the fuselage ready to be attached by the despatcher to the parachutes slung overhead. There would probably be three or four "Joes" aboard as well. On arrival over the dropping zone we would confirm our position with the radio beacon set up by the BATS party and the pilot would flash the night's pre-arranged signal on the downward recognition lamp. If we were lucky we would receive an answer immediately from the ground – usually from hand torch. The hand torch would then be kept on by the airfield controller as a marker beacon and we would make our first run over the zone at about 300 to 600 feet. The escape hatch was opened and the "Joes" would stand by to jump. When the despatcher saw the jump light turn on (switched by the pilot or navigator) he would tap the agent on the shoulder and if necessary, push him out. With luck we would send all our agents out on the first run and then start our supply-drop runs. Sometimes we would have to make as many as 6 to 8 runs to make sure our precious supplies were dropped in the very limited area.

Another important job Wing 334 had to do was concerned with the Polish Resistance Movement in Warsaw. In August 1944 active rebellion flared up (prematurely, I regret to say, as it turned out). The Poles were isolated and beseiged in the middle of Warsaw and their only hope of survival lay in their being supplied with arms, ammunition and food from outside sources, so it was decided to drop supplies by parachute, at night. The dropping zone was very small and in order to ensure the supplies reaching the zone, aircraft had to drop from no more than 300 feet.

In order to reach Warsaw from Brindisi, in the south of Italy, the aircraft had to fly over 1800 miles each way, over rugged country, across several mountain ranges, across Yugoslavia, Hungary, Czechoslovakia and Poland. Large tracts of these countries were occupied by the advancing Russian armies and although we gave our so called Allies ample warning of our operations, the Russians put up heavy anti-aircraft fire against our aircraft over the whole route, on all occasions. In addition, the Russians were within a few miles of Warsaw, but they did nothing to assist the gallant Poles. In two nights in August 1944, over Warsaw, No 334 Wing sustained very heavy casualties, but they at least got some of their supplies through to the Poles before the rebellion was put down.

The month before I took over the Wing, a most outstanding mission was carried out to Poland by a DC3 from 267 Squadron, piloted by a New Zealander, Flight Lieutenant Stan Culliford, with Flying Officer Szajer from 1536 Polish flight as co-pilot.

An experimental missile fired from Peenemunde, the German development establishment, had gone off course and landed intact in Poland where a Polish professor, Chmielewski, assisted by partisans, had dismantled it.

Culliford landed after his 1800-mile flight and the stores and personnel were unloaded in five minutes. In another five minutes the dismantled missile and the gallant professor (now travelling under the code-name Rafal) responsible for it were on board, together with several Poles who were due to be brought out, when it was discovered that the aircraft could not move because the wheels had sunk in the soft surface. The pilot persuaded the local partisans to dig the wheels out. In the meantime all passengers but the professor and his missile were off loaded. The Germans were only a mile away and the personnel detailed to hold the torches forming the flare path had gone to cover. Preparations were reluctantly made to destroy the machine but Culliford persevered (to the extent of cutting the brake hoses in case the brakes were locking) and finally freed the aircraft after two attempts.

By dint of taking off down wind (which was luckily also down hill) the DC3 just managed to stagger off the ground and safely delivered the missile and the professor to Brindisi. The missile (which was an early V2) was considered to be so important that it was almost immediately flown to England for detailed examination. "Rafal" had been told to stay with the missile and refused to let any part out of his sight - even when he reached London he would not release his parcels to British intelligence until a Polish Colonel arrived and told him all was safe.

Culliford was awarded a well deserved DSO for the courage and determination he had displayed.

The operations over Warsaw were very hazardous indeed. No 148 Squadron lost 12 aircraft over Poland and No 301 (Polish) Squadron(as No 1586 Flight had now become) lost 20. Most of these losses occurred in August and September 1944.

At the end of August, both squadrons were deplorably weak in both aircraft and crews. After frantic requests for replacements, 12 Stirlings were ferried out from Bomber Command. These aircraft were quite unsuitable for our operations and more than 50 per cent arrived requiring an engine change. After further urgent requests, they were replaced by Halifaxes.

At the end of August 1944, Wing Commander Pitt DFC, AFC handed over command of No 148 Squadron after eight months magnificent service to the Squadron and the Wing. His successor was Wing Commander "Dagwood" Hayward, a South African who had already completed three tours of bomber operations and after a brief "rest" at an Operational Training Unit, had come back to command 148 Squadron in which he had operated for a tour from North Africa as a Flight Commander.

We had known each other briefly in Malta in 1942 when he was flying Wellingtons that came from the Middle East to arm and refuel in Malta before carrying out their attacks on enemy aerodromes and installations in Sicily and Italy.

"Dagwood" and I became firm friends although he would never tell me the origin of his nickname if there was one. He was one of the most modest men I have known. To have completed and survived three tours of bomber operations and to quietly volunteer for a fourth tour after all the hazards he had gone through since 1939, was to say the least of it, impressive.

When I inspected his flying log book I saw that he had flown over 100 Operational Bomber sorties, a great achievement by any standards.

When he took over command of the Squadron, it was sadly depleted in aircrews and aircraft after the heavy losses over Warsaw on August 13 and 14, although the morale was high.

"Dagwood" quickly got into his stride and flew on operations almost immediately and showed himself to be a most determined pilot, so much so that I had to curb him from flying every night. I pointed out that with a tour of operations being laid down at 30 completed missions, I would have to apply for another squadron commander in little over a month.

However when he did fly, he always chose the most difficult and hazardous mission for himself and his crew, who needless to say, had unbounded faith in him as a "skipper."

In September 1944 it was found that the Germans were starting to withdraw from Greece and Albania and were slowly retreating up the Dalmatian coast.

To expedite and harass this withdrawal a wing of fighters was attached to the Wing at Brindisi and what was known as "Operation Ratweek" started (to drive the German "rats" out of the Balkans). By the end of October, the fighters based at Brindisi had flown 565 sorties in which they destroyed 67 locomotives, 40 railway wagons, 305 military transport vehicles and 19 enemy aircraft. These offensive operations were most effective and rewarding to us. By October, owing to the deteriorating night weather over the Balkans, we changed to daylight supply dropping and landing operations, escorted by fighters.

Of course Dagwood Hayward initiated and led these daylight operations which proved most successful.

The changeover to daylight operations over Greece, Albania and Yugoslavia entailed a large increase of our scale of effort, as well as a much larger percentage of successful missions.

Our commitments to Central Europe and Northern Italy still required night operations, so we were stretched to the limit of our resources. I found myself getting so little sleep that I applied for a second in command and the AOC quickly appointed Wing Commander Griffiths, DFC, to the position.

Little "Griff" (he was even shorter than I and rather "tubby") was an acquisition to the Wing and did a lot to reduce the load for me. Always cheerful and ready for a joke, he was an excellent "Wing Co Flying" and an able administrator.

The Lysanders have already been mentioned and their achievements deserve a special tribute.

In February 1944, six Lysanders commanded by Flight Lieutenant Vaughan Fowler DFC became known as C Flight 148 Squadron.

Vaughan Fowler and most of his pilots had previous experience in clandestine operations from Tangmere to occupied France (as has been described in Chapter 11).

In May 1944, four Lysanders landed in Greece and brought out seven valuable "Joes." In June 1944, operating from an advanced base in Corsica, agents were landed into Central France and others evacuated. These operations entailed crossing the Alps at about 16,000 feet, which was no ordinary accomplishment for heavily-loaded Lysanders.

In October, Flight Lieutenant Franklin and Flying Officer Attenborough made many landings on aerodromes which had been evacuated by the retreating enemy in order to check on their serviceability for use by our fighters and heavier aircraft. These initial landings by Lysanders involved calculated risks because there was more than a possibility that the enemy had mined the runways.

In the same month Flight Lieutenant Franklin flew an official photographer over Athens and confirmed that the enemy had withdrawn from the capital.

In November 1944, Flying Officer John Rayns accomplished a tricky daylight pick up operation to northern Italy. As there were still a few enemy aircraft in this area, the vulnerable Lysander was escorted by P51 Mustangs from 3 Squadron RAAF. On the return flight, the slow Lysander with its weaving escort of fighters was seen by a squadron of American P51 fighters who were returning from a patrol. One of the P51's detached himself from the rest of his squadron, flew alongside our Lysander, apparently for a closer look. Our pilot was seen to wave in a friendly fashion to the American, who promptly carried out a steep turn to position himself astern of the Lysander and deliberately shot it down. The leader of our fighter escort frantically called the Americans on the RT when he realised what was happening, but as they were tuned to a different wavelength this had no effect.

This grievous and senseless killing of a British pilot and two valuable British agents was all the more incomprehensible because our Lysander carried proper

British markings, it took no avoiding action and was quite obviously being escorted by British fighters. When the United States C-in-C of Mediterranean Allied Air Forces (MAAF) received the report of this tragedy he flew down to Brindisi to apologise and informed us that the P51 pilot concerned had been flown back to the United States for court martial. As the pilot was reportedly a negro, we assumed he was from the "Tuskegee" Squadron with 332 Fighter Group

Another stout-hearted member of the Lysander team who must be mentioned was Flying Officer McCairns, DFM, MM. I had known McCairns when he was a Sergeant Pilot in No 616 Squadron in 1941 and I remember attending his 21st birthday party at the Unicorn in Chichester. After forced landing his damaged Spitfire after a sweep over Lille in July 1941, McCairns was taken prisoner and sent to prison camp in Germany, escaped, was recaptured and punished. He escaped again in the severe winter of 1941-42 and after many adventures which included crossing the Rhine into Holland in a blizzard, reached England via France and Spain. He was awarded the Military medal for this determined escape and was commissioned shortly afterwards. It did my heart good to meet him again with the Lysanders in Italy, where with the rest of the team he carried out so many difficult and dangerous missions.

When Italy collapsed after the invasion, some squadrons surrendered intact and volunteered to continue the fight on our side. Among these were No 1 and No 88 Italian Bomber Squadrons, armed with Savoia twin-engined aircraft based at Lecce, an aerdrome about 40 miles south east of Brindisi and they were placed under the operational control of 334 Wing. Shortly after I assumed command of the Wing, the Italian Colonel commanding these two squadrons came to call on me, so I asked him to lunch. He spoke fluent English and he related harrowing stories of the terrific battles his two squadrons had fought over Malta in 1942. I listened with interest, particularly when he stated that we must have been able to put at least a hundred fighters in the air at one time and was quite certain that Malta possessed vast underground hangars. He described the heavy losses the Italians had suffered when they bombed the island at night and then told how five Savoias with a large fighter escort had carried out high level bombing in daylight and three were shot down by 50 Spitfires who also destroyed several Italian fighters. He claimed that he was flying one of the Savoias that returned. Then in a hushed voice, he told how five more bombers were sent over on a similar raid a day or two later and none returned. I then told him that I had been there and remembered both interceptions perfectly. When I assured him that on each occasion the attacking British force consisted of only four Spitfires he just would not believe me.

It seemed a strange quirk of fate that the survivors of the same two Italian Squadrons who had taken such heavy punishment over Malta in 1942 should now be under my operational command.

These two "co-belligerent" squadrons were not much of an asset to the Wing. Their serviceability was very poor, because they had no spares and new parts could not be obtained because the Savoia aircraft factory in northern Italy was still in German-held territory. Morale of the Italians was low and they were willing co-operators providing they were not asked to be "belligerent." Although the theatre of operations they were committed to in the main was Albania, which involved the shortest flight from their base at Lecce, their record of successes was low.

In justice, I must say that the partisans in northern Italy fought hard and more than justified the assistance we gave them, but then the northern Italians were almost a different race and breed.

Squadron Leader Count Czernin who fought with the Italian Partisans in the Udine gave them the highest praise. Czernin, who I believe had a Tyrolean father and an American mother, was a naturalised Englishman who was awarded the DFC in the Battle of Britain and he and I had served together briefly at Tangmere. He spoke German and Italian perfectly and because of his knowledge of the language and the country he volunteered to be parachuted in to organise the partisans. In November 1944 one of our Lysanders landed in the Udine and brought Czernin back to Brindisi with very valuable information. For his achievements in organising and leading the partisans in their flight he was awarded a well-earned DSO.

By November the Germans were on the run. Greece and Albania were evacuated by the enemy as they withdrew northwards up the Dalmatian coast. On November 28 the inhabitants of Tirana the capital of Albania celebrated their freedom and on that day, six Halifaxes of No 148 Squadron led by Wing Commander Hayward, flying in close formation dropped 15 tons of food over the city. Our mission in Tirana reported that this gesture was very enthusiastically received by the Tiranians.

The advance of the Allies in France and in northern Italy increased rather than diminished the tasks that 334 Wing had to undertake, in spite of adverse weather conditions. As the Germans retreated they took with them all the stocks of food they could lay their hands on, leaving the inhabitants facing starvation. Many mercy missions were carried out to supply food to isolated communities and large numbers of wounded were flown out to Italy. At the same time, long-distance missions were flown to Poland, Czechoslovakia and Austria by the heavy aircraft of Nos 148 and 301 Squadrons.

An achievement which all ranks in the Wing took pride in was the building of our church. Although most of the Wing personnel were Protestants, our Church of England Padre could find nowhere to hold services so we decided to build him a church. Our very capable Administrative Officer, Squadron Leader Good was largely responsible for this. What gave us the idea was that I discovered that one of our airmen was a stained-glass artist in civil life, so that it can be said that the church almost grew round a stained-glass window.

Using Perspex and aluminium strips from crashed aircraft, our artist designed and built a magnificent window depicting a Biblical subject. Volunteers from the Wing, working in their spare time built the church of stones from a bomb-flattened building. Our carpenters built the altar, the pews, the pulpit, lectern the lot, from salvaged timber and then we heard that Doctor Garbett, Archbishop of York, was visiting Italy. I sent a letter to him, informing him of what we had done and he immediately agreed to come down and consecrate the church and hold a confirmation service afterwards.

When the day came, we were most impressed by the dignity and sincerity of the Archbishop who was truly a grand old gentleman. It was fitting that Squadron Leader Good who had done so much to build the church should be the first person to be confirmed in it. It was heart-warming to have the unqualified approval that the Archbishop expressed to all concerned and the window was especially admired. I wonder what has become of our church now.

Early in 1945, the Wing was called on to carry out a new type of operation. This was to parachute the SAS (Special Airborne Service) into northern Italy complete with their jeeps. Two Halifaxes of No 148 Squadron had their bomb bays specially modified to accommodate the jeeps and six jeeps with their tough SAS crews were dropped into enemy territory where they successfully hastened the collapse of the retreating Germans.

In February 1945, I had great pleasure in recommending Wing Commander "Dagwood" Hayward for the immediate award of the DSO and at the same time nominated him to attend the next RAF Staff College course. "Dagwood" had by then completed far more than the quota of missions laid down as constituting his fourth tour of operations. He had taken over No 148 Squadron at a most difficult time, just after the heavy losses over Poland and by his example and personal leadership he had helped to make history. He was awarded the DSO early in March and almost immediately afterwards he was appointed to the Staff College.

"Dagwood" was loathe to leave the Squadron and plaintively told me that he could not possibly survive a Staff College course without putting up a "black." However, I told him that he had been sticking his neck out quite long enough; that Wing Commanders with four tours of operations and a DSO to their credit were scarce and that with his operational experience he should be able to contribute as much to the Staff College as he would gain from it. Besides, said I, it's time you moved up in the queue and let someone else have a turn, so Squadron Leader Hewitt DFC, the Flight Commander of B Flight was promoted to Wing Commander and assumed command of the Squadron.

We threw a farewell party for "Dagwood" which was, to say the least of it, memorable and was a fitting send off for a very gallant officer.

A very small incident and an apparently unimportant one at the time. A Dakota with Russian markings was being loaded up and a "Joe" in British Army battledress was being offensively an blasphemously rude to one of our aircraftmen who was doing his best to help the agent into the aircraft in the dark. The "Joe" was being so offensive that I had shone my torch on him while I told him in no measured terms that I would not allow anyone of whatever rank to use such language to any airman under my command. The "Joe" had replied civilly enough and apologised but as he turned away into the interior of the aircraft he said something in Russian which sounded full of expletives and caused a titter to come from the Russians already aboard. I had taken time to see this particular aircraft loaded because I had been told it was taking an English agent into southern Serbia. The normal rule was that the Russians never had any contact with us except through their liaison officer. They never asked us to their mess, nor would they enter ours. Although they made full use of our weather and intelligence reports, they aseemed to be fighting a separate war.

I was surprised therefore when the Russian liaison officer, an Englishman who had been born in Russia and educated partly in Russia and partly in England, rang from Bari to say the aircraft would land at Brindisi to pick up an agent being sent direct from the training school at Lecce. I knew that the training school at Lecce, a very hush-hush establishment, specialised in training Joes to be dropped into Northern Italy and the Russians were not supposed to know of its existence. The Russian Dakota was supposed to be on a mission to a landing strip near the Russian HQ in Serbia. This particular Joe was driven into the aerodrome in a Jeep with British markings by a conducting officer whose credentials seemed perfect. This procedure was normal as all agents going behind enemy lines would obviously leave any British or allied papers behind and the conducting officer vouched for them on arrival at the aircraft. I would have thought no more about it if the man had not drawn attention to himself. However, the pilot, whose engines were already ticking over, took off without waiting for the green affirmative from the Watch Office, at the same time smothering me with dust. I looked around for the conducting officer but he had driven off and was already past the perimeter barrier.

By this time I was thoroughly suspicious and drove straight to the Operations Room and asked Radar to track the aircraft as long as possible. Immediately, the track showed something unusual. Instead of flying almost due east towards Monastir in Serbia as briefed, the aircraft was steering a south-easterly course which would take it to Greece. I immediately telephoned the mission operating in Northern Italy and asked them to check up on who had been sent from the Lecce training school, giving them the name of he conducting officer. Within half an hour I got the reply that no-one had been sent and they knew no conducting officer of the name given. Furthermore, they were amazed and horrified to hear that the Russians even knew of the Lecce establishment.

I then rang the duty officer at Balkan Air Force HQ, told him the whole story and asked him to seek an explanation from the Russians as soon as possible. By this time it was 0300 so I turned in order to snatch a couple of hours sleep before collecting the reports from the aircraft which would be returning from their various missions about 0500. The last radar plot of the Russian aircraft showed it crossing the Greek coast at about 5000ft.

At 0730, I rang the Air Officer Commanding the BAF, Air Vice Marshall William Elliot, with the customary resume of the night's operations and then told him what had happened with the Russian aircraft. Bill was very interested and more than a little angry and said he would send for the Russian colonel and demand an explanation. Later that day I flew up to Bari for a conference on other matters and the AOC told me that the Russian colonel had at first pretended on the "No spik Eenglish" principle that he knew nothing , but then he gave a beaming smile and said "But the aircraft is reported missing, so it is all finish, no?" That was all that could be got out of the Russians and we never found out where the Joe or his conducting officer had come from. Some months later, however, after the liberation of Greece, when Communist guerrillas were doing their worst to seize control of the country, we heard some nasty stories from escaped prisoners (some of them British) of atrocities massacres and the like by a band of guerrillas lead by a tall Englishman.

With the end of the war in sight, we began to be plagued by Labour politicians who somehow managed to be transported by the RAF and arrived demanding VIP treatment. Worse, they expected hard-worked commanding officers to order special parades of their units so that a vote-catching speech could be made in readiness for the general election which would undoubtedly be held at the end of hostilities. This appeared to me to be dangerously similar to the compulsory indoctrination methods adopted alike by the Nazis and the Communists, particularly if discipline was made use of to force men to listen to political speeches. Also in a Wing like ours, where most of the personnel were working and flying round the clock a parade, even of those off-duty or resting was an unjustifiable infringement on the men's free time.

So, as far as our Wing was concerned, the only men who attended the vote-catchers political talks were volunteers whose numbers were so small and proved that our refusal to hold a parade for political purposes was more than justified.

During a blizzard which covered much of the southern end of Italy we received a signal to the effect that two of these political VIP's would be leaving Naples the following morning to fly to Brindisi. Visibility at Brindisi was down to 200 yards and the weather forecast predicted worse conditions for the next day. As soon as I received the message I sent off a priority signal to Naples to say that landing at Brindisi was impossible.

To our horror, we learnt the next day that the aircraft, a small twin-engined communications type, had taken off from Naples in spite of adverse weather reports. We were told that the VIP's had persuaded the pilot against his better judgement to try to get them through. Unfortunately, the aircraft flew into a mountain in the bad visibility and they were all killed.

After this regrettable and unnecessary accident, no more politicians came to bother us. The war in Europe was nearing the end. The Germans were retreating on all fronts, but we could not reduce our efforts, because there were still starving people to be fed and wounded to be evacuated.

Our indefatigable Squadron Leader Good made plans for an all-ranks peace celebration however, so when the final collapse of Germany was announced, we were prepared. With great ingenuity, Good had organised a beer garden within the Station bounds, with a stage, a band, coloured lights and a dance floor surrounded by tables and seats. We managed to stockpile a fair quantity of beer and plenty of the local wine and paid for them out of our accumulated canteen funds.

When VE Day came, our celebration party was much appreciated by everyone and although the drinks were plentiful and free, there were no incidents. When chatting to Squadron Leader Arciuszkiewicz and some of the Polish officers, I noticed that they were very subdued so I said "Cheer up, Archie, the war's over and you will soon be back in your own country. Aren't you pleased?"

With a twisted smile he replied "For you the war is over, you go back to England. We Poles have nowhere to go we go to Poland, is Russia now, for us only Siberia or worse." When I protested that Russia was supposed to be our ally, he replied "When we fly 1800 miles to Warsaw and back to help Polish rising against Germans in Warsaw Russian army only two miles away, do nothing, only try to shoot us down. Is not future for Poles who fight in British forces. Only slavery for Poles now. You see!" How right he proved to be.

By the end of May 1945, the Americans had withdrawn their squadrons, the Polish Squadron returned to England for disbandment and it was decided to move the Wing Headquarters and No 148 Squadron to Foggia by the end of June.

I was glad to hand over the Wing to my successor before this move took place. Sometime in July, after a few days in a transit camp in Naples, I sailed in the Athlone Castle for Southampton.

On the five day voyage I spent most of the time asleep it had been a long war and I was very tired.

Woody as a Royal Marine subaltern. A portrait taken in June 1916 only a few days before he left for action in France. *ABW Collection.*

Woody's 824 Squadron Swordfish at Seletar Airfield, Singapore, January 1938. *ABW Collection.*

This photograph is obviously a copy from a magazine or newspaper. It was captioned "Working party at Beaumont Hamel, November 1916." *ABW Collection.*

824 Squadron Swordfish from HMS Eagle on Coronation Flypast over Hong Kong, May 12, 1937 (Happy Valley racecourse is in the background). The pilot of 945 with black flight leader's marking on tail is Squadron Leader AB Woodhall and his crew is Leading Telegraphist Faulkner and Lieutenant Gardner. *ABW Collection, Crown Copyright.*

"The Staffordshires with all their equipment formed a considerable clutter on the forward end of the lower flying-off deck." The scene on HMS Courageous on August 27, 1929 as the carrier set off from Malta to Haifa to deal with "trouble between the Jews and Arabs". *ABW Collection, Crown Copyright.*

An informal group of personnel at a Duxford party during 1940. *ABW Collection.*

Group Captain Woodhall with Air Vice Marshal Sir Trafford Leigh-Mallory at Tangmere, 1941. *ABW Collection.*

A photograph of Duxford Wing pilots of the Battle of Britain that went round the world in 1940 with varying patriotic captions. Sitting on the wing, from left to right are:- Squadron Leader 'Sandy' Lane, Flight Sergeant 'Grumpy' Unwin and Flying Officer Francis Brinsden (New Zealand). The two dogs are Unwin's 'Flash' and Brinsden's 'Rangi' (right). Standing (from left) Sergeant Bernard Jennings, Flight Lieutenant Colin MacFie, Flight Lieutenant Howard Burton and Pilot Officer Phillip Leckrone (USA). The last three named are 616 Squadron pilots, the rest being 19 Squadron. *ABW Collection, Crown Copyright.*

The Duxford Operations Room, July 1940. In this original print, documents have been inked over (by Woody as CO) to indicate that such items should be painted out on the negative before prints are released for publication. *ABW Collection, Crown Copyright.*

A sector station generated plenty of paperwork - the Duxford Orderly Room, 1940. *ABW Collection, Crown Copyright.*

Squadron Leader Douglas Bader with Dorothy Stanbury (Woody's youngest sister) early in 1940. *ABW Collection.*

"Hello Woody, how are you?" Douglas Bader ignores the official welcome party and greets his former Duxford and Tangmere CO. AB "Woody" Woodhall at Harewood Airport, Christchurch NZ in 1956. *George Weigel photo.*

Hurricanes of 87 Squadron in Lille Marc, France March 1940. Hurricane LK-L of Pilot Officer Roland "Bee" Beamont is the only aircraft with a 3-blade variable-pitch propellor. Squadron Leadderr Dennis David's machine is closest to camera. *ABW Collection, Crown Copyright.*

Pilot Officer Wallace Cunningham, Sub Lieutenant AG "Admiral" Blake FAA and Flying Officer Frank Brinsden (NZ) plus Rangi, a very fat spaniel that made more photo-shoots than many pilots. Fowlemere 1940. *ABW Collection, Crown Copyright.*

Sergeant Alois Dvorak, 310 Squadron, on the wing of his Hurricane at Duxford. This was another of those photos that were sent worldwide as part of the patriotic effort. It appeared in New Zealand newspapers with the caption "A Czechoslovak fighter pilot is congratulated by his comrades after a successful sortie." Dvorak died on September 29, 1941 after crashing in fog while on a formation flight from Dyce to Montrose. *ABW Collection, Crown Copyright.*

19 Squadron pilots pose for a briefing photo, Duxford, 1940. *ABW Collection, Crown Copyright.*

At the age of 31, Captain A.B.Woodhall R.M. in his cabin on *HMS Courageous*, Malta 1928. *ABW Collection.*

An early photograph of 19 Squadron Mk 1 Spitfires, over Duxford. Photo probably among those taken on Press Day at Duxford, May, 1939. *ABW Collection, Crown Copyright.*

An informal photo of the Queen at Duxford, January 16, 1941. She was being shown how to play "Shove ha'penny" by the station medical officer, Dr Apley. *ABW Collection.*

Wing Commander AB Woodhall as Commanding officer and senior sector controller, Duxford, 1940. *ABW Collection, Crown Copyright.*

Malta, July 1942. Woody and Squadron Leader Stan Grant and two members of his control staff shortly before he left the island. *ABW Collection.*

The WW1 destroyer, *HMS Shikari*, entering Grand Harbour, Malta. *HMS Shikari* was the last Royal Navy ship to safely leave Dunkirk during the evacuation and served the rest of the war on escort duties in the North Atlantic and Mediterranean. *ABW collection.*

Fighter pilots relaxing between raids at Luqa, June 1942. *ABW Collection.*

Aircrew taking a breather during work preparing aircraft pens for the second reinforcement of Spitfires from USS Wasp on May 9, 1942. *ABW Collection.*

Flying officer Buck Buchanan DFC, 249 Squadron, on the wing of Spitfire, Takali, May 1942. Buchanan, a Rhodesian who had been with 41 Squadron during the Tangmere Wing days, was one of the Hurricane pilots from the early days of 249 Squadron on Malta. *ABW Collection.*

The Rhodesian pilot, Flight Lieutenant "Johnnie" Plagis DFC, one of the top-scoring Malta fighter pilots. This portrait was taken in England in 1943 when Plagis became godfather to Martin Woodhall. *ABW Collection.*

Pilots and other officers relaxing outside the Xara Palace mess in March 1942. At left is Warby - Flight Lieutenant Adrian Warburton, and next to him the Canadian Flight Lieutenant 'Buck' McNair. *ABW Collection.*

Squadron Leader Brian Lane, 19 Squadron CO, watches as ground crew rearm and refuel a Hurricane at Fowlmere during the Battle of Britain. *ABW Collection, Crown Copyright.*

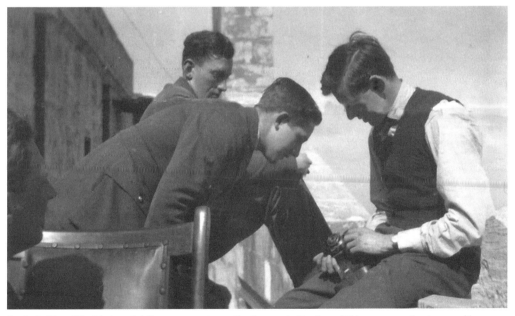

A pilot's (Raoul Daddo-Langlois') camera captures the focus of attention of this group on the terrace, Xara Palace, probably May 1942. Buck McNair is at right rear. *ABW Collection.*

An American and British mission commander being briefed at Brindisi before a supply dropping mission over northern Yugoslavia. *ABW Collection, Crown Copyright.*

Spitfires of 253 Squadron undergo maintenance on 19 July 1944, Italy. (Photo taken on July 19, 1944 judging by chalk writing on foreground machine). Caption (as released to Press) reads: "Specially selected partisans from Marshall Tito's forces in Yugoslavia were recently chosen to make the journey to Italy to train with RAF ground crews on Spitfires. Their instructional classes are taken by RAF non- commissioned officers. Yugoslave Partisans and men of the RAF work on Spitfires on an airfield in Italy. *ABW collection. Crown Copyright.*

A 148 Squadron despatcher checking supplies on a Halifax ready for dropping to partisans in Yugoslavia. *ABW Collection, Crown Copyright.*

Two Handley - Page Halifax aircraft with 148 Squadron, Brinidisi, July 1944. Halifax JP246 'FS-B' suffered a collapsed undercarriage on return from a mission over Yugoslavia on October 8, 1944. *ABW Collection, Crown Copyright.*

Pesonnel from 148 Squadron packing supplies for dropping to partisans in Yugoslavia, August 1944. *ABW Collection, Crown Copyright.*

The prototype Gloster Gladiator in its final configuration with Bristol Mercury IX engine, sliding hood and faired tailwheel, On 1 July 1935 the allocation of the name Gladiator was officially announced and an initial contract placed for 23 aircraft. This aircraft was flown by Flight Lieutenant Woodhall at the Hendon air display. *ABW Collection, Crown Copyright.*

Taken in 1937, this photograph was recirculated to newspapers in 1940 with the caption "A Baffin returning to the aircraft carrier Eagle after a search for enemy craft." *ABW Collection, Crown Copyright.*

Douglas and Thelma Bader and Margot and Woody Woodhall at Christchurch Airport, November 1956. *ABW Collection, Green & Hahn photo.*

Woody, Margot, and family members at the entrance to their house "Boray" in Waterrow, Kent. April 20 1941. At left is Woody's brother Herbert and on the right are nieces Frieda and Peggy. *ABW Collection.*

Proud father - Woody with his 18-month-old daughter Jennifer, on the Thames barge '*Swiftsure*', November 1947. *ABW Collection.*

Postscript

Woody wrote a large part of "Soldier Sailor and Airman Too" in 1956 to 1958 but the chapter on Malta was originally drafted in his off-duty time at Brindisi in 1944-45. Some of his stories were broadcast on the Radio New Zealand national programme as a series of tapes he recorded in 1958 and he also made tapes for the Returned Services Association around the same time. He had made a number of unsuccessful attempts to find a publisher both in New Zealand and in the United Kingdom. After his death in 1968, two publishers who had rejected the manuscript came forward and tried to obtain the rights from Margot (our mother). She was furious and locked the book away. I was eventually given access, but only after I had promised that nobody outside the family would rewrite or edit his words.

Like so many of his generation and profession, Woody has left out much detail about himself. His main manuscript ended with his retirement in 1945 although he did intend to write a postscript with a little of his post-service activities.

The picture that emerges from these writings is largely of a "man's man", a gentleman adventurer who was most at home in a service environment with the men of his Royal Marine detachment at the Somme, then later with his squadrons in the Fleet Air Arm or the Royal Air Force. Little mention is made of women in his life – but more of that later.

He spoke very fondly of his 1916 comrade Joe Thorold who so boosted their spirits and entertained with his renditions of Kipling's "Barrackroom Ballads". What he failed to mention was that he himself took up this mantle, teaching himself to play the piano by ear and there was rarely a party in the mess where at some time in the evening, Woody would sing and play at least one number from his extensive repertoire of often bawdy songs. He had a particular way of delivering certain songs that conveyed both seriousness and humour at the same time and there was also an air of experience and wisdom. Some particular songs seemed almost to be about him rather than merely sung by him.

If there was no piano available, Woody could usually find a banjo or a ukelele (sometimes , if only to play one of his signature tunes "Song of the Banjo" and this would invariably also launch him into a selection of songs by the Australian, Banjo

Paterson.) He was a great admirer of Rudyard Kipling and he remained a loyal supporter long after it was fashionable to do so. When he became a sector controller at Duxford during the Battle of Britain it was from Kipling that he drew his call-sign. ("Beetle" from Stalky and Co.)

The two songs I most remember him singing are "Foggy Foggy Dew" (an old Irish folksong and music hall ballad) and "The Ladies" (Kipling). Both songs were always delivered in a comic fashion but also in such a way that listeners believed they were about real events in his life.

Woody was also a skilled and enthusiastic saxophone player and there many who remember him playing Glen Miller songs at wartime parties. There are other references to his playing "a very expensive piano accordion" or accompanying himself on a humble 'squeezebox'.

When he returned to England after his two-year cruise to China and the Far East in HMS Hawkins, Woody married his first wife, Dorothy Seymour Wingfield at St Simons Church, Southsea, on November 17, 1921. At the time of writing this, I have only the details on the marriage certificate. Dorothy was the daughter of a Royal Navy Fleet Engineer, Henry Eggleton Wingfield (deceased) and the marriage was conducted by Howard J Marshall, Chaplain to HM Forces. Witnesses were Laura Rider, Jane Wingfield and Richard F. Darff.

The honeymoon was apparently cut short. While not referring to the marriage in his manuscript, Woody states that his leave was curtailed in December 1921 when his Royal Marine battalion went into training for deployment to Ireland. It is my belief that Dorothy was the night sister at Haslar Hospital referred to in Chapter 3, but I have so far been unable to substantiate this. I (along with my brother and sister) were totally unaware of any previous relationships involving our father until the early 1960's when Woody's cover was well and truly blown because we all three received letters from a London solicitor stating "your father's second wife" had left each of us 100 pounds in her will. At the time, Woody somehow glossed over the issue without giving any details, on the grounds that he did not speak of such things out of loyalty to our mother. On my part, I found the concept of two previous wives merely slightly interesting but very remote and irrelevant to my life as a young university student, so I did not pursue the question. By the time I was keen to research the matter, all the paperwork had disappeared. I did discover, however, that my Aunt Dorothy (Woody's youngest sister) had secretly introduced me to this second wife in 1961. I was visiting England with a party of high school cadets and stayed with my aunt in her St John's Wood Rd apartment for several days. She told me that no visit to London would be complete without taking tea at a Lyon's corner teashop and duly took me to the cornerhouse on The Strand one afternoon. I vaguely remember her "surprise" meeting at a neighbouring table with a woman who she introduced as an old friend who "knew Woody before the war". The old friend was really Mrs Helen Bruce who married Woody on September 16, 1935 at Alderton Parish Church, Suffolk. Helen was born Helen Kayler and had been formerly married to Harold E.B. Holden "from whom she obtained a divorce" according to the marriage certificate. The decree absolute was granted to Woody's first wife only four days prior to the second marriage which was performed by F.E.Doughty, honorary RAF chaplain.

That meeting was obviously a set-up. With Dorothy as a sister, Woody had also been able to slip out of an earlier moment of confrontation. In 1957, I was reading his flying logbook covering his time on Malta with HMS Courageous and saw an entry in red ink marked "Private flying in Glen Kidston's Moth". There were two dates, June 30 and July 4, 1928 and the passenger was listed as D.S.Woodhall. When I quizzed him about this he airily replied "Oh that was my sister Dorothy who came out to Malta for a short holiday."

(In his manuscript, Woody speaks of "a lady friend who had never been flying and who was unable to understand my love of flying.") Thirty years were to pass before I even thought about further questioning that statement, but it was obviously his wife, Dorothy Seymour Woodhall, who had travelled to Malta with him in a very adventurous journey in an Austin 7 they affectionately called "Pimple." (See appendix.)

In his narrative, Woody speaks of the journey without mentioning a wife but says he wrote an article which was published in the Austin Magazine. Using the resources of the Internet, I contacted vintage Austin clubs in New Zealand and the U.K. and was delighted to receive Part 2 of the article from Barry Davis in Worcestshire, England. (See appendix). Several months later, Barry contacted me again with Part 1 of the article in the March 1928 Austin Magazine and even came up with a complete issue of the May 1928 publication which is now in my "Woody Archive." Woody does not directly describe his wife and gives no details abut her. But judging by the article, she was quite obviously resourceful, adventurous and attractive and along with many other British service wives set up a flat in Malta in support of her husband and doubtless became a patron of the vaunted and feared Ladies bar at the Union Club. The car apparently returned to England as "personal luggage" on HMS Courageous when Woody returned with the carrier to Gosport in June 1930. Serving officers obviously made use of such facilities at the "Captain's discretion" – Lieutenant Glen Kidston transported his private aircraft out to Malta in the same way. Dorothy apparently travelled back to England by steamer and presumably at he same time. I have no clues as to when and why the marriage fell apart but Woody did once tell me that the belief that "absence makes the heart grow fonder" was a load of rubbish. "Take it from one who knows!" (This could have obviously have applied to either of the first two marriages.)

Dorothy served a divorce summons on Flight Lieutenant A.B.Woodhall on September 16, 1935. At that time he was officer commanding 'A' Flight with the RAF performance testing section at Martlesham Heath. For some information on his second wife, I am indebted to Heather Prins in Melbourne, Australia, who responded (also via the Internet) providing me with background on the Kayler family. It seems very likely that Woody and Helen shared an interest in sailing from Torquay in Devon and probably met at the local yacht club. Heather Prins also very kindly researched my family history and went to a great deal of effort in providing a detailed family tree.

The second marriage officially ended with a decree absolute on May 22, 1940. There was a lesson handed down from this marriage too. My mother warned me about the dangers of surprise returns from afar when I was about to come back to the New Zealand mainland from a crayfishing foray in the Chatham Islands. "Don't be silly and think it would be amusing to arrive on your girlfriend without warning. Your father did that to his second wife but he was the one that got the surprise because he discovered that an Army officer had moved in with her while he was away." In response to the Abyssinian crisis, Woody had been posted to Khormaksar, Aden, with 41 Fighter Squadron only a month after the marriage and he was invalided home from there in November with a torn cartilage. When he was promoted to Squadron Leader a year later (December 1, 1936) he was then posted to HMS Eagle as commanding officer of 824 Squadron which meant a prolonged time away from home. It was after his night-flying crash on Eagle that he made the unheralded trip back on the SS Somersetshire and surprised both wife and rival. (He had been in Malta, Singapore and China from January 1937 until June 1938.) In the way the story was told, the worst aspect of the unfaithfulness was that it was with an Army officer – there was some implication that the affair would have been more understandable (and forgivable) if it had involved either a naval or air force officer. Apparently, however, both men behaved impeccably, as officers and gentlemen should; they shook hands and settled future matters over a drink at the local pub. Following the divorce from Woody, Helen married Major Nigel Bruce on December 7, 1940.

After that unsatisfactory homecoming, Woody spent his foreign service leave with his brother Herbert and family. In a letter written just after Woody's death, Herbert's elder daughter Frieda wrote: "During my childhood and when I was a young woman he was a very favourite uncle and it was always a very happy time for me when he was home on leave. We had some very happy times together and I used to adore him.

"He was, of course, always a wanderer in those days, in more ways than one.."

Efforts on my part to contact relatives of either Woody's first two wives or even any of his family relatives have been unsuccessful. I am sure that either Dorothy or Helen would have received both letters and photographs from him and hopefully stored them safely. He kept in touch with both his sisters prior to the war and I would also expect both of them would have photographs from the pre-World War 2 years. We have albums and photographs from the date of his marriage to my mother, Margot (nee Robinson) who was W.A.A.F. Section Officer at Duxford when they met. (They married on January 9, 1941, Woody's 44th birthday.) Three wives. Once we knew that, my brother and I were convinced there was a fourth relationship somewhere, basing our suspicions entirely on the grin on Woody's face when he sang "The Ladies". "I've 'ad me pickin' o' sweet'earts. An' four o' the lot was prime"

In retrospect, I believe that was an understatement. There was yet another cautionary tale told (in extreme confidence, mind) by both Woody and Margot. When Woody was in Shanghai in 1920, his role as a Royal Marine officer brought with it a number of ceremonial and ambassadorial responsibilities and he was in frequent contact with influential Chinese authorities. At some point he was in almost daily contact with a very important family and as Woody put it, he developed a "fondness" for a daughter of the official he was dealing with. (Margot said simply, they fell in love with each other.) Protocol and culture meant, however, that the match was forbidden. The attraction was noticed by both the girl's family and Woody's superiors and temptation was quietly removed – Woody's duties were altered and she was sent away to stay with relatives outside Shanghai. The moral of course was "East is east and west is west and never the twain shall meet" so yet another of Kipling's songs were sung with a personal input. When I heard all this in the 1960's, I was horrified by what I saw as the racism portrayed and with all the confidence of a student of the time said so in no uncertain terms. While allowing me the confidence and principles of youth, both parents quietly pointed out the changes in mores from 1920 and Woody also said it was her family that would have been most outraged at any relationship.

"She was effectively a princess within her society. And on top of the perceived class difference, there was a huge cultural and religious barrier between us."

Apparently, the girl was among the first in family to be allowed to grow up with her feet unbound, a detail that does give further credence to the term "princess." The picture remains of a very pretty and finely-dressed Asian girl and a dashing young Royal marine officer in his white ceremonial uniform, both exchanging polite pleasantries at a distance, while adoring each other. "But I didn't do such. 'Cos I loved her too much. And I learned about women from her.." (More from "The Ladies".)

He also told me that on his return to China on MS Eagle 1937 he had made some attempts to contact the family but believed the whole family had been slaughtered by the Japanese.

For an example of Woody's sense of humour and theatre in a social setting, I cannot do better than quote in full a letter from Mariquita Westinghouse received in 1997: She titled the anecdote "Introduction to a Lady". (Mariquita Dunkley was a British servicewoman who married Tom Westinghouse, one of the United States pilots operating out of Brindisi while Woody was there in 1945.)

During World War 2 in the service in Italy (1945), a sister unit down the coast from me invited me to a special party. 'Transortation and an escort will be provided.'

The escort, they said, would be Group Captain Woodhall, whom I had never met. I was, however, familiar with his fame as a director (from the ground) of the aerial dog-fights over Malta where my fiancée had been staioned in the Artillery (Heavy Coastal Defence) for nearly three years. In my acceptance, I asked that my escort be warned that when he came to pick me up, I would be rather slow in making an appearance and please to wait patiently! This was not owing to a false sense of grandeur but that, as I lived on the top floor of an apartment building and the Germans had removed the working parts of the elevator, I would have to hang out of the window until I saw my ride appear and then run madly down eight floors of stairs, 64 short flights.

At the appointed time, I duly hung out of the window and was greatly impressed to see a long, low-slung, shiny black Lagonda glide up to the door. I practically fell down the stairs. Seated at the wheel was the great Group Captain, service cap right down over his nose (Like any good ex-Royal Marine.) Seated next to him was his driver, who hopped out, put me in his seat and then retired to the back seat where he sat smartly at attention with his arms folded at chest level.

The officer under the cap explained that he had to deal immediately with an urgent telegram so we must detour to Balkan Air Force HQ. The driver and I waited until he reappeared a short time later and he started off for the party. Remember, I had never met nor even seen this officer before. Without preliminary, in the darkness, out from under the cap came these immortal words:-

'Ullo dearie, Lash me up to a whisky an' soda
An Oi'll tell yer the story o' me life, Me farver was a vicar in Kent
'Ow Oi did 'ate that man.
Oi was hengaged to an orficer in the Guards Pa shot 'im (Gawd 'ow 'e did bleed) Thank you ducky, mine's a Creamy de Menthey
Whisky makes me burp so..

He then extended his hand, and introduced himself. Needless to say we had a wonderful time at the party, he was a great man and a marvellous companion and I always valued his friendship."

I should make it very clear, however, that there was never any unfaithfulness within marriage. Woody had a very high sense of duty and morals and if there was any virtue he prized above all, it was loyalty.

"It had been a long war and I was very tired." With these words, Woody rang down the end of his service career. He had been in uniform for six months short of 30 years and spent two months longer in the Royal Air Force than in the Royal Marines.

The reasons for his voluntary retirement are not given but within the family we were told that the government, forseeing the end of the war in the Pacific against the Japanese had already been offering "Golden Bowlers" to regular service officers in the service. Woody's decision to accept a lump sum payment plus a full retirement pay was also coloured by the fact that early in 1945 he had been told that a promotion to Air Commodore was on its way and that he should consider himself acting in that rank. This offer was withdrawn just before hostilities ceased against Germany and in one version of his manuscript Woody wrote "so for the second time I was glad that I hadn't put up the stripe for air rank."

He returned to England and rejoined Margot and his two sons, then aged four and two, at a cottage in Waterrow, Kent. As the two-year-old, who had reportedly run a little rampant without fatherly discipline, I was not initially amused. After a few weeks of facing up to Woody, I plaintively asked my mother "When is that man going away?" But within a few months I was already learning outside the nursery for during an afternoon tea party an aircraft flew overhead and the local vicar (it had to be that, of course) asked me "Look, an aeroplane, is it a Spitfire?" Based entirely on the sound, I replied "No. It's just a little pisser." The aircraft was in fact a Miles Magister.

Once in civilian life, Woody lost no time in returning to his first love, the sea. He bought an old Thames sailing barge, "Swiftsure", at Conyer Creek near Sittingbourne, Kent, and almost immediately moved the family aboard and started converting it into a sailing house-boat. The 76-foot vessel had been built around the turn of the century and as with all her class was yawl-rigged and designed for coastal sailing – there was no engine and despite the fairly tall rig, she could be handled by two men. The rig on these barges included a "sprit", an extremely large spar like a gaff that went from the peak of the 'leg o' mutton' mainsail to the foot of the mast. Considering the weight and size of this spar, Woody replaced it with a more conventional (and modern) gaff and had the sprit sawn into planks from which he built a 13ft sailing dory. He also installed a diesel auxiliary motor, doing all the engineering and carpentry himself.

After such a career, how did he settle into retirement? The simple answer is like so many of his contemporaries, even those servicemen who had only joined up for the duration of the war, he found peacetime and civilian life in England restrictive and possibly boring.

Kipling put it all into words following the Boer War in his poem Chant-Pagan, which we were to become familiar with.

"Me that 'ave been what I've been,
Me that 'ave gone where I've gone,
Me that 'ave seen what I've seen
'Ow can I ever take on
With awful old England again?"

Like the subject of the piece (members of the English Irregular Army 1899-1902) Woody loved his England and had returned hopefully but he had also met so many personnel from so many faraway and to him enticing and more free countries. Rationing was still very tight in post-war Britain and the two countries he found most alluring were New Zealand and Canada. Now with a family of three children, he apparently favoured New Zealand at the outset, based largely on the pilots he had served with, and duly applied for emigration to that country. He was turned down because with his retired pay he was considered too well off for acceptance for an assisted passage. Canada welcomed him, but with predicted high unemployment threatening among all the returning servicemen, made him sign papers saying he would not seek paid employment for ten years.

We travelled to Canada on the Empress of Canada and arrived via Halifax in October 1947. Following a memorable steam-train trip right across Canada on the famed Canadian Pacific railroad, we then took the ferry from Vancouver and joined a group of ex-RCAF personnel at the little settlement of Genoa Bay on Vancouver Island. Lead by the Gould brothers, members of the community refurbished several houses that had been part of a saw-milling village and the Woodhalls moved into one of the first completed. While using his woodworking and carpentry skills for the group, Woody also built a 19-ft Lightning sailing dinghy. This little yacht, a design still in popular use today, was chosen as an ideal compromise as both a racing dinghy and family knock-about.

The Royal Canadian Air Force was still operating from Sidney and Woody joined the reserve and for a brief time was able to fly again, becoming a pilot officer in the RCAF (service number 205038) on May 14, 1948.

After a couple of years at Genoa bay, the family moved to Schwarz Bay and became neighbours of Randall and Brenda Mathews who ran a little boat-hire and fishing business at Randall's Landing. My brother Jeremy and I both started school at Deep Cove School a few miles away.

The cottage at Schwarz Bay was tiny for a family of five and Woody immediately started building an extension to provide an extra bedroom and what was termed a rumpus room. Money was tight so he made his own moulds and hand-cast concrete blocks. He had almost completed the work when he became seriously ill from what was originally diagnosed as asthma and believed to be a reaction to the concrete he was handling. Later, the diagnosis was emphysema and a form of silicosis which was thought largely due to the prolonged exposure to the dust of Malta during the wartime bombing. Whatever the cause, the illness was prolonged and if it was not for the charity of the local Seventh Day Adventist hospital Woody may well have died because being without medical insurance (as he was not working in Canada) he was initially unable to get treatment. Once out of hospital he made a good recovery (although the asthma/emphysema was chronic) but sadly was unable to re-qualify for his pilot's license. With the house extension completed, he built a little Yachting World Cadet for the children to sail. (We were allowed out alone once we had proved we could swim from the middle of the bay to the shore.)

One of the frequent visitors to the Woodhall house in those days was "Poppy" Pope, by then a retired Air Commodore but still very outgoing and exuberant personality. (see Chapter 7) He became Uncle Poppy to the children and I can vividly remember being carried around the house on his shoulders at parties – he was still about 6ft

6in tall – and the trick was to swing sideways and down when being taken through doorways. Woody thought then I might have a future at rodeo events.

Another occasion remembered vividly was the day we heard a screech of tires on the main highway above our house. A car, which had stopped suddenly, then reversed down our drive and a three-day party ensued. The driver of the car was none other than Stan Turner, possibly one of Woody's staunchest and best friends, although the two had hardly seen each other since leaving Malta in 1942. The famed eagle-eyes of Stan had spotted the name A.B.Woodhall on the letterbox as he drove past, until then he had no idea Woody was in Canada. (Stan was by then living in Toronto and was on holiday on Vancouver Island) Our house became the centre of an ongoing reunion and ex-aircrew were summoned from near and far. This was the first time I had an inkling that my father had "been in a war."

The two Christmases of 1949 and 1950 were also memorable, particularly for the children. We travelled by car and ferry to Seattle and spent Christmas with Tom and Mariquita Westinghouse and family on Bainbridge Island. Tom and his twin brother Geoff were also pilots and Mariquita of course introduced herself above.

The idyllic existence on the island came to a sudden halt early in 1950. I remember being told that we had to leave Canada because a man named "Sir Stifford Bloody Crapps" had devalued the pound sterling against the United States and Canadian dollars. (Sir Stafford Cripps, Chancellor of the Exchequer in the post-war British Labour Government of Clement Attlee, devalued the pound from US$4.03 to US2.80 in September 1949.) Now, Woody could no longer support a family on his retired pay and New Zealand became the only viable option - apparently we were now poor enough to gain admission. To raise money for the fares, practically everything had to be sold and I'm told we only just raised enough, the last vital amount coming from the sail of our beloved YW Cadet sailing dinghy to the family of pioneer Vancouver Island aviator, Aubrey Westinghouse (cousin of Geoff and Tom Westinghouse).

We travelled to New Zealand on the S.S. Aorangi. The journey took 21 days with brief stops at Hawaii and Fiji and we arrived at Auckland on May 16, 1950. We rented houses briefly at Mairangi Bay and Browns Bay on Auckland's North Shore but eventually moved to a house with 4 acres of land at Stanmore Bay on Whangaparoa Peninsula. Woody's woodworking skills were put to good use when he was employed as a cabinetmaker by a local builder and for several months he was happily working with his hands at constructing built-in furniture in houses in Orewa. He also borrowed a crawler tractor and equipment from a local farmer and cultivated most of the 4 acres and planted a large crop of potatoes and some carrots. After a year of working for the builder ("a gentleman named Snow" was all he ever told us later), Woody went into partnership with him with plans to build motels at Orewa and Warkworth. To raise capital for his share in the venture, Woody "commuted" his retired pay i.e. he took a lump sum payment in advance and effectively went on to half the income from that source. His "partner" promptly disappeared to Australia with the money - about 5000 pounds which was a considerable sum in those days. Woody laid a complaint with the police but was told that he would have to take civil proceedings to recover the money and he was unlikely to succeed as there was little in the way of formal paperwork. The service background where a promise could be sealed with a handshake did not work so well in civilian life - a lesson Woody was to learn several times.

With his retired pay halved, Woody took temporary work on the Auckland waterfront as a tally clerk – he was among a number of ex-servicemen employed in an attempt to break the 1951 Watersiders' Strike. Within a few months , however, he moved the family to Plimmerton, near Wellington, and spent three years as administrative assistant to the Controller of Airways (Sir Arthur Nevill) with the New Zealand Civil Aviation Administration. This job did involve quite a large amount of being flown to various aerodromes throughout New Zealand and such places as Fiji, Rarotonga and the Chatham Islands.

While in Plimmerton, Woody built two more sailing dinghies. The first was a GP 14 ("General Purpose 14ft") and the second and 11ft Heron. Both were Yachting World magazine sponsored designs. He built the GP 14 from scratch using double-diagonal kauri planking but the Heron was a plywood-skinned kitset that had been imported by a CAA colleague, Douglas Cooper, who sold when he decided to return to England.

A visit to Queenstown in 1954 and a resultant party of former air force pilots at the Shotover Hotel had a two-year sequel. Fred "Popeye" Lucas immediately offered Woody employment as Operations Manager of Southern Scenic Air Services. A little airline with several ex-air force aircraft such as Tiger Moths, Percival Proctors, an Auster and two de Havilland Dominie among its fleet as well as a staff of mainly ex-service personnel – it was almost like returning to active duty. The company was heavily involved in the fledgling topdressing industry (using Tiger Moths) and was also opening up tourist flights to Fiordland and the West Coast as well as running a passenger, mail and freight service between Queenstown and Dunedin. Tiger Moth aircraft were also used to drop poisoned carrots in the extensive fight against the rabbit in Central Otago. A very popular service with both pilots and clients was the ferrying of whitebait in 4-gallon tins from the West Coast to various destinations. The growth potential of such pioneer flying soon attracted bigger business and in 1956, Mount Cook Airlines bought out Southern Scenic Air Services. Although they employed several of the pilots, they did not need an operations manager so Woody was unemployed again. His private view was that Mount Cook's interest was only in the lease of Queenstown Airport.

The family then moved to Dunedin where Woody, after unsuccessfully trying to sell insurance, became secretary to the National Party in Dunedin.

As a father, I always remember Woody seemed to spend more time with his children than most other dads, wherever we lived. He was as old as some of the grandparents of my contemporaries and that possibly was a factor. When I started high school (Kings' High School, Dunedin) he enthusiastically entered us in the father-son shooting competition . He insisted on all contestants being allowed two "sighting shots"

(and nobody argued with him). He fired first and it was obvious that the sniping training from 40 years ago had not been forgotten, after stating that the rifle was firing high and at 10 o'clock, he scored three bullseyes and then told me to shoot for the 4 o'clock position on the outer ring of the target. I did exactly as asked and scored two bullseyes and one inner – we won the competition.

His social life in Dunedin revolved around the RSA and the Otago Officers' Club and there was rarely a couple of months would go by without him arriving home on a Friday evening with some old friend (or friends) from his service life. He invariably opened introductions by saying to Margot "Look who I've found." Such evenings usually resulted in other friends being contacted and very often the piano would be opened up and several Kipling songs sung. Unfortunately, the family have been unable to find any recordings of such parties although I am sure some tapes were made.

In 1960, Woody was honoured to be invited to attend the 20th Anniversary of the Battle of Britain as a VIP guest and he spent a memorable two months in the UK in August and September of that year. As well as staying with Douglas Bader and Johnny Johnson (by then an Air Commodore) and a number of other comrades from the war, Woody also visited his two sisters, Dorothy and Mabel.

Woody's health deteriorated in the later 1960's and in his latter years he was often short of breath. He died in Dunedin Hospital at the age of 71 on June 11, 1968. A full military funeral was held for him and after cremation, his ashes were scattered off Otago Harbour from the RNZN launch, HMNZS Toroa.

In researching his career, I found one particular question kept surfacing. Why was the man who many considered the outstanding RAF fighter controller of the war, posted to a Special Duties Wing in Italy? I suspected the answer was perhaps a partial side-effect of the loss of Air Chief Marshal Sir Trafford Leigh-Mallory in 1944 but the dates did not tally (Leigh-Mallory died in November 1944 some months after Woody was posted to Brindisi). The "patronage" of air marshals often effected the career of RAF officers and by being identified with Leigh-Mallory from the Battle of Britain, Woody was seen as in the wrong camp as far as Air Chief Sir Keith Park was concerned. That Park was known to bear grudges has been well documented – there was the famous case of Stan Turner (another of Woody's close allies and friends in Malta and Group Captain Desmond Scott wrote in "Typhoon Pilot" about the effective side-lining of Group Captain Lord David Douglas-Hamilton after a disagreement with Sir Keith Park.)

Air Marshall Sir Hugh Lloyd was another close friend and supporter of Woody and his relationship with Sir Keith was also known to be frosty so there seemed a good chance that the appointment to Brindisi (which was specifically "sorted-out" by Lloyd) was perhaps a result of what Laddie Lucas termed "the Lloyd-Park Axis in a chapter of "Malta- A Thorn in Rommel's Side." Further investigation turned up a clipping from The Times dated October 14, 1943. This stated that the findings of the court martial at Exeter in August on Squadron Leader W.G. Dreschfield had not been confirmed by the RAF higher authority to which they were referred.

"The Court announced after a three-day hearing that Squadron Leader Dreschfield had been found Not Guilty of knowingly making false statements without having any reasonable grounds for supposing they were true, and that findings would be promulgated on charges that his former station commander, Group Captain A.B.Woodhall, was more often than not under the influence of drink, and of engaging in conduct prejudicial to good order and Air Force discipline.

Squadron Leader E.Cudden submitted in defence that only a small part of the document in which the statements were alleged to have be made was the subject of the charges. It was written to secure an interview with the Area Officer Commanding and was confidential . A Court of Enquiry should therefore have been held before a court-martial was considered."

Shades of the Royal Oak Affair. Woody had been accused and then damned by his accusers' trial although he never at any stage was actually charged with anything. His views on strong drink were shown in his dealing with Johnny Johnson and Hugh Dundas, but he was also a great believer in the positive aspects of alcohol in relieving stress and like many other officers was always happy to " buy the troops a drink" after a heavy action. (Sir Hugh Lloyd also records how he presented Woodhall with his last bottle of gin after the action in which the three Italian Cant bombers were shot down over Malta in 1942.) Woody may well have decided he was over-doing things at this time, I note that while photographs on Malta often show him with a glass in his hand, pictures at Brindisi, while including a caricature of him on the wall of the officers' mess, usually show him with a bottle of CocaCola (obviously a bit of foreign aid from the United States deployment on the other side of the airfield). His change in role to a bomber station commander was in fact, much appreciated by the United States forces – I remember one American pilot visiting our house who told me very solemnly "we had any number of goddamn officers sending us out on dangerous missions but it was Woody that got us home again." On May 5, 1945, the President of the United States, Harry Truman , awarded Woody with the Legion of Merit (Officer).

Bibliography

249 at War (1997) by Brian Cull.

All the Fine Young Eagles - In the Cockpit with Canada's Second World War Fighter Pilots (1996) by David L. Bashow

A Pair of Silver Wings (2007) by James Holland.

Bader, The Man and His Men (1990) by Michael G. Burns.

Bader's Duxford Fighters (1997) by Dilip Sarkar.

Bader's Tangmere Spitfires (1996) by Dilip Sarkar.

Briefed to Attack (1949) by Air Marshal Sir Hugh Lloyd.

Carve Malta on My Heart and Other Wartime Stories (1994) by Frederick Galea

Clouds of Fear (1975) by Roger Hall

Douglas Bader - A Biography (1983) by Robert Jackson.

Elephant Island and Beyond - the Life and Diaries of Thomas Orde Lees (2003) by John Thomson

Fight for the Sky - The Story of the Spitfire and Hurricane (1973) by Group Captain DRS Bader.

Flying Colours - The Epic Story of Douglas Bader (1981) by Laddie Lucas.

Flying Start - A Fighter Pilot's War Years (1988) by Group Captain Sir Hugh SL Dundas.

Fortress Malta (2003) by James Holland.

Full Circle - The Story of Air Fighting (1964) by JE 'Johnnie' Johnson.

Hess - A Kiwi Malta Ace (2000) by James Sutherland.

Hurricanes Over Malta (2001) by Brian Cull and Frederick Galea.

Kiwi Spitfire Ace (2001) by Jack Rae.

Malta - The Thorn in Rommels Side (1992) by Laddie Lucas.

Malta Spitfire - The Story of a Fighter Pilot (1943) by Flying Officer George Beurling and Leslie Roberts.

Malta: The Spitfire Year 1942 (1991) by Christopher Shores, Brian Cull and Nicola Malizia.

Martlesham Heath (1975) by Gordon Kinsey.

My Boy Jack - The Search for Kipling's Only Son (1998) by Tonie and Valmai Scott

Nine Lives (1959) by Alan C. Deere.

One Man's Window (1956) Denis Barnham

Reach For the Sky (1954) by Paul Brickhill.

Reggie - The Life of Air Vice marshall Reggie Marix (1994) by John Lea.

Spitfires Over Malta (1943) by Pilot Officers Paul Brennan and Ray Hesselyn with Henry Bateson

Spitfires Over Malta: The Epic Air Battles of 1942 (2005) by Brian Cull with Frederick Galea.

Tattered Battlements - A Malta Diary by A Fighter Pilot (1943). The author was Wing Commander Tim Johnstone and this book was later republished with his name on the cover.

Ten Fighter Boys (1942). Edited by Wing Commander Athol Forbes and Squadron Leader Hubert Alan.

Thanks for the Memory (1989) by Laddie Lucas.

Chapter Notes

Chapter 1:

P. 1: In describing his leaving South Africa to join up for war service, Woody didn't mention that he was effectively running away from home. His parents were strict Quakers and therefore strongly opposed to warfare as a means of settling political or religious differences.

P. 14: In the original handwritten version of his manuscript, Woody made only a passing reference to Captain Bamford and his VC but stated simply "he was a very fine fellow indeed." As a teenager, I was horrified at the lack of detail and the simplistic accolade and it was only then that Woody provided this passage on the action at Zeebrugge.

P. 28: The action at Beaumont Hamel at this time was recorded only very succinctly in the 2nd Battalion RMLI War Diary: "November 13th 1916 Bn. attacked according to attached orders. 2nd Lt. Stokes, Welman & Dewar killed. November 14th 1916 Capt. & Adjt. CG Farquharson, Capt. Edwards, Capt. Staughton, Capt. Goldring, Capt. Bisset, Lt. Thorold, Thomas, 2nd Lts. Holloway, Grayson, Wrangham, & Garnett wounded. Surgeon J MacB. Ross RN wounded, remained at duty." The entry for December 6 simply records "2nd Lt AB Woodhall officially declared wounded." Woody's Royal Marine service records that he "received s. wound and buried by shell blast, Beaumont Hamel" and makes no mention of the later evacuation. It is my belief that he continued to fight with his unit while in a state of shock after being dug out of the mud on November 13 and it was not until the wound in his back was badly infected that he was declared wounded some 23 days later.

Chapter 2:

P. 30-31: For an excellent book on Orde Lees and the Shackelton Expedition, see "Elephant Island and Beyond: The Life and Diaries of Thomas Orde Lees". By John Thomson (2003).

P. 37: This fairly detailed and loving description of th history of HMS Agincourt was one of the talks prepared for a series entiled "Woody Woodhall Remembers" broadcast by the National Programme on Radio New Zealand in the late 1950's. Those wishing to know more would be rewarded by reading "The Big Battleship or the curious career of HMS Agincourt" by Richard Hough, London, 1966.

Chapter 3

P. 50-51: Woody was alaways suspicious about the total lack of survivors in the sinking of the Robert S. Holt, particularly as Wodehouse had been a strong swimmmer and had been awarded a Humane Society medal for a sea rescue before the First War. For the German version of events read Jost Metzler's "The Laughing Cow" originally published in 1955.

Chapter 4

P. 61-62: The names and basic details of this episode are verified in The Online Dictionary of Canadian Biography. Woody had cuttings from the St John's Telegram newspaper as quoted.

P. 63-68: These two stories, Revolution in Mexico and Emigrant Ship Mutiny were broadcast in the "Woody Woodhall Remembers" talks on the Radio New Zealand National Programme in 1958.

P. 68: "Or startin' a Board School mutiny along o' the Onion Guards" is the line referred to in Rudyard Kipling's "Soldier and Sailor Too" which is of course also the inspiration for the title of this book. The battle-cruiser, HMS *Repulse*, was too large to travel up the St Lawrence seaway from Quebec to Montreal. HMS *Repulse* had the unfortunate distinction of being the first capital ship sunk at sea entirely by aircraft attack. (December 10, 1941).

Chapter 5

P. 74: Woody fails to record that he was the only pilot on his course to be awarded "Special Distinction" on gaining his wings.

P. 75: In spite of the "near miss" recorded with the submarine, HMS M1, Woody did later volunteer to test fly a Parnall Peto off the M2 which had the 12inch gun replaced by an aircraft hangar. Perhaps luckily, his offer was not taken up, M2 sank with all
hands of Portland in 1932 after flooding through the hangar doors.

Chapter 6

P. 83: In two Atlantic Journal articles, "Loot for the Master Race" (September, 1946) and "Hitler's Capital" (October, 1946), James S. Plaut told the story of Nazi art theft in occupied Europe. As director of the Art Looting Unit of the O.S.S., Plaut investigated what he called "the most extensive and highly organized series of thefts devised by a nation in modern times." In France alone a special Nazi task force seized 203 privately owned French art collections that together contained nearly 21,000 works of art. Copies of both these articles are available from The Atlantic Journal.

P. 84: See "Reggie - The life of Air Vice Marshall RLG Marix CB DSO" by John Lea (1994).

P. 85-87: See "The Royal Oak Courts Martial" by Leslie Gardiner (1965) and "The Royal Oak Affair" by Robert Glenton (1991). The Times (London) had this announcement on August 8, 1924: "The marriage of Baron Kurt von Behr of Munich, and Joy Clarke, daughter of Mrs Godfrey Clarke, of Venice, and the late Godfrey Clarke, of Halden Hall , Kent, took place in London on August 7, from the home of her aunt, Miss de Guzman Youl."

Von Behr and his wife were reported to have suicided at the Schloss Banz in 1945 by drinking Prussic acid in Champagne. (Source: The Activity of the Einstatzstab Rosenberg in France, 25 August 1945 by J. S. Plaut,

Lieutenant, USNR. Further reference in the Atlantic Journal 1946 (same author) and numerous other references in more recent histories including The Faustian Bargain: The Art World in Nazi Germany By Jonathan Petropoulos.

P. 88: The "lady friend" was Woody's first wife, Dorothy - see Postscript.

P. 90-92: "Palestine Incident" was another of the talks broadcast on the Radio New Zealand National programe. In Woody's service record under Special Notations there is the citation "Name brought to notice by the Commander in Chief, Mediterranean, for services rendered between 28.8.29 - 9.9.29 in connection with the disturbances in Palestine."

Chapter 8

P. 106: The book "Martlesham Heath" by Gordon Kinsey has the following passage: "The M1/30, Blackburn's bid for a torpedo-bomber specification crashed into the trees where the Black Tiles restaurant now stands (1975) after engine failure just after take-off, but the crew got away with a shaking and bruises." For verification of Jim Skyrme's service career, I have to thank his son, David Skyrme (contacted via website).

P. 109: The Airspeed Courier was first flown on April 10, 1933 and Woody's first flight in this aircraft is recorded in his logbook as July 1, 1933 as handling tests with a Mr Osborne as passenger.

P. 118: When 824 Squadron was formed on HMS Eagle, it had no squadron badge. With collaboration from fellow officers, Woody designed the badge that was carried by the squadron until the end of the torpedo-bomber era. The original badge, hand-carved from mahogany, showing an Eagle carrying a torpedo, was presented to the Otago Officers Club, Dunedin, on Woody's death.

P. 120: In spite of numerous enquiries, the identity of the British Charge d'Affairs evacuated from Tientsen on HMS Eagle has not been established.

Chapter 9

P. 126: Woody had avoided using the real name of the villian in this piece but a quick search of "The Times" archives brought forth the name.

Chapter 11

P. 162: "Cocky Dundas" desribes the lecture from Woody in his autobiographical "Flying Start (1989). Johnnie Johnson also mentioned the drinking lecture in a telephone conversation in 1997 when he added "They were often hard and desperate times but I must say that we also had a lot of fun with Woody."

P. 164: The photograph on the cover endpaper is the one taken for the "civilian" passport issued to Mr Alfred Basil Woodhall on February 2, 1942 for transit to Malta. His occupation is described as "Foreign Office official". All other pasports issued in his name since 1916 had his service rank (including those issued after retirement - as a regular officer he was entitled to keep his rank after leaving the service and he was always on the retired list and subject to recall).

Chapter 12

P. 179: In one of those wonderful coincidences, Bob McManus is now living in Christchurch, New Zealand. He has been a tireless campaigner to have a plaque mounted on the Christchurch Bridge of Remembrance to commemorate those who died defending Malta. He told me that his worst job on Malta was cleaing out the rear turret of Wellington bombers. The aircraft tended to return after taking the most horrendous fire, but invariably the rear gunner had been killed by fighter cannon.

P. 189· The Great Siege of Malta, one of history's bloodiest battles, took place in 1565.

P. 189: In "Malta Spitfire Ace" (2001), Flight Lieutenant Jack Rae records the destruction of these three Cant 1007 bombers on July 4, 1942. "Woody's vectors proved immaculate." AVM Sir Lloyd also records it, saying "Woodhall excelled himself" and notes "I gave him my last bottle of gin that day"! ("Briefed To Attack" by Sir Hugh Lloyd, 1949).

Chapter 13

P. 200: In his notes about the Atcherley twins, Woody had pencilled "Dick Atcherley's Report on German build-up to War - 1936??" (This note was in the margin of text now on P109) At the time of checking this manuscript there was no verification for this annotation but I have since uncovered the article by Vincent Orange "The German Air Force is Already 'The Most Powerful In Europe' : Two Royal Air Force Officers Report on a Visit to German, 6-15 October 1936". In it, the author recounts how Squadron Leader Richard Rowley and Flight Lieutenant Richard Atcherley flew privately to German to see what they could discover about the Luftwaffe. Their 44 page typewritten report went apparently unread but a summary was subsequently forwarded to Sir Winston Churchill. The Vincent Orange article was published in The Journal Of Military History 70 (October 2006).

P. 202: The reference to "at least one enemy" is perhaps in reference to Squadron Leader W.G. Dreschfield - see P252.

P. 205: The story of Squadron Leader Geoff Warnes and Pilot Officer Tuff was another of the "Woody Woodhall Remembers" talks on the Radio New Zealand National Programme in 1958.

P. 212: Details about the Bari Raid and the subsequent medical research are contained in an article in the US Army Chemical Review July 1990. "Bari Harbor and the Origins of Chemotherapy" by Dr Stewart Alexander.

From England to Malta in an Austin Seven.

By A. B. Woodhall

(as published in March 1928 issue of The Austin Magazine)
The Account of a Trip across a Continent

This is the story of a journey undertaken in a hurry, after the minimum amount of preparation, by two people who knew nothing about Continental motoring.

My wife and I were on leave in the Lake District when I received orders to join a ship stationed at Malta. We were so delighted with our little car's performance on the Lake District hills that we at once said, "Let's go overland in 'Pimple,'" 'Pimple' is a standard Austin "Seven" touring model, and being our first car, is the darling of our hearts. We christened her 'Pimple' because although she is so very small, she refuses to be ignored.

The Decision is Made

When we made the momentous decision 'Pimple' was just 4 ½ months old and had done 7,500 miles. I was recalled from leave and in order to reach my headquarters at Gosport had to travel 351 miles in one day. My average for the whole distance was 28.3m.p.h. This excellent performance sealed our decision to go out to Malta in the car, so we consulted the A.A., who very ably arranged all formalities about triptiques, carnets, etc., and supplied us with the necessary route card and maps. On our way through Birmingham we called at the Austin works and asked their advice as to what spares we should carry, and we were very much impressed by the efficiency of their Service Department. We ordered a spare magneto, spare springs (one front and one rear), two spare valves and a spare brake cable. We never had to use them, but as Austins said, their presence in the car would give us moral support! Altogether, Austins treated us with as much deference and courtesy as if we had come to order a fleet of their most expensive models, and we left saying what nice people they were.

Exactly ten days after we decided to undertake the trip, we landed at Boulogne, complete with "Pimple" and about 200lbs, of luggage on the back seat. The little car looked puny and frail alongside her late shipmates of the Channel steamer – two Rolls-Royces, a Packard, a Buick and Sunbeam, and we were given one or two pitying smiles when we mentioned how far we were going. One optimist told us that the most we could hope to do with a large car (which we didn't possess!) would be 150 miles a day.

An Unfortunate Start

However, full of enthusiasm, we set off cautiously along the quay, being careful to remember the Continental rules of the road, particularly the one which says that you must give way to traffic approaching from the right. We had gone about 500 yards when we came to a cross-roads. We slackened speed to about 5 m.p.h. in second gear over these, when a taxi shot over a bridge on our left and rammed us hard on the near side.

Our hearts were in our boots. Here we were, right at the very beginning of our journey, apparently hopelessly crippled. The driver of the taxi – an Englishman – was humble at first, admitting that he was to blame and that he wasn't looking. Then he consulted with his fares (also Englishmen, I'm sorry to say) and became truculent, saying that we ran into him, and his fares seemed to think that their mission in life was to insult my wife. If only we could have spared the time, I would have given at least one of the said fares in charge for using obscene and insulting language.

England the Happiest Country for an Accident!

By this time of course we were surrounded by the usual chattering French crowd, amongst whom was a young and very ignorant gendarme who completely lost his head and his temper. At this juncture, an Englishman who saw the accident came up and offered himself as a witness on our side. How we yearned for the good old English constable though, who would have proved beyond a shadow of doubt that we were in the right, because the position of the cars showed that the taxi driver and his friends were lying.

Eventually, having exchanged names and addresses all round, we found that the poor old "Pimple" was still capable of proceeding under her own steam, so we decided to push on to Abbeville. As soon as we were under way, I discovered that the steering had been damaged by the crash, but we reached Abbeville in two hours in spite of this.

Very depressed, we went to bed after deciding that no repairs could be done until daylight. Early next morning I took the car to a garage, where they roughly straightened out the wing and running board, and under my directions trued up the front wheels, all for the very reasonable sum of 19 francs. They decided that they were not expert enough to deal with the dents in the body.

By 8.45am we were on the road again, feeling considerably cheered that our "Pimple" had suffered no serious damage. Our route took us through Pontoise, Versailles, and the beautiful forest of Fontainebleau, then by Sens and along the valley of the Yonne to Auxerre, which we reached by 8.20pm having covered 246 miles. The roads as far as this were good on the whole, with the exception of some very bad patches of pavé near Versailles and at Ris-Orangis.

Next day we left Auxerre at 8.30am. and followed the banks of the Yonne and the Cure to Avallon. This was a very pleasant run through low wooded hills along a road with a fair surface, then over roads that became gradually worse through Dijon and Pontarlier to the Swiss frontier at Jougen, which we reached at 5.30pm. The Customs formalities only occupied about half-an-hour, so we decided to make Lausanne our stopping place for the night.

The First Puncture

Just before reaching Orbe we had our first puncture, caused by a large flat-head nail. We became very familiar with these nails before we reached the end of our journey! However, we changed the wheel and reached Lausanne in a thunderstorm at 8.30pm. and foolishly went to a large hotel which was on our list.

This hotel might be a good place to stay at if only some kind person could explain to the manager the meaning of the word "Service." As it was, we arrived looking rather dirty and dishevelled. A very unwilling porter showed me where the garage was. Whilst I was putting the car away, the manager asked my wife what sort of a room we would like, and being a truthful sort of person she answered, "The cheapest you've got." He at once looked down his nose and lost all interest in us – and so did the rest of the hotel staff. We asked for a call at 6am, and were assured that we would be duly awakened at that hour. We were not called, our shoes were not cleaned, 7a.m. appeared to be too early an hour to provide us with coffee, and we even had to carry our own suitcases down three flights of stairs. For this I found that we were charged 10 per cent on an exorbitantly high bill for "Service." After this experience we came to the conclusion that large and fashionable hotels were to be avoided.

Rain!

At 7.30 a.m. on the 24th we left Lausanne in a steady downpour of rain and went on to Vevey, where we breakfasted and had our punctured spare wheel repaired. My impression of Switzerland was unfortunate, as the whole time we were there (less than 24 hours I admit) it rained steadily and all the mountains and the lake of Geneva were obscured by mist. My wife had been promising me wonderful views in

Switzerland (she had stayed in Lausanne before and had seen it at its best) so that when I likened the view of the lake of Geneva to that of Gosport Hard on a rainy day, I found that I had "struck rather a low note!"

After leaving Vevey we encountered very bad roads between Martigny Ville and Brigue. Just beyond, we passed two large landslides; workmen were still clearing enormous boulders from the road.

The Simplon Pass held no terrors for our little car, and she accomplished about half the climb on second gear, and never boiled. When we got above the clouds the scenery was grand, the mountains rising out of vast seas of cloud, the latter giving the impression of huge valleys filled with snow.

At the top of the Simplon we passed a party, obviously English, who had climbed the pass on foot, When they saw our little Austin they were vastly astonished and pleased, giving us a cheer as we passed. The road surface was quite good, and we never encountered any hairpins acute enough to make us reverse, as we had been led to expect, either here or elsewhere on the trip.

An Armed Escort

We followed the steep descent through very wild and rugged scenery to Gondo on the Italian frontier, arriving there about 4 p.m. There we were stopped by some Bersaglieri, who examined and stamped our passports. We were then sent under an armed escort of one man (I saw his officer issue him with six rounds for his revolver before we left the post!) to the Italian customs three kilometres further on. We had a little difficulty in dealng with the transport of the escort, because he apparently was not allowed to travel on the running board. We solved the problem by my wife driving with the escort alongside her and myself on the running board. I didn't like that escort - because his objection to riding on the running board meant that I got wet instead of him! However, our apparent consideration for the comfort of the escort favourably impressed the Customs people so that they did not open any of our luggage and signed our carnet without even troubling to check the engine and chassis numbers.

From here onwards a lot of interest was taken in our "Pimple"; it seemed that ours was the first Austin " Seven " that had been seen in these parts. We learnt amongst other things that the proper pronunciation of Austin was "A-oosteen," with the accent on "oo."

After Gondo the roads grew steadily worse, and to make things more cheerful a thunderstorm seemed to keep pace with us. Just after leaving Domodossola we picked up another nail and I had to change a wheel in the pouring rain. We went on over dreadful pot-holes, in second gear much of the time, with the mud splashing right up to the wind-screen. At Cuzzago we were stopped by a distracted woman whose child had fallen and injured itself badly, and we were debating as to how we could possible help the poor kiddie to a doctor when a larger car drove up and solved the problem.

More Rain!

We reached Stresa at 8.45 p.m. thoroughly downcast by the appalling weather and worse roads, but we cheered up a little after a meal; and weary, went early to bed.

At 8 a.m. the next day we left Stresa, after repairing our puncture, and, in almost the first sunshine we had seen since leaving Boulogne, proceeded along the shores of Lake Maggiore to Arona, then joined the Autostrada at Sesto Calende. Just after arriving on the Autostrada we collected yet another nail!

We had heard a lot about this Autostrada, but on seeing it we were not impressed. By comparison with the roads we had encountered elsewhere it was wonderful ; but in comparison with, say, our Great West Road, its surface is poor and it is only about half the width.

A Good Road at Last!

However, our little car was pleased. She fairly purred with joy with her speedometer needle steady between 40 and 45 all the way to Milan. In Milan we ate a belated breakfast while our latest puncture was being mended, and on leaving there we were very much encouraged by a good stretch of road as far as San Donato Milanese; but, alas for our hopes, this was the last good road we encountered in Italy.

to be continued...

Part 2 – As published in the may 1928 issue of The Austin Magazine

We left Pianoro at 7 a.m. and crossed the Etruscan "Apennincs by the Raticosa andFuta Passes in Florence. We breakfasted at Baglia in a restaurant whose walls were decorated with the autographs of Lloyd George, several princes and princesses, Charlie Chaplin, Douglas Fairbanks and other famous people. As they had the signatures of so many notabilities we decided that they did not need ours!

The roads had by now become so bad that we had no time to admire the scenery, being much too busy trying to avoid potholes. After leaving Florence, the engine developed a thump at low speeds, so we stopped at Barberino-de-Val d'Elsa, had lunch, then having diagnosed the trouble as a sticking valve, I took off the cylinder head and found that somehow or other grit had found its way into one of the valve-guides, preventing the valve from seating properly. I cleaned the valve guide, ground in the valve and we were under way again in 2 ½ hours. After Siena we found ourselves in a barren hilly country with very winding and extremely dusty roads.

We arrived at San Quirico d'Orcia at 8 p.m., after only 124 miles, owing to our stop for repairs and the bad roads we had encountered. Here, encouraged by our experience of the previous night, we went to the local Albergo, and found it be a dirty, foul-smelling place, with a cow-shed immediately under the bedroom. However, we were too tired to be fussy, so put up with these discomforts.

Owing to a slight misunderstanding about our call, we did not get away until 8 a.m. We passed over steep hills to Montefiascone and crossed the barren plain of the Campagna to Rome.

There I thought it advisable to report to the British Naval Attaché, as I realised that it would be impossible for me to reach Malta by the 29th, the date I had been told to arrive. I rang up the Embassy and found that nobody would be there until 5 p.m., so we went and had a much-needed lunch.

Trouble at the Police Station!

I had rather a quaint adventure here. When buying some cigarettes, I carelessly left by wife's attaché case in the tobacconist's shop. Leaving my wife in the restaurant, I went back for the case and found that they had sent it to the police station, so I went there. I tried to explain by trouble with no success, so I was taken to a plain clothes detective who seemed to think that I was a potential criminal, for having failed to understand me, he refused to let me go and fetch my wife to explain matters. After keeping me for about half-an-hour while he wrote a report, he took me to an hotel near by, where the porter spoke English. During this journey I felt, and most of the passers-by certainly thought, that I was under arrest! On realising my trouble, however, the detective was very affable and took me to another police stations, where the lost case was found.

On going to the Embassy at 5 p.m., we were told that the Attaché had gone away for the week-end, so rather sick at having delayed several hours for nothing, we had tea and proceeded. After leaving Rome we felt it incumbent on us to go on until at least midnight to make up for lost time. By 12.20 midnight to make up for lost time. By 12.30 we were about 10 kilometres beyond Arce and were so sleepy that we decided to sleep "a la belle étoile," so parked the car just off the road and prepared for bed.

Sleeping Our in the Car

Having taken the luggage out of the back seat, we arranged our beds as follows: We put the rear cushion fore and aft, first taking out the front seats, and with an attaché case to fill the gap at the forward end, one bed was made. For the other bed we used the back of one of the front seats and the two front seat cushions. The whole arrangement, with the help of a cushion, a rolled up dressing gown and a rug, was surprisingly comfortable and infinitely preferable to a dirty, evil-smelling hotel.

After rather limited ablutions in a nearby stream, we replaced the seats and luggage and were on the road by 6 a.m. We made fairly good time as far as Capua and then encountered the worst road it is possible to imagine. The potholes were the worst we had encountered; they were so deep that at times our rear number-plate scraped along the ridges between, and the dust was axle deep. We still have nightmares about this stretch of road! We arrived at Naples smothered in dust; out hair was white with it, and even the inside of the car was smothered.

We thought Naples beautiful from a distance, but found that it would not bear close inspection. The roads in the town were vile; many of the paving stones which were about a foot square, were either missing or else were standing on end; the buildings all seemed to be on the point of collapsing, and the smells in the streets were well-nigh unbearable. They say, I believe, "See Naples and die" we saw (and smelt) Naples and only just got away with our lives! If I ever have to visit Naples again I will take a gas mask!

A Little Trouble About Our Whereabouts

When we were apparently in the middle of Naples we asked the way to Pazzigno, the next place on our route card, and were sent back the way we had come. After going back about a mile we asked again and were turned about. Thinking we must have missed a turning, we went in the original direction and enquired again and our informant again pointed back the way we had come. It then dawned on us that were in Pazzigno all the time! I couldn't say what I wanted to, owing to my wife's presence, but I thought a lot!

We eventually proceeded along the coast past the ruins of Pompeii, with Vesuvius emitting the usual cloud of smoke overhead. We left the coast shortly after, then passed through Salerno to Eboli, where we had a slight contretemps. We went to a garage which advertised Shell and asked for 10 litres to top up our tank, and the man produced what I thought to be a 10-litre tin. He tried by temper to begin with by pouring it so fast that about a quart was spilt over the engine, in spite of my caution to pour slowly. I then found that the tin was an 18-litre one and the tank would only take 11 litres. The proprietor insisted on charging us for the whole tin, and when I tried to reason with him an unpleasant-looking individual stepped out of the crowd and said, "He wanta doity tree" I looked blank and asked him to repeat it, whereupon he got quite angry and said, "Doity tree, doity tree – you no on-stand English?"

I told him that I couldn't think why he should want a dirty tree- then it dawned on my wife (who is good at cross-word puzzles and riddles and such things!) that he meant thirty-three! I then got angry at such obvious profiteering – the price for 11 litres, according to the advertisement, should have been 22 lire – and after a little heat from both sides we gave him thirty lire and left him cursing. After Eboli the roads became mountainous again, and when we had nearly come to grief by encountering an unfenced bridge over a chasm on the blind side of a hairpin in the dark, we decided to put up at the first village we came to. This happened to be a tiny place called Polla. We found the local Albergo, and having put the car into a barn, we were conducted into the dining (?) room, where two Italian soldiers were enjoying their evening meal. They were eating with such noisy enjoyment (in spite of the fact that they were obviously troubled by several hollow teeth) that we were quite put off our food and were content to go to bed on a cup of black coffee each.

The next morning we left Polla with no regrets and, having breakfasted off raw eggs (the waiter said they were boiled) and black coffee at Sala Consilina, proceeded through Lagonegro to the Campotenese Pass. It is worthy of note that we found it impossible to obtain either milk or butter anywhere south of Naples, and the Italians do not know how to boil eggs.

Our stout-hearted little "Pimple" climbed the Campotenese Pass without fuss, in spite of very steep gradients and nasty corners.

From here to Coscenza the roads consisted of bullock cart tracks with enormous sharp flints between the ruts. As our little car's track was about 6 inches narrower than the ruts, driving became a real strain, with one wheel in a rut and the other on the flints, between the rut tracks.

Punctures in the Dark

A mile beyond Spezzano Albancsi we had another puncture and I hopefully put on our spare wheel, but this punctured about five miles further on. I started to mend it, and having discovered the puncture could not find my patches in the dark. Just then, a party of Italians in a large Fiat came along, and very kindly gave us a patch. Having mended the puncture, we reached Cosenza about 9 p.m., had a much-needed supper,, then pushed on until 11 p.m., when we selected a suitable site and again slept in the car.

Next morning I arose at 5 a.m. mended the puncture in the spare wheel, greased the car, then, having restowed the luggage, we washed rather sketchily in a neighbouring stream and got under way at 6.40a.m.

About 9 o'clock we were passed by our Italians friends of the night before, who looked rather surprised at finding we had got ahead of them. They looked more surprised still when we passed them in Monteleone, where they had stopped for some refreshment. They evidently thought it astounding that so small a car could have been so close behind them for all that distance. We arrived at Villa San Giovanni at 6 p.m., and after many troubles we managed to get the car on to the ferry for Messina.

Short of Cash!

Our troubles arose out of the fact that we had run short of Italian money and there were no banks open where we could change English money. A porter took us all over the town trying to find someone to change our money, and we eventually managed this by running a bank manager to earth in his house.

Apparently it is impossible to ship a car on these ferries unless one first pays out large sums to the porters, and the annoying part about this is that the porters do nothing beyond buying the tickets. I will say that our porter had to work hard in order to change our money, so we did not grumble. The captain of the train ferry was very kind to us and took us on the bridge o admire the lights of the Straits of Messina, and we arrived in Messina at 8.30 p.m.

Main Roads that Disappear

In Sicily we found the roads to be worse than ever, and to make matters more difficult we now encountered a lot of unmarked open drains. We struck the first of these after a stretch of comparatively decent road, and how the springs withstood the awful bump I do not know. Anyhow, the little car didn't seem to mind and went on as stoutly as ever. Another thing that tried us was that the road would suddenly end and we would have to go across country for about half-a-mile before we found it again!

Very much chastened by our encounter with the drain we went on until 1 a.m., by which time I felt I could not drive any further, so we parked the car in the only suitable place we could find – a quarry by the roadside and slept in her as before. After a night made dreadful by myriads of mosquitoes we were awakened by curious workmen peering in at 5 a.m., so we got under way with all speed and started the last lap of our journey.

In Catania we stopped to have another punctured mended and to fill up with petrol, and found that there was no charge made for mending the puncture. We were only expected to tip the boy who did the job. When the garage-man saw our engine he grinned and called it "motoletto." He looked at it with more respect though when we told him how far we had come!

We went wearily on, over a road that beggars description, enveloped in a cloud of dust and in heat that I would not have imagined possible outside of the tropics, until we were about 15 miles from Syracuse. Here we struck quite a good road and we kept up a steady thirty rest of the way, arriving at 2.30 p.m.

A Dash for the Boat

On enquiry we found that the mailboat left at 3 p.m., so I cashed on board and interviewed the purser, who turned out to be a perfect brick. We were in rather a predicament because our supply of ready money had given out, but the purser told me to get the Customs formalities over with and the car on board, and we could discuss finance afterwards. He sent the shipping company's agent with us to show where the Customs offices were, but this individual, as soon as we got out of earshot of the purser told us he hadn't got time to help us, and so that we should miss the boat and give him no more trouble, deliberately misdirected us.

However, in spite of this, we eventually unearthed the customs people, and leaving my wife to get the carnets signed, I drove the car on to a lighter and by 3 p.m. she was safely transhipped to the mailboat. In the meantime, my wife had cleverly got all the documents signed (our friend the purser said that he had never known the Italian customs move so quickly before). I gather that she worked this miracle entirely by means of a pleasant smile and an appearance of helplessness!

Having paid the robbers who owned the lighter, the purser threatened his minions with instant death if they did not get us everything we wanted and was perfectly happy to accept my cheque in payments

When we arrived at Malta we found that we were rather celebrities; people thought that it was a wonderful feat to have come from England to Malta in just over ten days in a car the size of "Pimple."

I must say that the little car behaved marvellously well under most difficult conditions. We only had one involuntary stop apart from those caused by punctures, and the only attentions we gave the car were to fill her with petrol, oil and water and to grease her before each day's run.

The total distance covered was 1,804 miles and we did this on 40 gallons of petrol, making and average consumption of over 45 m.p.g. The oil used on the journey amounted to exactly a gallon.

The little car is now running as well as ever in Malta and is still the joy of our lives; proving itself a boon for shopping, picnics and social outings.

Index

SQUADRONS AND UNITS

NAMES

GENERAL - INCLUDING PLACES, EVENTS, NON-HM SHIPS

ROYAL NAVY VESSELS